23,268

Fourth Edition, Revised

TAX RESEARCH TECHNIQUES

A publication issued by the Tax Division

Robert L. Gardner, PhD
Brigham Young University

Dave N. Stewart, CPA, PhD
Brigham Young University

American Institute of Certified Public Accountants

Credits

Pp. 105, 114: Reprinted with permission from *Standard Federal Tax Reporter*. Published and copyrighted by Commerce Clearing House, Inc., 4025 W. Peterson Avenue, Chicago, IL 60640.

Pp. 115–120 and 155–157: Reprinted with permission from *U.S. Tax Reporter*. Published and copyrighted by Research Institute of America, Inc., 90 Fifth Avenue, New York, NY 10011.

CCH ACCESS® is a registered trademark of Commerce Clearing House.

LEXIS® is a registered trademark of Mead Data Services, Inc.

WESTLAW® is a registered trademark of West Publishing Company.

Library of Congress Cataloging-in-Publication Data

Gardner, Robert L.
     Tax research techniques / Robert L. Gardner, Dave N. Stewart.—
4. ed.
        p. cm.
     "A publication issued by the Federal Taxation Division."
     Includes index.
     ISBN 0-87051-133-5
        1. Taxation—Law and legislation—United States—Legal research.
I. Stewart, Dave N.   II. Title.
KF241.T38G35   1993
343.7304'072—dc20
[347.3034072]   93-454
                                                                          CIP

To our wives,
JANICE and JANE

Preface

Tax Research Techniques is designed to aid tax advisers in the development of their research skills. The book employs a systematic approach to tax problems based on four steps, namely: the critical role of facts, the elusive nature of tax questions, locating and assessing appropriate authority, and communicating the findings. Included are specific examples explaining in detail the four steps employed by successful tax advisers.

Since its original publication in 1976, the book has become a helpful tool for the practicing tax adviser and for classroom instruction. The fourth edition updates the examples and illustrations to reflect the changes that have taken place in the tax law over the past four years. Also, chapter 9 has been revised to reflect advances in the technology of computer-assisted tax research.

The authors express appreciation to Ray M. Sommerfeld and G. Fred Streuling who were coauthors of the earlier editions of this book. The authors also thank Russell Beeton, Barbara Fillmore, Laura Lewis, Melanie Livingston, and J. Brooks Peacock, who served as research assistants for this project.

Contents

1

...scientific method, like science itself, defies definition. It is made up of a number of operations, some mental, some manual. Each of these, in its time, has been found useful, first in the formulation of questions that seem urgent... and then in the finding, testing, and using the answers to them.

J.D. BERNAL

Tax Research in Perspective

This study is designed to provide a working knowledge of tax research methodology for the certified public accountant who is not already a tax specialist. After a careful reading of this study and many hours of experience in implementing the procedures suggested here, the reader should be capable of solving most of the tax problems encountered in a public accounting practice.

This study also introduces the reference volumes necessary for a tax library. It suggests both minimal library requirements and methods of utilizing the more important tax reference works. This study is not primarily intended to increase knowledge of specific substantive tax provisions *per se*, but, as a secondary benefit, it may teach readers more than they previously knew about some tax provisions as they study the examples offered as problem-solving illustrations. When solving similar problems of their own, however, readers should not rely on the conclusions reached in these examples without updating them. Although this AICPA tax study is periodically revised, it was never intended as a substitute for a current tax-reference service.

Meaning of Research in General

Ideally, a book devoted to tax research would begin with an unambiguous definition of the word *research*. Unfortunately, no such definition has come to the authors' attention; therefore, we will have to be satisfied with a general description rather than a precise definition. This general description should adequately reveal the nature of the process envisioned within the phrase *tax research* as it is used here.

The word *research* is used to describe a wide variety of diverse activities. For example, at one extreme it can include the search for anything not presently known by the person making the search. In that context, looking up an unknown telephone number in a directory would constitute research. At the other extreme, a scientist might restrict his or her use of the word *research* to exhaustive experimentation under tightly controlled conditions solely for the purpose of revising previously accepted conclusions in light of recently determined facts. Between the extremes lie infinite alternative definitions.

Thus, this tax study does not purport to deal with all forms of tax research; except for a few introductory comments in this chapter, this study is restricted to a description of the procedures commonly utilized by a diverse group of professionals—including certified public accountants—to determine a defensibly "correct" (and in some instances an optimal) conclusion to a tax question. Totally different kinds of work undertaken by these individuals or by other persons might be properly included within the meaning of the phrase *tax research*. Our objective is neither to define nor to reconcile conflicting definitions. We desire only to place the general characteristics of the different types of tax research in perspective. Very few persons become expert in each of the research methodologies noted. Nevertheless, anyone deeply engaged in any facet of tax work should at least be generally aware of what other individuals working in the same general field are doing. Often, those expert in one facet of taxation are asked to express an informed opinion on a wholly different aspect of taxation. In these circumstances, it is especially desirable that the expert be aware of what others have done, and thereby move with appropriate caution in dealing with tax matters with which he or she is not intimately familiar.

Perhaps the easiest and most desirable way to place the different types of tax research in meaningful perspective is to create a general classification system based on the purpose of the inquiry. Although other possible classification systems are evident—for example, one could easily construct a classification scheme based on the character of the methodology employed—one based upon the purpose behind the research effort seems to be most useful for this statement of perspective. At least three distinct purposes for tax research come immediately to mind: implementation of rules, policy determination, and advancement of knowledge.

Research for Implementation of Rules

A great deal of tax research is undertaken to determine the applicability of general tax laws to specific fact situations. After a tax law is enacted, implementation of the law is the responsibility of the taxpayer. Although we have what purports to be a self-assessment tax system in this country, both tax rules and business practices have become so complex that many taxpayers seek the assistance of specially trained individuals to ensure not only their compliance with the tax rules, but also their achievement of that compliance at minimal tax cost.

Five elementary steps constitute a total research effort: (1) establishing the facts, (2) from the facts, determining the question, (3) searching for an authoritative solution to that question, (4) determining the import of the frequently incomplete and sometimes conflicting tax authorities located, and (5) communicating the conclusion to the interested party. Although a thorough examination of what each of these five steps involves must be deferred to later chapters, we can briefly describe each step at this juncture.

Establishing the Facts. Most tax laws and related administrative regulations are necessarily written in general terms. Effective rules must be stated in terms that adequately describe the vast majority of factual circumstances envisioned by those who determine the rules. Rules stated too broadly invite conflicting interpretation; those stated too narrowly often fail to achieve their intended objective. However, no matter how carefully the words of a statute are selected, general rules cannot possibly describe every conceivable factual variation that might be subject to the intended rules. Consequently, the first step in implementation-oriented research necessarily involves the process of obtaining all of the facts so that the researcher can determine which tax rule or rules might apply to those particular events.

Determining the Question. Questions arise when specific fact situations are examined in light of general rules or laws. Complex tax questions frequently evolve through several stages of development. Based on prior knowledge of tax rules, a researcher usually can state the pertinent questions in terms of very general rules. For example, the tax researcher may ask whether the facts necessitate the recognition of gross income by the taxpayer, or whether the facts permit the taxpayer to claim a deduction in the determination of taxable income. After making an initial search of the authorities to answer the general question, the researcher often discovers that one or more specific technical questions of interpretation must be answered before the general question can be resolved. These secondary questions frequently involve the need to determine the exact meaning of certain words and/or phrases as they are used in particular tax rules. For example, the tax researcher may have to determine if the fact situation under consideration is "ordinary," "necessary," or "reasonable" as those words are used in various sections of the code. Alternatively he or she may have to determine the meaning of the word "primarily" or, perhaps, the meaning of the phrase "trade or business." Once the general question is restated in this more specific way, the researcher often must return briefly to the process of collecting more facts. From a study of the authorities, the researcher learns that facts initially not considered important may be critical to the resolution of the revised question. After obtaining all necessary facts and resolving the more technical questions, the tax researcher may discover that the general question is also resolved. Often an answer to a related question must be resolved before the researcher can proceed to a conclusion. For example, even if a tax researcher determines that a particular expenditure is not tax deductible, he or she may have to determine whether or not the expenditure can be capitalized (that is, added to the tax basis of an asset) or whether it must simply be ignored in the tax determination procedure.[1] In effect, raising collateral ques-

---

[1] In a tax-planning situation, of course, the tax adviser may recommend an alternative way of structuring the transaction to achieve the most desirable tax result.

the discipline of economics. Often econometric models are constructed and much aggregate data obtained to formulate tax policy.

Similarly, our government representatives should have factual information about voter preferences. They should know, for example, whether a majority of the voters prefers to deal with problems of pollution through fines and penalty taxes, through incentive provisions in the tax laws, or through nontax legislation. Those who enact laws should know how the voters feel about funding public medical care, employee retirement programs, mass transit systems, interstate highways, and a host of other government projects. The research methodology common to determining voter preferences draws heavily on survey techniques developed by sociologists, demographers, and other social scientists.

Every change in tax law has a direct impact on the federal budget and on monetary policies, the magnitude and direction of which should be determined as accurately as possible before the law is finalized. Operations research techniques and computer technology are useful in making such determinations. Some of the research techniques used to make these predictions are similar to those used by the econometrician in building models that tell us whether or not a law can achieve its intended objectives. In other ways the techniques utilized are quite different. The point is simply that, even within the confines of the work that must be undertaken to provide tax policy prescriptions, the procedures that must be utilized to make those determinations vary substantially. Yet all of these diverse procedures are commonly referred to as tax research.

Research for Advancement of Knowledge

Another purpose for undertaking tax research is the advancement of knowledge in general. Research undertaken to determine a preferable tax policy, as well as that undertaken to implement tax rules, has a pragmatic objective. The researcher in each instance has a very practical reason for wanting to know the answer. Some research, on the other hand, is undertaken solely for the purpose of disseminating general knowledge. There is, however, no single common methodology for such research. Rather, the methodology selected depends entirely upon the nature of the investigation being undertaken. If it involves economic predictions, economic modeling is necessary. If it involves taxpayer attitudes and/or preferences, surveys based on carefully selected statistical samples are equally mandatory. And if it involves compliance considerations, a studied opinion of pertinent authority is just as essential.

Tax practitioners, as well as academicians, government employees, and foundation personnel, often engage in tax research work intended solely for the advancement of knowledge. The results are published in journals and presented in proceedings that appeal to two fundamentally different audiences. Policy-oriented journals and proceedings primarily attract persons who are economists by education and training. Implementation-oriented journals and proceedings primarily attract those who are either accountants or lawyers by education and training. Academicians are found in both camps.

Examples of Tax Research

Chapter 7 is an example of implementation-oriented tax research. The objective of chapter 7 is simply to illustrate how a tax researcher might determine the "correct" tax treatment of the act of incorporating a sole proprietorship under stated fact conditions. Chapter 8 demonstrates how tax planning can be utilized to minimize the tax dangers and maximize the tax opportunities implicit in a different fact setting.

Before we turn all of our attention to the details of implementation-oriented research in subsequent chapters, however, let us pause very briefly to note some examples of policy-oriented tax research.

The AICPA issued its first statement of tax policy in 1974.[2] Eight additional statements were issued in the next seven years. At the beginning of 1993, the AICPA issued an exposure draft of *Statement of Tax Policy 10, Integration of the Corporate and Shareholder Tax Systems*. In addition, the AICPA publishes various studies that address tax issues.

Tax-policy-oriented research has also been done at the National Bureau of Economic Research and the Brookings Institute. An example is Brookings' Studies on Governmental Finance, which is

---

[2] See *Taxation of Capital Gains* (New York: American Institute of Certified Public Accountants, 1974), 28 pages.

devoted to examining issues in taxation and public expenditure policy. One book in this series is *Federal Tax Policy* by Joseph A. Pechman.[3] This book discusses individual and corporate income taxes, consumption taxes, payroll taxes, estate and gift taxes, and state and local taxes. The emphasis of the book, however, is on other issues such as the effects of taxation on economic incentives and changes in fiscal relations between the federal and the state and local governments.

In recent years, the AICPA and individual CPA firms have become more active in their efforts to shape tax policy by committing significant resources to support policy-oriented tax research. These efforts include funding tax research symposia for academicians and practitioners, research grants for established academicians, and dissertation awards for aspiring researchers. In addition, the AICPA Tax Division is becoming more aggressive by regularly responding to tax policy issues considered by Congress. For example, in 1987, the AICPA Tax Division successfully spearheaded a specific effort to pass federal tax legislation allowing partnerships, S Corporations, and personal service corporations to use a fiscal year for tax reporting purposes. Another recent example of the AICPA's efforts to shape tax policy is the release of the exposure draft of its tenth statement of tax policy dealing with the integration of the corporate tax system. This issue is one which Congress has expressly directed Treasury to study.

In summary, the phrase *tax research* is commonly used to refer to widely divergent processes. All are legitimate, socially productive endeavors that may be included in a definition of tax research. A broad outline of the different processes are mentioned in this perspectives chapter for two reasons: first, to give the reader some idea of what is and what is not to be described in the study, and second, to suggest to accountants and others, who by their own inclination are implementation-oriented, the kinds of efforts that should be included in policy-oriented projects they might undertake.

In closing this chapter, the authors join many others who have called for a broader participation and cooperation of tax-interested persons in the determination of tax policy. In the past, the tax

---

[3] This 420-page book, published in 1987 (5th ed.), is available from the Brookings Institution, 1775 Massachusetts Avenue, Washington, D.C. 20036.

research efforts of theoreticians have all too often wholly ignored all practical consequences, including the behavioral adaptation of those most directly affected by their recommendations. On the other hand, the policy prescriptions rendered by the implementation-oriented groups have often overlooked important empirical evidence accumulated in the more theoretical studies. An important first step in this hoped-for cooperation is the acquaintance of each with the aims and the methodologies of the other. This volume should help to describe the tax research methodology commonly utilized by the more implementation-oriented group.

2

The Moving Finger writes; and having writ,
Moves on; nor all your Piety nor Wit
Shall lure it back to cancel half a Line,
Nor all your Tears wash out a Word of it.

OMAR KHAYYAM

The Critical Role
of Facts

A tax result is dependent upon three variables: the pertinent facts, applicable law, and an administrative (and occasionally judicial) process. Often, an accountant not trained in the practice of law is apt to underestimate the significance of facts to the resolution of a tax question. Most laypersons' study of law, including the accountant's study of business law, tends to concentrate on general rules. For the accountant turned tax adviser, however, general rules will not suffice. It is essential that every tax adviser understand why a thorough knowledge of *all* the facts is critical to the resolution of any tax question.

The Importance of Facts to Tax Questions

As used here, the word *fact* means an actual occurrence or an event or thing; facts are the who, what, when, why, where, and how of daily existence. Questions arise from facts. A tax adviser must be able to distinguish a conclusion from a fact. For example, a statement that an individual is married really is a conclusion rather than a fact. The facts that support such a conclusion may include such real-world events as these:

- On June 9, 1993, that person appeared with a member of the opposite sex before a third person duly authorized to perform marriages.
- That person exchanged certain oral vows with the specified member of the opposite sex.
- The person authorized to perform marriages made certain declaratory statements to those present.
- The exchange of vows and the declaratory statements were made in the presence of a designated number of witnesses.
- Certain documents were signed by designated parties to this ceremony, and those documents were filed in a specified repository.
- No events that might change this relationship have subsequently transpired.

Change any one of these facts, and the conclusion—that is, that a person is married—may no longer be valid. A statement of pertinent facts is virtually always much longer and clumsier than is a simple statement of the conclusion drawn from them. Consequently, most of the time our conversations and thoughts are based on conclusions rather than on elementary facts.

In tax work it often is necessary to pursue facts at length to be certain of the validity of a particular tax conclusion. To continue the foregoing illustration, a person cannot file a "joint income tax return" unless he or she is married. Obviously, most people know if they are married or not, and most tax advisers accept their client's word on this important conclusion. If, in the course of a conversation or in an investigation related to the preparation of a tax return, it becomes apparent that there is reason to doubt the validity of the client's conclusion, then a full-scale investigation of all the facts is necessary. For example, a client may state that he or she has recently been divorced. This simple statement should be sufficient to cause an alert tax adviser to make further investigations, because a person may be deemed to be married for tax purposes even after that person believes that he or she once again is single. By the same token, the tax adviser must know that persons who have never exchanged marriage vows may be deemed to be married for tax and other purposes by virtue of their actions (that is, by virtue of "the facts") and the law of the state in which they reside. The tax adviser also knows that persons married to nonresident aliens may not be eligible to file joint income tax returns, even though they are obviously married.

Tax work is often made difficult and risky precisely because the taxpayer may not understand the significance of the pertinent facts, and a tax adviser often cannot spend the time to verify every alleged fact without charging an exorbitant fee. When a tax adviser is (or reasonably should be) alerted to the possibility that a further investigation of the facts may lead to a significantly different conclusion in a tax determination, however, it is the tax adviser's professional obligation to investigate those facts in sufficient depth to permit a correct determination of a tax conclusion. In situations involving aspects of the law beyond the confines of taxation—as in the marriage example—the accountant may very well find it necessary to advise a client to engage legal counsel before proceeding with the client's tax problem.

No one engaged in tax practice should ever underestimate the importance of factual detail. Virtually every authoritative reference on tax practice stresses this important conclusion. Bickford says, "It would be impossible . . . to overemphasize the importance of knowing *all* the facts of a case, down to the last detail, figure, and date."[1] Freeman and Freeman put it this way: "Facts determine the law. Law is really facts. Shape the facts and you have planned the law. Facts have to be found. Be a detective. Find not some of the facts but all of the facts."[2] Implied in the latter quotation is the important distinction between events that have already taken place and those that are yet to occur. Tax planning is based on this critical distinction.

---

[1] Hugh C. Bickford, *Successful Tax Practice*, 4th ed. (Englewood Cliffs, N.J.: Prentice-Hall, Inc., 1967), p. 14.

[2] Harrop A. Freeman and Norman D. Freeman, *The Tax Practice Deskbook* (Boston: Warren, Gorham & Lamont, 1973), p. 2-1.

Facts—Established and Anticipated

Taxpayer compliance and tax planning constitute two major portions of any successful tax adviser's work. The initial and critical difference between these two phases of tax practice is simply a difference in the state of the facts. In compliance work, all of the facts have already transpired, and the tax adviser's only task—assuming that he or she already knows what the facts are—is determining the tax result implicit in those facts. In planning work, the tax adviser researches alternative ways of achieving established goals and recommends to a client those actions that will—considering all operational constraints, personal and financial objectives, and personal and business history—minimize the resulting tax liability. In other words, the tax planner must determine an optimal set of facts from the standpoint of tax results, given certain personal and financial constraints. The operational procedures applied in these two phases of tax practice are quite different.

After-the-Facts Compliance

The first step in taxpayer compliance work is a determination of the facts that have already taken place. The procedures used to determine facts differ significantly depending upon the relationship existing between the tax adviser and the taxpayer. The less personal the relationship, the greater the amount of time that must be devoted to a discovery of facts. In most instances, the fact discovery process can be divided into at least four distinct steps: initial inquiry, independent investigation, additional inquiry, and substantiation.

Initial Inquiry. At one extreme, the tax adviser will not have known the taxpayer prior to the request for services. In that event, if the initial request is for tax return preparation services, it is common for the tax adviser to complete a predetermined checklist of facts during (or immediately following) an initial interview. Many firms have devised their own forms to facilitate this information-gathering process; others use standard forms prepared by tax return computer services or other agencies. If the initial request is for assistance in an administrative proceeding, a less structured interview is typically used. In every instance the objective of the inquiry is the same: to establish all of the facts essential to an accurate determination of the tax liability.

Tax advisers who are intimately familiar with their clients' affairs often are able to extract sufficient facts from existing files and personal knowledge without extended personal contact with the taxpayer while making an investigation comparable to the initial inquiry. For example, the certified public accountant who regularly maintains and/or audits all of a client's financial records will require only minimal additional contact with the client to establish the information necessary to determine the correct tax liability.

Independent Investigation. Regardless of the extent of personal contact involved in the initial inquiry, all but the simplest taxpayer compliance engagements require some independent investigation on the part of the tax adviser. The specific reason for undertaking such an independent investigation varies from one situation to another, but all stem from the need for additional facts to determine a tax result. Sometimes the impetus for obtaining more facts comes from something the client said; at other times, from what he or she did not say. At still other times, the need for further facts becomes apparent when the tax adviser begins to examine the client's financial records. For example, a canceled check made payable to an unknown Dr. Fred Jones may or may not be tax deductible. The return preparer must determine what kind of doctor Jones is and what service he rendered to the taxpayer before deciding whether or not the payment can be deducted.

Whatever the cause, the tax adviser frequently does detective work to determine necessary facts. An independent investigation may involve a detailed review of financial records, old files, correspondence, corporate minutes, sales agreements, bank statements, and so forth. It may involve interviews with friends, family, employees, business associates, or others. In some cases, that search may extend to reviews of general business conditions and practices. Because of the relatively high cost of some investigations, it is common to defer incurring those costs until they are absolutely necessary. Usually this means deferring them from the time of the initial act of taxpayer compliance to the time of a dispute, that is, from the time of filing the tax return to the time at which the Internal Revenue Service challenges a tax conclusion previously reported by the taxpayer on the basis of rather tenuous facts. Because less than 1 percent of all tax returns filed are challenged in an average year, the reason for delaying a costly in-depth investigation is obvious. Nevertheless, the competent tax adviser should always be alert for situations that are apt to require further investigation later. Often it is easier and cheaper to obtain facts and to assemble related evidence at the time events transpire than it is to reconstruct them at a later date; occasionally facts may become impossible to determine if too much time has elapsed between the events and the inquiry. A tax adviser's services are often more efficient and less costly if the client collects much of the necessary evidence to support the facts. Again, the probability of the client's doing this successfully is much greater if facts relate to recent events. Deferring an investigation of pertinent facts nearly always increases the costs. The trade-off is clear: incur a smaller cost now at the risk of its being unnecessary, or incur greater cost later in the unlikely event that it is needed.

Additional Inquiry. Even in those situations in which an in-depth investigation of the facts has been completed, the tax adviser frequently will need to make further factual inquiries after beginning a search of the law. A search for the tax law applicable to a given set of facts often uncovers the need for information not originally deemed relevant by the taxpayer or the tax adviser. By reading revenue rulings and judicial decisions in situations similar to that of the client, an adviser may become aware of the importance of facts not originally considered. Being alerted to their possible importance, the tax adviser must return to the fact determination process once again. In highly complex situations, this process of moving between finding facts and determining the law may repeat itself several times before the tax question is finally resolved.

Substantiation of Facts. Determining what the facts are and proving those facts are two entirely different things. The nature and quality of the proof that is required varies significantly, depending on who is receiving proof. In tax matters, the person who must be convinced of the authenticity of the facts can be anyone from an Internal Revenue Service agent to a Supreme Court justice. The methods used to substantiate facts vary tremendously. Generally, fact substantiation procedures are much less formal in dealings with an administrative agency such as the IRS than in dealings with a court. Even with the judicial system, the rules of evidence vary from one court to another. Obviously, the closer one moves to formal litigation the greater the need for the opinion and the assistance of a qualified trial attorney. Only such a professional can adequately assess the hazards of the litigation procedure, including the rules of evidence and the burden-of-proof problems.

The certified public accountant engaged in tax practice should not lose sight of the fact that the vast majority of all tax disputes are settled at the administrative level. Therefore, it is necessary for the CPA to be fully prepared to determine, present, and substantiate all of the facts critical to the resolution of a tax dispute in any administrative proceeding. In doing this, the CPA must exercise caution to avoid stipulation of any fact that might be detrimental to the client in the unlikely event that a dispute should move beyond administrative hearings and into the courts. Because of this ever-present danger, the CPA should consult with a trial attorney at the first sign of significant litigation potential.

Before-the-Facts Planning

If events have not yet transpired, the facts have not yet been established, and there is opportunity to plan anticipated facts carefully. As noted earlier, tax planning is nothing more than determining an optimal set of facts from the standpoint of tax results. The procedures followed in making such a determination differ significantly from the procedures utilized in taxpayer compliance work.

Determination of the Preferred Alternative. The first step in the determination of the tax-preferred alternative involves a client interview. In this instance, however, the purpose of the interview is not to determine exactly what has happened in the past but, rather, to determine (1) the future economic objectives of the client and (2) any operative constraints in achieving those objectives. If the tax planner is to perform successfully, *all* of the client's hopes, dreams, ambitions, prejudices, present circumstances, and history must be fully understood. That kind of information can seldom be obtained in a single interview. Ideally, it is derived through a long, open, and trusting relationship between client and tax adviser. When tax planning is based on such an on-going relationship, any particular client interview may be brief and directly to the point. Even relatively major plans can sometimes be developed, at least initially, with no more than a simple telephone conversation.

When the tax adviser fully understands a client's objectives and constraints, he or she should spend a considerable amount of time simply thinking about alternative ways of achieving the objectives specified by the client before beginning the research. Generally, there are diverse ways to achieve a single goal; failure to spend enough time and effort in creative thinking about that goal usually results in taking the most obvious route to the solution. In many instances, the most obvious route is not the preferred alternative. A vivid imagination and creative ability have their greatest payoff in this "thinking step."

Although in all probability no one can do much to increase his or her native imagination or creative ability, many people simply do not take advantage of that which they already possess. By far the most common cause of unimaginative tax planning is the failure of the adviser to spend sufficient time *thinking about* alternative ways to achieve a client's objectives. A common tendency is to rush far too quickly from the initial inquiry to a search of the law for an answer. By rushing to a solution, we very often completely overlook the preferred alternative.

An example of creative imagination appears in *John J. Sexton*, 42 T.C. 1094 (1964), where a taxpayer successfully defended the right to depreciate a hole in the ground. The facts of the case are both interesting and instructive. The taxpayer was an operator of refuse dumps. He acquired land with major excavations primarily to use in his dumping business, and he allocated a substantial portion of the purchase price of the land to the holes. As the holes were filled, he depreciated the value so allocated. Because the taxpayer carefully documented all the pertinent facts in this case, the court allowed the deduction. Many less imaginative persons might have totally overlooked this major tax advantage simply because it is unusual and because they did not spend enough time just thinking about the facts of the case.

After a tax adviser has determined a client's objectives, and after thinking about alternative ways of achieving those objectives, the tax adviser should systematically go about researching the tax rules and calculating the tax result of each viable alternative. The preparation of a "decision tree" is very often helpful in determining which of several alternatives is the tax-preferred one (see chapter 8). It forces the adviser to think through each alternative carefully, and it demonstrates vividly the dollar significance of the tax savings in the preferred set of facts. Obviously, however, it is up to the client to implement the plan successfully.

Substantiation of Subsequent Events. The client and the tax adviser, working together, must take every precaution to accumulate and preserve sufficient documentation of the facts to support the tax plan selected. In relatively extreme circumstances, a court will not hesitate to apply any one of several judicial doctrines—most notably the doctrine of substance-over-form—to find that an overly ambitious tax plan is not a valid interpretation of the law. If, however, the tax adviser exercises reasonable caution against plans that lack substance, and if he or she takes sufficient care to document each step of the plans, the chance of succeeding is considerably improved. Of course, the process of substantiating carefully selected facts is primarily the responsibility of the taxpayer. The tax adviser, however, will often supervise the process of implementation to make certain that the intended event actually transpires in the sequence intended, and that the proof of these events will be available when and if it is needed.

Some Common Fact Questions

Most tax disputes involve questions of fact, not questions of law. In working with fact questions, a tax adviser's job is to assemble, clarify, and present the facts in such a way that any reasonable person would conclude that they conform to the requirements outlined in the tax law. Demonstrating the facts so clearly is often next to impossible. Some fact questions are necessarily much more involved and difficult to prove than others. Following are brief examples of common but difficult questions of fact.

Fair Market Value

The determination of the fair market value of a property is probably the most commonly encountered fact question in all of taxation. It arises in connection with income, estate, and gift taxes. The applicable law common to many of these situations is relatively simple if we could but determine the fair market value of the properties involved. For example, section 61 of the code provides that "gross income means all income from whatever source derived," and Treas. Reg. Sec. 1.61-2(d)(1) goes on to state, "The fair market value of the property or services taken in payment (for services rendered) must be included in income." Generally, the application of this law is simple enough once the valuation question is settled.

The legal definition of *fair market value*, stated concisely in Estate Tax Reg. Sec. 20.2031-1(b), follows:

> The fair market value is the price at which the property would change hands between a willing buyer and a willing seller, neither being under any compulsion to buy or to sell and both having reasonable knowledge of relevant facts.

Fact problems are involved in making that brief definition operational. What is a willing buyer? A willing seller? A compulsion to buy? A compulsion to sell? Reasonable knowledge? A relevant fact? Only in the case of comparatively small blocks of listed securities and in the case of selected commodities do we have access to an organized market that will supply us with ready answers to those questions. In all other instances we must look to all of the surrounding facts and circumstances to find an answer.

Books have been written to delineate the circumstances that must be considered in determining fair market value. Unfortunately, even a cursory review of those books must remain outside the scope of this tax study.[3] Suffice it to observe here that valuation is a fact question and that, ordinarily, the party to any tax valuation dispute who does the best job of determining, clarifying, and presenting all of the pertinent facts is the party who wins that dispute.

Reasonable Salaries

The determination of what constitutes a reasonable salary has long been a troublesome tax problem. As usual, the applicable law is

---

[3] See J. R. Krahmer, *Valuation of Shares of Closely Held Corporations*, Tax Management Portfolio 221–2nd, and M. F. Beausang, Jr., *Valuation: General and Real Estate*, Tax Management Portfolio 132–3rd.

relatively simple if we could only determine what is reasonable within a particular fact setting.

In determining reasonableness, both Internal Revenue Service agents and judges often look, for comparison, to such obvious facts as salaries paid to other employees performing similar tasks for other employers, any unique attributes of a particular employee, the employee's education, the availability of other persons with similar skills, and prior compensation paid to the employee. In addition, tax authorities trying to determine the reasonableness of salaries also look to the dividend history of the employer corporation, the relation between salaries and equity ownership, the time and method of making the compensation decision, the state of the economy, and many other facts. Again, we cannot examine here all of the detailed facts that have been important to reasonable salary decisions in the past.[4] We need only observe that the question of reasonableness is a fact question. The taxpayer who marshals all of the pertinent facts and presents them in a favorable light stands a better chance of winning an IRS challenge of unreasonable salaries than does the taxpayer who ignores any critical facts. The best reason for carefully studying regulations, rulings, and cases in such a circumstance is to make certain not to overlook the opportunity to determine and prove a fact that could be important to the desired conclusion.

Casualty and Theft Losses

Noncorporate taxpayers frequently lose their right to claim a casualty or theft loss deduction for income tax purposes because they did not take sufficient care to establish the facts surrounding that loss. The law authorizes a tax deduction for losses sustained on property held for personal use only if the property is damaged or destroyed by a casualty or theft. Thus, the loss sustained because of the disappearance of a diamond ring will not give rise to a tax deduction unless the taxpayer can prove that the disappearance is attributable to a casualty or theft, rather than to carelessness on the part of the owner. If the taxpayer has photographs, news-

---

[4] See J. G. Bond and P. W. Kretschmar, "The Reasonable Compensation Issue," 18 *The Tax Adviser* 897 (Dec. 1987); Gary L. Maydew, "Reasonable Compensation: How Much Is Too Much?" 36 *The National Public Accountant* 31 (August 1991); and G. A. Kafka, *Reasonable Compensation*, Tax Management Portfolio, 390-2nd.

paper accounts, police reports, testimony of impartial persons, and/or other evidence that a casualty or theft has occurred, he or she will have relatively little trouble in convincing a skeptical internal revenue agent or a judge of the right to claim that deduction. It is the facts that count, and the taxpayer generally has the burden of proving the facts in a tax dispute.

Gifts

Section 102 provides that receipt of a gift does not constitute taxable income. In many situations, however, it is difficult to determine whether a particular property transfer really is a gift or compensation for either a past or a contemplated future service. Once again the facts surrounding the transfer are what will control that determination. Facts that demonstrate the intent of the transferor to make a gratuitous transfer—that is, one without any expectation of something in return—are necessary to the determination that the transfer was a gift. Relationships existing between the transferor and the transferee may be important; for example, it generally will be easier to establish the fact that a gift was made if the two involved persons are closely related individuals (for example, father and son). On the other hand, if the two are related in an employer-employee relationship, it will be especially difficult to establish the presence of a gift. Although the broad outline of many other abstract but common fact questions could be noted here, let us consider in somewhat greater detail a few examples of some real-world tax disputes that were based on fact questions.

Illustrative Fact Cases

To better illustrate the critical role of facts in the resolution of tax questions, examinations of four previously litigated tax cases follow. The four cases can be divided into two sets of two cases each. One set deals with the question of distinguishing between a gift and income for services rendered; the other set deals with the propriety of deducting payments made by a taxpayer to his parent. None of the four cases is particularly important in its own right, but together they serve to illustrate several important conclusions common to tax research and fact questions. The court decisions in these cases are relatively brief, and the facts involved are easy to comprehend.

Gifts or Income?

The 1939, 1954, and 1986 Internal Revenue Codes include a rule providing that gifts do not constitute an element of taxable income. The present rule is stated in section 102 as follows: "(a) General Rule.—Gross income does not include the value of property acquired by gift, bequest, devise, or inheritance." The first two cases to be examined consist largely of judicial review of the facts necessary to determine whether or not particular transfers or property constitute gifts or taxable income for services rendered.

The first case involves a taxpayer named Margaret D. Brizendine and her husband, Everett. The case was heard by the Tax Court in 1957, and the decision, rendered by Judge Rice, reads in part as follows:

Case 1. Everett W. Brizendine, *T.C.M. 1957-32*

Findings of Fact

Petitioners were married in 1945 and throughout the years in issue were husband and wife and residents of Roanoke, Virginia. They filed no returns for the years 1945 through 1949, inclusive, but did file returns for 1950 and 1951 with the former collector of internal revenue in Richmond.

Prior to the years in issue, petitioner, Margaret D. Brizendine, was convicted and fined on five separate occasions for operating a house of prostitution, or for working in such a house. Petitioner, Everett W. Brizendine, prior to the years in issue, had served a term in the penitentiary. During the years in issue, he was convicted and fined seven times for violation of the Roanoke City Gambling Code, for operating a gambling house, and for disorderly conduct.

Prior to the years in issue, petitioner, Margaret D. Brizendine, met an individual in a Roanoke, Virginia, restaurant with whom she became friendly. The individual promised her that if she would discontinue her activities as a prostitute he would buy her a home and provide for her support. In 1945, the individual paid Margaret $2,000 with which sum she made the down payment on a house; he also arranged for her to secure a loan to pay the balance of the purchase price. From 1945 and until the time of his death in March 1950, the individual provided money with which Margaret made payments on such loan. In addition, he paid her approximately $25 per week in cash and also paid her money to provide for utilities, insurance, furniture, and clothing. In 1946, he paid her $500 which she used to buy a fur coat.

In determining the deficiencies herein, the respondent arrived at petitioners' adjusted gross income by adding annual estimated living expenses in the amount of $2,000 to the known expenditures made by them. The amounts of adjusted gross income so determined were as follows:

1945	$4,784.80
1946	3,300.70
1947	2,645.00
1948	2,978.62
1949	2,763.37
1950	4,812.82
1951	3,641.57

Petitioners' living expenses did not exceed $1,200 in addition to the known personal expenditures made by them during each of the years in issue.

Petitioners' failure to file returns for the years 1945 through 1949 inclusive, was not due to reasonable cause. The deficiencies in issue were due to petitioners' negligence or intentional disregard of rules and regulations. The petitioners' failure to file declarations of estimated tax was not due to reasonable cause and resulted in an underestimate of estimated tax.

Opinion

Petitioners contended that the amount received by Margaret from the individual, with which she made a down payment on a house, as well as all other amounts received from him until the time of his death in 1950, were gifts to her and, therefore, did not constitute taxable income. The respondent, while accepting petitioner's testimony as to the source of the sums, argues that she has not established that the amounts received from the individual were really gifts. He further points out that Margaret testified that the payments received from the individual were in consideration of her forbearance to refrain from engaging in prostitution, and to grant him her companionship, and argues that her promise constituted valid consideration for the payments which causes them to be taxable as ordinary income.

Both petitioners testified at the hearing in this case. Their demeanor on the stand, coupled with their long criminal records, leaves considerable doubt in our mind that the payments from the individual to Margaret were the only source of petitioner's income during the years in question, or that such amounts as the individual paid to Margaret were gifts. Since petitioners thus failed to establish that those amounts were in fact gifts, we conclude that such amounts were correctly determined by respondent to be taxable income which petitioners received during the years in issue. We further think that there is considerable merit to the respondent's argument that Margaret's promise to the individual to forbear from engaging in prostitution, and to grant him her companionship, constituted sufficient consideration for the money received from him to make it taxable to her.

We think, on the basis of the whole record, that respondent's estimate of personal living expenses in the amount of $2,000 was excessive. Many of the known expenditures which petitioners made during the years in issue were for living expenses, and pursuant to our findings we are satisfied that an additional $1,200 adequately covers all of their personal living expenses.

The second case involves a taxpayer named Greta Starks. The case was heard by the Tax Court in 1966, and the decision, rendered by Judge Mulroney, reads in parts as follows:

Case 2. Greta Starks, *T.C.M. 1966-134*

Findings of Fact

Petitioner, who was unmarried during the years in question, lives at 16900 Parkside, Detroit, Michigan. She filed no federal income tax returns for the years 1954 through 1958. She was 24 years old in 1954 and during that year and throughout the years 1955, 1956, 1957, and 1958 she received from one certain man, amounts of money for living expenses, and a house (he gave her the cash to buy it in her name), furniture, an automobile, jewelry, fur coats, and other clothing. This man was married and about 55 years old in 1954.

Respondent in his notice of deficiency stated that he determined that the property and money petitioner received each year constituted income received by petitioner "for services rendered" and in his computation he held her subject to self-employment tax. He explained his computation of the deficiency for each year by reference to Exhibit A which was attached to the notice of deficiency. Page 13 of this Exhibit A is as follows:

Analysis of Living Expenses and Assets Received
for Services Rendered

Year 1954
1955 Oldsmobile automobile	$ 3,000.00
Weekly allowance ($150.00 × 20 weeks)	3,000.00
Total	$ 6,000.00

Year 1955
16900 Parkside	$22,211.08
Roberts Furs	5,038.00
Saks Fifth Avenue	828.18
Piano and furniture	6,000.00
Weekly allowance ($150.00 × 52 weeks)	7,800.00
Total	$41,877.26

Year 1956
Roberts Furs	$ 1,570.00
Saks Fifth Avenue	3,543.17
Miscellaneous household expense	1,500.00
Total	$ 6,613.17

Year 1957
Furs by Roberts	$ 121.00
Saks Fifth Avenue	1,353.19
Living expenses	4,000.00
Total	$ 5,474.19

Year 1958
Furs by Roberts	$ 35.00
Saks Fifth Avenue	978.79
Living expenses	4,000.00
Total	$ 5,013.79

The money and property received by petitioner during the years in question were all gifts from the above described man with whom she had a very close personal relationship during all of the years here involved.

Opinion

The question in this case is whether the advancements made by respondent's witness were gifts under section 102, Internal Revenue Code of 1954, or in some manner payments that would constitute taxable income. The question is one of fact.

There were two witnesses in this case. Petitioner took the stand

and testified she was not gainfully employed during the years here involved except for an occasional modeling job in 1954 for which her total receipts did not exceed $600. She said she had no occupation and was not engaged in any business or practicing any profession and had no investments that yielded her income during the years in question. She in effect admitted the receipt of the items of money and property recited in respondent's notice of deficiency but said they were all gifts made to her by the man she identified as sitting in the front row in the courtroom. She testified that this man gave her money to defray her living expenses, and about $20,000 cash to buy the house at 16900 Parkside in 1955. She testified that she mortgaged this house for about $9,000 and she and this man lived for a time off of the proceeds of this loan. She said that this man gave her the furniture, jewelry, and clothing but she never considered the money and property turned over to her by this man as earnings. She said she had during the years in question, love and affection for this man and a very personal relationship.

The only other witness in the case was the alleged donor who sat in the courtroom during all of petitioner's testimony. He was called to the stand by respondent. He admitted on direct examination (there was no cross-examination) that he had advanced petitioner funds for the purchase of a house, clothes, fur coat, and furniture for the house. He was asked the purpose of the payments and he replied: "To insure the companionship of Greta Starks, more or less of a personal investment in the future on my part." The only other portion of his testimony that might be said to have any bearing on whether the advancements were gifts or not is the following:

Q. In advancing Greta Starks monies to purchase the properties I previously mentioned, what factors did you take into consideration pertaining to your wish or desire of securing the permanent companionship of Greta Starks?

A. The monies were advanced as I considered necessary. The purchase of a house was considered a permanent basis to last ten, twenty years not for a short while.

Respondent, of course, asks us to believe the testimony of his witness for respondent's counsel stated he was not to be considered a hostile witness. The witness was only asked a few questions. He had heard all of petitioner's testimony to the effect that the money, home, car, furniture, clothing, etc. were gifts by him to her. It is somewhat significant that he was not asked the direct question as to whether the advancement of money and property, which he admits he made, were gifts by him to her. We have quoted the only two statements he made that throw any light at all on the issue of whether the advancements were gifts or earnings. Such passages in his answers to the effect that he was making a "personal investment in the future" or the house purchase was "considered a permanent basis" are incomprehensive and rather absurd as statements of purpose. His testimony, in so far as it can be understood at all, tends to corroborate petitioner. He gives as his purpose for making the advancements "to insure the companionship" of petitioner. This can well be his purpose for making the gifts. It certainly serves no basis for the argument advanced by respondent on brief to the effect that her "companionship" was a service she rendered in return for the money and property she received. Evidently respondent would argue the man paid her over $41,000 for her companionship in 1955 and $5,000 or $6,000 for her companionship in the other years.

We are not called upon to determine the propriety of the relations that existed between petitioner and her admirer during the five years in question. He testified he had not seen her for five or six years. Petitioner was married in 1961 and is now living with her husband and mother. It is enough to say that all of the circumstances and the testimony of petitioner and even of respondent's witness support her statement that she received gifts of money and property during the five years in question and no taxable income.

A Comparison of Facts. Even a cursory examination of these two Tax Court memorandum decisions reveals that the two cases have many facts in common. In both instances, a female taxpayer received substantial sums of money and other valuable property each year for several years, from a specific male person, in exchange for the taxpayer's companionship.

On the other hand, the two decisions also suggest several fact differences between the two cases. For example—

1. The names, dates, and places of residence of the principal parties differed in the two instances.
2. The woman involved in the one case was, throughout the years in question, married; the other woman was single.
3. One of the male companion/transferors had died prior to the legal action; the other was alive and testified at the trial.
4. One of the taxpayer/transferees had a criminal record as a prostitute prior to the years in the question; the other had no such record.

Because the pertinent tax issue is the same in both cases, the question is whether the facts common to the two cases are sufficiently alike to demand a common result or whether facts are sufficiently dissimilar to justify opposite results. Ms. Brizendine had to report taxable income; Ms. Starks was found to have received only gifts and, therefore, had no taxable income to report. The law was the same in both instances; therefore, the different results must be explained either by the differences in the facts or by differences in the judicial process. Theoretically, the judicial process should work equally well in every case; if so, the different results can only be explained by different facts.

An Analysis of the Divergent Results. The published decision rendered by any court is, quite obviously, much less than a complete transcript of judicial proceeding. It is, at best, a brief synopsis of those elements of the case deemed to be most important to the judge who has the responsibility of explaining why and how the court reached its decision. A review of the two judicial decisions under consideration here suggests at least two hypotheses that might explain adequately the divergent results reached in these two cases.

On the one hand, the fact that Margaret Brizendine was found to have received taxable income rather than gifts may be attributable primarily to the fact that she had a record of prior prostitution. The fact that during the years 1945 through 1951 she elected to "discontinue her activities as a prostitute" may suggest that the taxable status of her receipts really had not changed all that significantly. Prior to 1945 her receipts apparently were derived from numerous persons; thereafter, from one individual. If the same explanation for the receipts is common to both time periods, the tax results should not differ simply because of the number of transferors involved. If, however, the explanation for those transfers differed materially during the two time periods, a history of prostitution should have no material impact on the present decision.

An alternative hypothesis that might also adequately explain the divergent results in these two cases would emphasize the differences in the judicial process rather than the differences in the facts. In most tax litigation the taxpayer has the burden of proving that the tax liability determined by the commissioner of internal revenue is incorrect. If the taxpayer fails to present such proof, the contentions of the IRS are deemed to be correct. Perhaps the attorney for Ms. Brizendine simply failed to *prove* the client's case.

Two adjacent statements in *Brizendine* support each of the above hypotheses. Judge Rice first says, "Since petitioners thus failed to establish that those amounts were in fact gifts, we conclude that such amounts were correctly determined by respondent to be taxable income which petitioners received during the years in issue." This sentence clearly suggests that Ms. Brizendine's primary problem was one of inadequate proof. In the next sentence, however, the judge suggests the alternative hypothesis in the following words: "We further think that there is considerable merit to the respondent's argument that Margaret's promise to the individual to forebear from engaging in prostitution, and to grant him her companionship, constituted sufficient consideration for the money received from him to make it taxable to her."

The ultimate basis for a judicial decision often is not known with much certainty. Any impartial reading of *Brizendine* could not pass lightly over the judge's observation that the taxpayers' "Demeanor on the stand, coupled with their long criminal records, leaves considerable doubt in our mind that the payments from the individual to Margaret... were gifts." Although initially it may be difficult to understand how courtroom behavior or criminal records relate to the presence or absence of a gift, those facts may help to establish the credibility of any statements made by a witness. The process of taxation is, after all, not a laboratory procedure but a very human process from beginning to end. Any attempt to minimize the significance of the human element at any level of the taxing process runs the risk of missing a critical ingredient.

Starks may be viewed as further evidence of the importance of the human element in the taxing process. This time, however, the record suggests that human sympathies were running with the taxpayer and against the IRS. Judge Mulroney seems to have been less than pleased with the performance of the government's attorney. The judge, commenting on the government's interrogation of the male transferor, observes, "He was not asked the direct question as to whether the advancements of money and property, which he admits he made, were gifts by him to her. We have quoted the only two statements he made that throw any light at all on the issue of whether the advancements were gifts or earnings. Such passages in his answers to the effect that he was making a 'personal investment in the future' or the house purchase was 'considered a permanent basis' are incomprehensive and rather absurd as statements of purpose. His testimony, in so far as it can be understood at all, tends to corroborate petitioner." In summary, even though the taxpayer technically once again had the burden of proving the IRS wrong, the failure of the government's attorney to ask the obvious question and to pursue related questions when a witness gave "incomprehensive" answers seems to have influenced the judge in this instance. In any event, the court did conclude that "all of the circumstances and the testimony of petitioner and even of respondent's witness support her statement that she received gifts of money and property during the five years in question and no taxable income."

Lessons for Tax Research. Even though the specific technical tax content of these two cases is trivial, a tax adviser can learn several things from these two cases. History—that is, facts that took place well before the events deemed to be critical in a given tax dispute—may significantly influence the outcome of the decision. Therefore, in gathering the facts in a tax problem, the tax adviser can never be too thorough in getting all of the facts of a case.

A study of these two cases also reveals the intricate balance between facts and conclusions. If the trier of facts—IRS agent, conferee, or judge—can be convinced of the authenticity or even the reasonableness of the facts presented for consideration, he or she has ample opportunity to reach the conclusion desired by the taxpayer. If those facts are not presented or are presented inadequately, the decisionmaker cannot be blamed for failing to give them full consideration. Disputes are often lost by the party who fails to capitalize on the opportunity to know and present all pertinent facts in the best light.

Finally, some further reflections on these two cases are instructive for tax planning generally. If the parties to this litigation had correctly anticipated their subsequent tax problems, what might they have done to reduce the probabilities of an unfavorable result? For example, would the results have differed if neither party had included a "weekly allowance" in their financial arrangements? Or if all transfers had been made on such special occasions as a birthday, an anniversary, Christmas, Yom Kippur, Saint Valentine's Day, or some other holiday? If gift cards had accompanied each transfer and those cards saved and "treasured" in a scrapbook? If gift tax returns had been filed by the transferor? Obviously, each of the additional facts suggested here would lend credence to the conclusion that the transfers were indeed gifts. At some point, the evidence—perhaps the filing of the gift tax return—would be so overwhelming that no one would question the conclusion in anything but the most unusual circumstances.

The important point of this review is, of course, that the tax adviser often plays a critical role in settings very remote from the courtroom. If the tax adviser correctly anticipates potential problems, it may be easy to recommend the accumulation of supporting proof that will almost insure the conclusion a client is interested in reaching, without going to court. Even when the tax adviser has been consulted only after all of the facts are "carved in stone," the thoroughness with which those facts are presented is often critical to the resolution of the tax question. And no one can make a good presentation of the facts until all of the facts are known, down to the very last detail. A study of two more cases can yield additional insight into the critical role that facts play in tax questions.

Deductible or Not?

In general, we know that income earned from the rendering of a service must be reported by the person who rendered the service and that income from property must be reported by the person who owns the property. If a taxpayer arranges for someone else to pay to one of his parents a part of the value that was originally owed to him for services rendered, generally that payment would still be taxed to the individual rendering the service, and the payment would not ordinarily be deductible by him. Payments made to parents, like payments made to anyone else, would be deductible for income tax purposes only if the parent had rendered a business-related service to the child and the payment made for such a service were reasonable in amount. But what exactly do those words mean?

The third case to be reviewed here involves a professional baseball player named Cecil Randolph Hundley, Jr. The case was heard by the Tax Court in 1967, and the decision, rendered by Judge Hoyt, reads in part as follows:

Case 3. Cecil Randolph Hundley, Jr., *48 T.C. 339 (1967)*

Findings of Fact

The stipulated facts are found accordingly and adopted as our findings.

Cecil Randolph Hundley, Jr. (hereinafter referred to as petitioner), filed his 1960 income tax return with the district director of internal revenue, Richmond, Va.; Martinsville, Va., was his legal residence at the time petitioner filed the petition herein. Petitioner is a professional baseball player and at the time of trial was a catcher for the Chicago Cubs of the National League.

Petitioner's father, Cecil Randolph Hundley, Sr. (hereinafter referred to as Cecil), is a former semiprofessional baseball player, and he has also been a baseball coach. Cecil played as a catcher throughout his baseball career, and received numerous injuries to his throwing hand while using the traditional two-handed method of catching. This is a common problem of catchers. A few years before Cecil retired from active participation in baseball as a player, he developed a one-handed method of catching which was unique and unorthodox. This technique was beneficial because injuries to the catcher's throwing hand were avoided. Cecil became actively engaged in the construction and excavation business in 1947 and was still engaged in that business at time of trial.

Petitioner attended Basset High School near Martinsville, Va., from which he graduated in June of 1960. During 1958 petitioner was a member of his high school baseball team and the local American Legion team. He played catcher for both teams and was an outstanding player. In the spring of 1958, while a sophomore in high school, petitioner decided that he wanted to become a good major league professional ball player. Petitioner believed that Cecil was best qualified to coach and train him for the attainment of this goal. After discussing his ambition with Cecil, an oral agreement was reached between petitioner and Cecil. Cecil agreed to devote his efforts to a program of intensive training of petitioner in the skills of baseball, to act as petitioner's coach, business agent, manager, publicity director, and sales agent in negotiating with professional baseball teams for a contract. His role may best be described in petitioner's own words when he first asked Cecil to handle things for him in 1958: "Daddy, do the business part and let me play the ball."

As compensation for Cecil's services, it was agreed that Cecil would receive 50 percent of any bonus that might be received under the terms of a professional baseball contract if one should later be signed. This contingent payment agreement was thought to be fair and reasonable by the parties since it was unknown at that time whether petitioner would ever develop into a player with major league potential or sign a professional baseball contract or receive a bonus for signing. Moreover, petitioner could not sign a baseball contract while still a minor without his parent's consent or until he graduated from high school. The size of baseball bonuses obtainable at some unknown time, years in the future, was extremely conjectural. A rule limiting bonuses to $4,000 for signing baseball contracts had been suspended in 1958 and its reinstatement was a definite possibility before 1960. It was not expected by petitioner or Cecil at that time that an exceptionally large bonus would ever be received. Later on they estimated that at most $25,000 might be paid to petitioner as a bonus.

Between the spring of 1958 and petitioner's graduation from high school in 1960, Cecil devoted a great deal of time to petitioner's development into the best baseball player possible. Cecil became petitioner's coach and taught petitioner the skill of being a one-handed catcher. While this method is advantageous, it is difficult to master because it is contrary to natural instincts. The perfection of this unorthodox technique therefore required an inordinate amount of time and effort by the teacher and the pupil. Cecil also taught petitioner to be a power hitter in order to enhance petitioner's appeal to professional baseball teams. Petitioner weighed only 155 pounds during his high school days which was a decided handicap for him both as a hitter and a catcher hoping to break into the big leagues.

Cecil attended every baseball practice session and every home and away game in which petitioner participated between 1958 and 1960. On many of these occasions he met with scouts for big league teams. By mutual agreement, Cecil relieved petitioner's high school and American Legion coach from any duties with respect to petitioner. It was agreed between the coach and Cecil that it would be in the petitioner's interest for Cecil to be in complete charge of the training program. Cecil supplied petitioner with baseball equipment at his own expense during this period.

In order to obtain the best possible professional baseball contract for petitioner, Cecil had many meetings with members of the press during the 2-year period from the spring of 1958 to June 16, 1960, to publicize petitioner's skill as a baseball player. Cecil handled all the negotiations with representatives of the many professional baseball teams that became interested in petitioner. This undertaking involved numerous meetings at home and out of town. Cecil left Sundays open for such negotiations for the entire 2-year period but negotiations often occurred on other days of the week. Cecil was never paid anything for the considerable expenses he incurred over the 2-year period.

The amount of compensation to be received by Cecil was contingent on the obtainment and size of a bonus to be paid petitioner for signing a professional baseball contract. In determining the percentage of the possible bonus to be received by Cecil, the parties also gave consideration to Cecil's increased expenses and the anticipated loss of time and income from his construction business. Cecil had to neglect his business and he lost several substantial contracts during the period of petitioner's intensive training. The amount of time he devoted to his grading and excavating business was substantially reduced during 1958, 1959, and 1960 with corresponding loss of business income.

Petitioner developed into an outstanding high school baseball player under Cecil's tutorage and by 1960 many major league clubs had become interested in signing him. Due to the rule requiring high school graduation before signing a baseball contract, extensive final negotiation sessions with representatives of the various major league baseball teams did not begin until after petitioner's graduation in 1960.

The final negotiation sessions were held at Cecil's home and after 2 weeks resulted in a professional baseball contract signed by petitioner on June 16, 1960. All of the negotiations with the many major league clubs bidding for petitioner's contract were handled by Cecil in such a way that the bidding for petitioner's signature was extremely competitive. Representatives of the various baseball teams were allowed to make as many offers as they wanted during the 2-week period, but the terms of any offer were not revealed to representatives of other teams. Cecil's expert and shrewd handling of the negotiations was instrumental in obtaining a most favorable contract and an extraordinarily large bonus for the petitioner.

The baseball contract finally signed by petitioner was with a minor league affiliate of the San Francisco Giants of the National League. The contract provided for a bonus of $110,000 to petitioner and $11,000 to Cecil, and a guaranteed salary to petitioner of not less than $1,000 per month during the baseball playing season for a period of 5 years. Cecil bargained for and insisted upon the minimum salary provision in addition to the large bonus because of his expectation that petitioner would be playing in the relatively low paying minor leagues for at least 5 years. Cecil also signed the contract because under the rules of professional baseball the signature of a minor was not accepted without the signature of his parent.

The baseball contract contained the following pertinent provisions:

1. The Club hereby employs the Player to render and the Player agrees to render, skilled services as a baseball player in connection

with all games of the Club during the year 1960, including the Club's training season, the Club's exhibition games, the Club's playing season, any official series in which the Club may participate, and in any game or games in the receipts of which the Player may be entitled to share. The Player covenants that at the time he signs this contract he is not under contract or contractual obligation to any baseball club other than the one party to this contract and that he is capable of and will perform with expertness, diligence and fidelity the service stated and such other duties as may be required of him in such employment.

2. For the service aforesaid subsequent to the training season the Club will pay the Player at the rate of one thousand dollars ($1,000) per month... after the commencement of the playing season... and end with the termination of the Club's scheduled playing season and any official league playoff series in which the Club participates.

• • • •

14. Player is to receive cash bonus of one hundred and ten thousand dollars ($110,000) payable as follows:

Eleven thousand dollars ($11,000) upon approval of this contract by the National Association of Professional Baseball Leagues. Also eleven thousand dollars ($11,000) on Sept. 15, 1961; Sept. 15, 1962; Sept. 15, 1963; Sept. 15, 1964.

The father, Cecil R. Hundley, is to receive eleven thousand dollars ($11,000) upon approval of contract by the National Association of Professional Baseball Leagues. Also eleven thousand dollars ($11,000) on Sept. 15, 1961; Sept. 15, 1962; Sept. 15, 1963; Sept. 15, 1964.

• • • •

The designation of $11,000 to be paid annually to Cecil for 5 years was a consequence of the agreement between Cecil and petitioner to divide equally any bonus received by petitioner for signing a professional baseball contract. The scout for the San Francisco Giants who negotiated the contract was aware of the aforementioned agreement before the contract was written, and the terms of the contract reflected the prior understanding of the contracting parties with respect to the division of the bonus payments. Petitioner's high school coach also knew of the 50-50 bonus agreement between petitioner and Cecil and had been aware of it since its inception in 1958.

During the 1960 taxable year which is in issue, petitioner and Cecil each received $11,000 of the bonus from the National Exhibition Co. pursuant to the terms of the contract. Petitioner did not include the $11,000 payment received by Cecil in his gross income reported in his income tax return for 1960. Cecil duly reported it in his income tax return for that year.

The notice of deficiency received by petitioner stated that income reported as received from the National Exhibition Co. was understated by the amount of $11,000. The parties are apparently in agreement that petitioner understated his income for 1960 in the determined amount, but petitioner contends that an offsetting expense deduction of $11,000 should have been allowed for the payment received by Cecil as partial compensation for services rendered under the 1958 agreement between petitioner and Cecil. Respondent's position on brief is that only a $2,200 expense deduction, 10 percent of the total bonus payment in 1960, is allowable to petitioner in 1960 as the reasonable value of services performed by Cecil.

The contract between Cecil and petitioner was made in 1958; it was bona fide and at arm's length, reasonable in light of the circumstances existing when made in the taxable year before us. The payment of 50 percent of petitioner's bonus thereunder to Cecil in 1960 was compensation to him for services actually rendered to petitioner. He received and kept the $11,000 of the bonus paid directly to him by the ball club.

Opinion

Respondent's determination that an additional $11,000 should have been included in petitioner's income for 1960 is based upon section 61(a) which provides that gross income includes compensation for services and section 73(a) which provides that amounts received in respect of the services of a child shall be included in the child's gross income even though such amounts are not received by the child.

It is beyond question and on brief the parties agree that the $11,000 received by Cecil actually represented an amount paid in consideration of obtaining petitioner's services as a professional baseball player. Petitioner, while agreeing with the foregoing conclusion, argues that a deduction in the amount of $11,000 should be allowed for 1960 under section 162 or 212. Respondent has conceded that such a deduction should be allowed but only in the amount of $2,200.

Section 162 provides that a deduction shall be allowed for an ordinary and necessary expense paid during the taxable year in carrying on any trade or business including a reasonable allowance for compensation for personal services actually rendered. Section 212 provides that an individual may deduct all ordinary and necessary expenses paid or incurred during the taxable year for the production or collection of income.

Respondent argues there is insufficient evidence to establish an agreement in 1958 to share any bonus equally and that even if there were such an agreement no portion paid for Cecil's services to petitioner prior to 1960 is deductible because prior to his graduation petitioner was not in the trade or business of being a baseball player. He contends that the only service performed by Cecil for which petitioner is entitled to a deduction was the actual negotiation of the June 16, 1960, contract. He concedes on brief that a reasonable value for the services rendered by Cecil during the 2-week period from graduation to signing the contract is $2,200, 10 percent of the total bonus paid in 1960.

Petitioner has introduced persuasive and convincing evidence that the agreement was in fact reached in the spring of 1958, and we have so found. This finding is essential to petitioner's position that a deduction for an ordinary and necessary business expense deduction in the amount of $11,000 should be allowed in 1960. He argues that a contingent right to 50 percent of any bonus obtained was a reasonable value for services rendered by Cecil between the spring of 1958 and the signing of the contract in 1960, and that payment for such services was therefore an ordinary and necessary expense associated with his business of professional baseball.

We agree that the 50 percent contingent compensation agreement was reasonable in amount. Section 1.162-7(b)(2) of the regulations sets forth a test for the deductibility of contingent compensation which we have accepted as correct in *Roy Marilyn Stone Trust*, 44 T.C. 349 (1965). We apply the test here.

The primary elements considered by petitioner and Cecil in determining Cecil's contingent compensation were the amount of time that would be spent in coaching, training, and representing petitioner during the uncertain period between 1958 and an eventual contract. Cecil's exclusive handling of all publicity and contract negotiations and the income that would probably be lost due to less time spent on Cecil's construction business were also important factors. In addition to the foregoing considerations, emphasis should be placed on the fact that the ultimate receipt of a bonus of any kind was uncertain and indefinite. The amount was indeterminable and in 1958 neither petitioner, Cecil, nor the high school coach who was aware of the agreement had any notion that an exceptionally large bonus would be paid 2 years hence. Petitioner might well never have become a professional ballplayer, nor was it at all certain that he would be paid a bonus in the future. Viewing the circumstances at the time the agreement was made in the light of all of the evidence before us we conclude and hold that the test of reasonableness has been met even though the contingent compensation may be greater than the amount which might be ordinarily paid.

• • • •

While it is true that an agreement of this sort between a father and his minor son cannot possess the arm's-length character of transactions between independent, knowledgeable businessmen and must be most carefully scrutinized, the agreement here stands every searching test. Independent and trustworthy witnesses verified its existence since 1958. It was in our judgment and in the opinion of both petitioner and Cecil, then and at trial, fair to both parties. See *Olivia de Havilland Goodrich*, 20 T.C. 323 (1953).

• • • •

Respondent contends further, however, that even if the bonus splitting agreement arose in 1958 and was intended to ultimately result in a reasonable amount of compensation for services rendered throughout the 2-year period, the full amount received by Cecil is still not deductible because petitioner was not engaged in a trade or business or any other income-producing activity until graduation from high school when he became eligible to sign a professional baseball contract. In order for an expenditure to qualify for deductibility under section 162 or 212, it must have been paid or incurred in carrying on any trade or business or for any other income producing or collecting activity. . . .

The contingent compensation agreement was so closely bound up with the existence of the petitioner's business activity of professional baseball that payments made thereunder must be considered as paid in carrying on a trade or business. If petitioner had never entered the business of professional baseball or had not been paid a bonus therefore, no payments would have been made to or received by Cecil. The whole basis of the agreement was the ultimate existence and establishment of the contemplated business activity and the collection of a bonus. We therefore conclude that payments made under the terms of the agreement were paid for services actually rendered in carrying on a business. The obligation to make the payments to Cecil was an obligation of the business since there would be no obligation without the business. If the business were entered without payment of a bonus there also would be no obligation to share it with Cecil. The unique relationship of Cecil's compensation to the professional baseball contract and petitioner's income derived therefrom in 1960 is most persuasive of the deductible nature of the compensation payment made that year.

Respondent's final argument, raised herein for the first time on brief, is based on the premise that the services rendered prior to high school graduation were basically educational in nature, and that educational expenditures are personal and nondeductible if undertaken primarily for the purpose of obtaining a new position or substantial advancement in position. See sec. 1.162-5(b), Income Tax

Regs. We have previously held that claimed deductions for educational expenditures of the foregoing type are not allowable. *Mary O. Furner*, 47 T.C. 165 (1966); *Joseph T. Booth III*, 35 T.C. 1144 (1961); and *Arnold Namrow*, 33 T.C. 419 (1959), aff'd. 288 F.2d 648 (C.A. 4, 1961).

However, petitioner is not claiming a deduction in the amount of $11,000 for educational expenditures, and indeed he could not. It is clear that a significant portion of Cecil's compensation was not for coaching and training petitioner in the skills of baseball, if that be deemed education, but for other services rendered throughout the 2-year period.

• • • •

We hold, therefore, that whereas respondent acted correctly in including the entire $22,000 bonus in petitioner's taxable income, petitioner should be nevertheless allowed a deduction in the amount of $11,000 in 1960 as a business expense for the portion of the bonus paid directly to Cecil for his personal services actually rendered with such rewarding financial results for both petitioner and his father.

The last case to be reviewed in this chapter involves another professional baseball player named Richard A. Allen. His case was heard by the Tax Court in 1968, and the decision, rendered by Judge Raum, reads in part as follows:

Case 4. Richard A. Allen, *50 T.C. 466 (1968)*

Findings of Fact

Some of the facts have been stipulated and, as stipulated, are incorporated herein by this reference along with accompanying exhibits.

Petitioners Richard A. and Barbara Allen are husband and wife, who at the time of the filing of the petitions and amended petitions herein resides in Philadelphia, Pa. Richard A. Allen filed his individual returns for the calendar years 1960, 1961, and 1962, and a joint return with his wife Barbara Allen for 1963, on the cash receipts and disbursements method of accounting, with the district director of internal revenue, Pittsburgh, Pa. Barbara Allen is a party to this proceeding solely by virtue of the joint return filed for 1963, and the term 'petitioner' will hereinafter refer solely to Richard A. Allen.

Petitioner was born on March 8, 1942. In the spring of 1960 petitioner, then age 18, was living with his mother, Mrs. Era Allen, in Wampum, Pa., and was a senior at a local high school. Mrs. Allen had been separated from her husband since 1957. She had eight children, of whom three, including petitioner, were dependent upon her for support during 1960. She received no funds from her husband, and supported her family by doing housework, sewing, or laundry work.

In the course of his high school years, petitioner acquired a reputation as an outstanding baseball and basketball player. He was anxious to play professional baseball, and had even expressed a desire to leave high school for that purpose before graduation, but was not permitted to do so by his mother. During the petitioner's junior year in high school, word of his athletic talents reached John Ogden (hereinafter "Ogden"), a baseball "scout" for the Philadelphia National League Club, commonly known and hereinafter referred to as the Phillies. Ogden's attention was drawn to petitioner through a newspaper article about petitioner which, while primarily describing him as a great basketball player, also mentioned that he had hit 22 "home runs" playing with a men's semiprofessional baseball team the summer before his junior year in high school, and that the player who had come closest to his total on the team, which otherwise comprised only grown men, had hit only 15 home runs. Ogden's function as a scout for the Phillies was to select baseball talent capable of playing in the major leagues, i.e., with the Phillies, and after reading this article he made up his mind to see petitioner.

Ogden had himself played baseball for around 16 to 18 years, was general manager of one baseball club and owner of another for 7 or 8 years, and at the time of the trial herein had been a baseball scout for the preceding 28 years—a total of about 52 years in professional baseball. After interviewing petitioner and watching him play basketball and baseball, Ogden determined that petitioner was the greatest prospect he had ever seen. He conveyed this impression to John Joseph Quinn (hereinafter "Quinn"), vice president and general manager of the Phillies, and told Quinn that petitioner was worth "whatever it takes to get him." Quinn thereupon gave Ogden authority to "go and get" petitioner, i.e., to sign him to a contract to play baseball for the Phillies.

From this point on, Ogden became very friendly with petitioner's family. He hired Coy Allen, petitioner's older brother of about 36 or 37 who had played some semiprofessional baseball in the past, as a scout for the Phillies. He also signed Harold Allen, another brother of petitioner to a contract to play baseball in the Phillies organization. He visited the Allen home often, and talked to petitioner about playing baseball. He did not, however, attempt immediately to sign petitioner to a contract because of a rule adhered to by the Phillies and other baseball teams prohibiting the signing of any boy attending high school to a baseball contract until after his graduation.

Ogden, as well as representatives of a dozen or more other baseball teams that also desired petitioner's services, discussed petitioner's prospects with his mother, Era Allen. She was the head of the family, and she made all the family decisions. Although petitioner discussed baseball with the various scouts, he referred them to his mother in connection with any proposed financial arrangements, and he felt "bound" to play for whichever club his mother might select.

Era Allen conducted all negotiations with Ogden in respect of the financial arrangements that might be made for petitioner if it should be determined that he would play for the Phillies. However, she knew nothing about baseball, particularly the financial aspects of baseball, and she relied almost entirely upon advice from her son Coy Allen. After petitioner had entered into a contract to play for the Phillies organization, as hereinafter more fully set forth, Era Allen paid Coy $2,000 in 1960 for his services out of the funds which she received under that contract, and she deducted that amount from her gross income on her 1960 individual income tax return.

One of the principal items of negotiation with Ogden was the amount of "bonus" to be paid for petitioner's agreement to play for the Phillies organization. Such bonus was in addition to the monthly or periodic compensation to be paid petitioner for services actually rendered as a ballplayer. The purpose of the bonus was to assure the Phillies of the right to the player's services, if he were to play at all, and to prevent him from playing for any other club except with permission of the Phillies. Scouts for other teams had made offers of a bonus of at least $20,000 or $25,000. During the course of the negotiations Ogden made successive offers of a bonus in the amounts of $35,000, $50,000, and finally $70,000. The $70,000 offer was satisfactory to petitioner's mother, but she wanted $40,000 of that amount paid to her and $30,000 to petitioner. She thought that she was entitled to a portion of the bonus because she was responsible for his coming into baseball by her hard work, perseverance, taking care of petitioner, and seeing that he "did the right thing." Although it had been informally agreed prior to petitioner's graduation that he would go with the Phillies, the contract was presented to and signed by petitioner some 30 or 40 minutes after he had received his high school diploma on June 2, 1960.

The contract was formally between petitioner and the Williamsport Baseball Club, one of six or seven minor league teams affiliated with the Phillies through a contractual arrangement known as a "working agreement" whereby, in general, the Phillies were entitled, in exchange for a stated consideration, to "select" the contracts of any of the players on the Williamsport Club for their own purposes and under which the Phillies further agreed, among other things, to reimburse the Williamsport Club for any bonus paid to a player for signing a contract with that club. The Williamsport Club was under the substantial control of the Phillies, and the contract between petitioner and the Williamsport Club was signed on behalf of the latter by an official of the Phillies, who was in charge of all the Phillies' minor league clubs, or what was called their "farm system," and who was authorized to sign on behalf of the Williamsport Club. The contract was on the standard form prescribed by the National Association of Professional Baseball Leagues. Since petitioner was a minor, his mother gave her consent to his execution of the contract by signing her name under a printed paragraph at the end of the form contract entitled "Consent of Parent or Guardian." Such consent was given explicity [sic] "to the execution of this contract by the minor player party hereto," and was stated to be effective as to any assignment or renewal of the contract as therein specified. She was not a party to the contract. The Phillies, in accordance with their usual practice, would not have entered into any such contract, through the Williamsport Club or otherwise, without having obtained the consent of a parent or guardian of the minor player.

In addition to providing for a salary of $850 per month for petitioner's services as a ballplayer, the contract provided for the $70,000 bonus payable over a 5-year period, of which $40,000 was to be paid directly to petitioner's mother and $30,000 to petitioner. The contract provided in part as follows:

1. The Club hereby employs the Player to render, and the Player agrees to render, skilled services as a baseball player in connection with all games of the Club during the year 1960. . . . The Player covenants that at the time he signs this contract he is not under contract or contractual obligation to any baseball club other than the one party to this contract and that he is capable of and will perform with expertness, diligence and fidelity the service stated and such other duties as may be required of him in such employment.

2. For the service aforesaid subsequent to the training season the Club will pay the Player at the rate of eight hundred fifty dollars per month.

• • • •

5. (a) The Player agrees that, while under contract and prior to expiration of the Club's right to renew the contract, and until he reports to his club for spring training, if this contract is renewed, for the purpose of avoiding injuries he will not play baseball otherwise than for the Club except that he may participate in postseason games as prescribed in the National Association Agreement.

(b) The Player and the Club recognize and agree that the Player's participation in other sports may impair or destroy his ability and skill as a baseball player. Accordingly, the Player agrees he will not engage in professional boxing or wrestling and that, except with the written consent of the Club, he will not play professional football, basketball, hockey or other contact sport.

· · · ·

Player is to receive bonus of $6,000 payable June 2, 1960
 Do .... $8,000 .. do ... June 1, 1961
 Do .... $8,000 .. do ... June 1, 1962
 Do .... $4,000 .. do ... June 1, 1963
 Do .... $4,000 .. do ... June 1, 1964

Mother, Mrs. Era Allen is to receive bonus of $16,000 payable June 2, 1960

Mother, Mrs. Era Allen is to receive bonus of $10,000 payable June 1, 1961

Mother, Mrs. Era Allen is to receive bonus of $6,000 payable June 2, 1962

Mother, Mrs. Era Allen is to receive bonus of $4,000 payable June 2, 1963

Mother, Mrs. Era Allen is to receive bonus of $4,000 payable June 2, 1964

Total bonus seventy thousand dollars guaranteed.

· · · ·

It was generally the practice in baseball to have the signature of a parent or guardian when signing a player under the age of 21 to a contract, and a contract lacking such signature would probably not have been approved by the president of the National Association of Professional Baseball Leagues.

The installments of the $70,000 bonus agreed to by the Williamsport Baseball Club in its contract with petitioner were actually paid by the Phillies under their "working agreement" with the Williamsport Club. The Phillies viewed such bonus arrangements as consideration to induce a player to sign a contract which thus tied him to the Phillies and prevented his playing baseball for any other club without the consent of the Phillies. These bonus arrangements represented a gamble on the part of the Phillies, for a player might not actually have the ability to play in the major leagues, or might decide on his own that he no longer wanted to play baseball. The Phillies could not recover bonus money already paid, and as a matter of baseball practice felt obligated to pay a bonus, once agreed to, in all events, even if some part of the bonus still remained unpaid when the player left or was given his unconditional release by the club. Nevertheless, in light of petitioner's future potential and ability, Ogden, who negotiated petitioner's bonus, and Quinn, who had the final say in these matters, felt that $70,000 was a fair price to pay to "get" the right to petitioner's services as a professional baseball player. It was a matter of indifference to them as to whom the bonus was paid or what division was made of the money. The previous year, in 1959, the Phillies had paid a bonus of approximately $100,000 to one Ted Kazanski and in 1960, at about the same time they signed petitioner, the Phillies paid a bonus of approximately $40,000 to one Bruce Gruber.

Following the execution of the foregoing contract in June 1960 with the Williamsport Club, petitioner performed services as a professional baseball player under annual contracts for various minor league teams affiliated with the Phillies until sometime in 1963. From that time, he has performed his services directly for the Phillies, and in 1967 his annual salary as a baseball player was approximately $65,000.

Petitioner (and his wife Barbara Allen in the taxable year 1963) reported as taxable ordinary income in his (their) Federal income tax returns for the taxable years 1960, 1961, 1962, and 1963 the bonus payments received by petitioner in each of said years, as follows:

1960	$ 6,000
1961	8,000
1962	8,000
1963	4,000

Petitioner's mother, Era Allen, reported as taxable ordinary income in her Federal income tax returns for the taxable years 1960, 1961, 1962, and 1963 the payments received by her in each of said years, as follows:

1960	$16,000
1961	10,000
1962	6,000
1963	4,000

In his notice of deficiency to petitioner in respect of the taxable years 1961 and 1962, and his notice of deficiency to petitioner Richard and his wife Barbara Allen in respect of the taxable year 1963, the

Commissioner determined that the bonus payments received by petitioner's mother in 1961, 1962, and 1963 represented amounts received in respect of a minor child and were taxable to petitioner under sections 61 and 73 of the Internal Revenue Code of 1954; he increased petitioner's taxable income in each of those years accordingly.

Opinion

1. *Inclusion of Bonus in Petitioner's Gross Income.* (a) Petitioner was only 18 years old when the event giving rise to the bonus payments in controversy took place. Accordingly, if the payments made during the years in issue (1961-63) by the Phillies to Era Allen, petitioner's mother, constitute "amounts received in respect of the services" of petitioner within the meaning of section 73(a), I.R.C. 1954, then plainly they must be included in petitioner's gross income rather than in that of his mother. Although petitioner contends that the statute does not cover the present situation, we hold that the payments made to his mother during the years in issue were received solely in respect of petitioner's services, and that all such amounts were therefore includable in his income.

Petitioner argues that the payments received by his mother, totaling $40,000 over a 5-year period, were not part of his bonus for signing a contract to play baseball for the Phillies organization, but rather represented compensation for services performed by her, paid by the Phillies in return for her influencing petitioner to sign the contract and giving her written consent thereto. But there was no evidence of any written or oral agreement between the Phillies and Era Allen in which she agreed to further the Phillies' interests in this manner, and we shall not lightly infer the existence of an agreement by a mother dealing on behalf of her minor child which would or could have the effect of consigning her child's interests to a secondary position so that she might act for her own profit. Moreover, we think the evidence in the record consistently points to the conclusion that the payments received from the Phillies by Era Allen were considered and treated by the parties as part of petitioner's total bonus of $70,000. This sum was paid by the Phillies solely to obtain the exclusive right to petitioner's services as a professional baseball player; no portion thereof was in fact paid for his mother's consent.

We note, first of all, that there was no separate written agreement between the Phillies and Era Allen concerning the payment of $40,000 to her, and that in fact the sole provision of which we are aware for the payment of this sum appears in the contract between petitioner and the Williamsport Baseball Club, a minor league baseball club

affiliated with the Phillies under a "working agreement" which entitled the Phillies to claim the contract and the services of any player on
the club at any time. Petitioner's contract, a uniform player's contract
standard in professional baseball, contained a paragraph requiring
the parties to set forth any "additional compensation" (aside from the
regular payment of salary) received or to be received from the club "in
connection with this contract" and it is in the space provided for such
"additional compensation" that all the annual installments of petitioner's bonus, both those payable to petitioner and those payable to
his mother, are set forth. After a description of all such installments,
identifying the payee (petitioner or his mother), the amount and the
date due, appear the words: "Total bonus seventy thousand dollars
guaranteed." Moreover, if further proof be needed that the Phillies
did not consider any part of the $70,000 bonus as compensation for
Era Allen's services it is provided by the testimony of John Ogden,
the baseball scout responsible for petitioner's signing a contract with
the Phillies' organization. Although Ogden resisted being pinned
down, the clear import of his testimony was that the total bonus paid
was determined solely by petitioner's ability to play baseball and his
future prospects as a player, that the Phillies considered $70,000 a fair
price to pay for the right to petitioner's services, and that it made little
difference to them whether petitioner's mother received any part of
the bonus so determined.

Era Allen herself did not claim to be entitled to $40,000 by virtue
of any services performed for or on behalf of the Phillies, and in fact
made clear in her testimony that she bargained, as one would expect,
"for whatever was best for my son." Rather, she insisted upon a large
portion of petitioner's bonus because she felt that petitioner would
never have reached the point at which he was able to sign a lucrative
contract with a professional baseball team had it not been for her hard
work and perseverance in supporting him. And indeed, as the
mother of a minor child, one who by the fruits of her own labor had
contributed to the support of her minor child without the help of the
child's father, she appears to have been entitled to *all* petitioner's
earnings under Pennsylvania law. Pa. Stat. tit. 48, sec. 91 (1965).

Prior to 1944, the Commissioner's rulings and regulations "required a parent to report in his (or her) return the earnings of a minor
child, if under the laws of the state where they resided the parent had
a right to such earnings," even if none or only part of the child's
earnings were actually appropriated by the parent. . . . Because parents were not entitled to the earnings of their minor children in all
States, and because even in those States following this common-law
doctrine the parents' right to the earnings of a minor child could be

lost if it was found that the child had been emancipated, the result of the Commissioner's policy was that:

> for Federal income tax purposes, opposite results obtain(ed) under the same set of facts depending upon the applicable State law. In addition, such variations in the facts as make applicable the exceptions to the general rule in each jurisdiction tend(ed) to produce additional uncertainty with respect to the tax treatment of the earnings of minor children.

H. Rept. No. 1365, 78th Cong., 2d Sess., p. 21 (1944); S. Rept. No. 885, 78th Cong., 2d Sess., p. 22. To remedy these defects, Congress in 1944 enacted the substantially identical predecessor of section 73 of the Internal Revenue Code of 1954, providing the easily determinable and uniform rule that all amounts received "in respect of the services of a child" shall be included in his income." Thus, even though the contract of employment is made directly by the parent and the parent receives the compensation for the services, for the purpose of the Federal income tax the amounts would be considered to be taxable to the child because earned by him." H. Rept. No. 885, 78th Cong., 2d Sess., p. 22, 23. We think section 73 reverses what would have been the likely result in this case under pre-1944 law wholly apart from the contract, and that the $70,000 bonus is taxable in full to petitioner.

Petitioner stresses the fact that the $70,000 bonus paid by the Phillies did not constitute a direct payment for his "services" as a professional baseball player, which were to be compensated at an agreed salary of $850 per month, for the $70,000 was to be paid in all events, whether or not petitioner ever performed any services for the Phillies organization. Therefore, it is argued, the bonus payments could not have constituted compensation for *services* which alone are taxed to a minor child under section 73. Cf. Rev. Rul. 58-145, 1958-1 C.B. 360. This argument misreads the statute, which speaks in terms of "amounts received *in respect of* the services of a child," and not merely of compensation for services performed. True, petitioner performed no services in the usual sense for his $70,000 bonus, unless his act of signing the contract be considered such, but the bonus payments here were paid by the Phillies as an inducement to obtain his services as a professional baseball player and to preclude him from rendering those services to other professional baseball teams; they thus certainly constituted amounts received "in respect of" his services.

(b) Even if amounts in issue were not received "in respect of the services" of a child under section 73, we think that the bonus install-ments paid to petitioner's mother during the tax years 1961–63 are nevertheless chargeable to him under the general provisions of section 61. It has long been established that one who becomes entitled to receive income may not avoid tax thereon by causing it to be paid to another through "anticipatory arrangements however skillfully devised." *Lucas v. Earl*, 281 U.S. 111, 114–115; *Helvering v. Horst*, 311 U.S. 112; *Helvering v. Eubank*, 311 U.S. 122; *Harrison v. Schaffner*, 312 U.S. 579.

As indicated above, the entire $70,000 bonus was paid as consideration for petitioner's agreement to play baseball for the Phillies or any team designated by the Phillies. We reject as contrary to fact the argument that part of that amount was paid to his mother for her consent to the contract. It was petitioner, and petitioner alone who was the source of the income and it is a matter of no consequence that his mother thought that she was entitled to some of that income because of her conscientious upbringing of petitioner. . . .

2. *Petitioner's Alternative Contention—Deduction of Bonus Payments From His Gross Income.* Finally petitioner argues alternatively that if his entire $70,000 bonus is includable in his income, he should be allowed to deduct the bonus payments received by his mother as an "ordinary and necessary" expense incurred in carrying on his trade or business as a professional baseball player. He places great reliance in this argument upon *Cecil Randolph Hundley, Jr.*, 48 T.C. 339, acq. 1967-2 C.B. 2, a case recently decided by this Court in which a professional baseball player was allowed to deduct that portion of his bonus for signing a baseball contract which was paid directly to his father, the result of an agreement entered into some 2 years before the contract was signed as a means of compensating the father for his services as a baseball coach and business agent. However, the special facts in *Hundley*, which supported a finding of reasonableness for the amount of the deduction claimed and warranted the conclusion that the amounts paid there in fact represented a bona fide expense incurred in carrying on the taxpayer's trade or business of being a professional baseball player, are almost entirely absent here.

It is unnecessary to determine the exact sum which would have constituted a reasonable payment to Era Allen for her services, though we note that only $2,000 was paid to her son Coy Allen for the advice she so greatly relied on, for we are certain that in any case it could not have exceeded the $16,000 received by her in 1960. Although the year 1960 is not before us in these proceedings, we can and do take into account the payment made to her in that year in determining whether the deductions now claimed by petitioner for payments made to her in the years 1961, 1962, and 1963 are reasonable in amount and deductible as "ordinary and necessary" business expenses. We think they clearly are not, and hold that petitioner is not entitled to deductions in any amount for payments made to his mother in those years.

A Comparison of the Facts. Once again, even a cursory examination of these two Tax Court decisions reveals that the cases have several facts in common. In both instances—

1. A professional baseball player arranged to have a portion of a sizable bonus paid to one of his parents.
2. Both the parent and the ball-playing minor child signed the professional contract.
3. The bonus payments actually were made by the ball club to the parent over several years.
4. The parent reported the amount received as ordinary taxable income and paid the tax liability thereon.

The two cases also differ in several factual respects.

1. The names, dates, amounts, and places of residence of the principal parties differed in the two cases.
2. The parent involved in one case was the baseball player's father; the other case involved his mother.
3. One parent was knowledgeable about, and deeply involved in, training the child in the skill of ball playing; the other parent knew relatively little about baseball.
4. One parent-child pair had a prior oral agreement about how they would divide any bonus that might eventually be received; the other parent-child pair had no such prior agreement.

Once again, it is pertinent to inquire whether or not the common facts are sufficient to require a common result or whether the different facts justify different results. The decisions of the court again were very different. Cecil Hundley, Jr., was allowed to deduct the portion of the bonus paid to his father; Richard Allen was denied the right to deduct the portion of the bonus paid to his mother. Because the law was the same in both cases, and because there is little basis in the reported decisions to conclude that differences in the judicial process had much influence on these results, we must conclude that the different facts adequately explain the divergent results.

An Analysis of the Divergent Results. Judge Hoyt makes it clear that the decision in *Hundley* is critically dependent on the existence of the oral agreement between the father and the son. He states, "Petitioner has introduced persuasive and convincing evidence that the agreement was in fact reached in the spring of 1958, and we have so found. This finding is essential to petitioner's position...." Judge Raum makes it equally clear in *Allen* that he could find no contractual agreement in that case. He states, "Petitioner argues that the payments received by his mother... were not part of his bonus for signing a contract to play baseball for the Phillies organization, but rather represented compensation for services performed by her, paid by the Phillies in return for her influencing petitioner to sign the contract and giving her written consent thereto. But there was no evidence of any written or oral agreement between the Phillies and Era Allen in which she agreed to further the Phillies' interests in this manner, and we shall not lightly infer the existence of an agreement by a mother dealing on behalf of her minor child...."

One cannot help but wonder exactly how it is possible for a person to present convincing evidence of an oral agreement made between a father and his tenth-grade son some nine years prior to the litigation. Two brief statements in the reported decision provide the only clues. One statement notes that the high school coach knew of the oral agreement since its inception; the other statement suggests that the scout for the San Francisco Giants, who negotiated the Hundley contract, also knew of the oral agreement since its inception. We can only conclude, therefore, that these statements are either based on an oral examination of witnesses at the trial or that written depositions were obtained from these persons and submitted as evidence at the trial to substantiate the existence of the oral contract.

Lessons for Tax Research. For the student of tax research, perhaps the most instructive aspect of the last two cases is their demonstration of the importance of favorable testimony by impartial witnesses.

Proper preparation of a tax file sometimes may include the need to provide supporting evidence available only from disinterested third parties. The longer one waits to locate such a party, the greater the difficulty in finding one capable of giving the testimony needed. To the maximum extent possible, considering economic constraints, the tax adviser should anticipate the imporance of all supporting documents, including sworn statements from third parties. If strong evidence of one or two critical facts can be provided to an IRS agent or to a conferee, the probability of litigation may be significantly reduced.

A careful reading of these two decisions also reveals that very similar facts or situations may sometimes be argued on radically different grounds. In other words, even though the facts are similar, the questions raised may be different. Although this observation really is more pertinent to the next chapter of this tax study than it is to the present chapter, and even though the more unusual argument did not prove to be fruitful in this instance, we observe in passing that *Allen* argues for a favorable result in the alternative. First, the taxpayer contends that the payments made to his mother were *not* for his services as a ballplayer. Only later, should the first argument fail, does he argue that the payments to his mother are deductible business expenses. In *Hundley*, on the other hand, the taxpayer never raised the former issue. The fact that both questions deserve consideration stems directly from a careful review of the facts and the law.

In *Allen*, the argument is made that a bonus payment really is not a payment for *services rendered*. At least in part, that payment really is to compensate the ballplayer for *not* rendering services (to a competitor club).

The pertinent statutory provisions refer to "amounts received *in respect of the services of a child*" [emphasis added]. The question raised, then, deals with whether a ballplayer's bonus properly falls within the meaning of the "in respect of" clause. After reviewing the congressional intent behind those words, the court determined that it did and thus rejected the taxpayer's first line of argument. Nevertheless, this observation should remind the tax adviser to consider the facts of a case in every possible way before selecting a single line of argument. The next chapter examines in greater detail the subtle relationship between the facts and a statement of the pertinent questions.

For the tax adviser, a knowledge of the statutes alone is insufficient. An adviser must carefully delineate facts important to the tax question and recognize the need to document significant facts in the event that they must be retrieved and substantiated during a later audit. The next chapter addresses the task of extracting or anticipating tax questions from the fact situation.

3

...there is frequently more to be learn'd from the unexpected Questions of a Child, than the Discourses of Men, who talk in a Road, according to the Notions they have borrowed, and the Prejudices of their Education.

JOHN LOCKE

The Elusive Nature of Tax Questions

Tax questions arise when a unique set of facts is examined in light of general rules of tax law. Learning to identify and phrase the critical tax questions implicit in any set of facts is no small accomplishment for, in many instances, the most important questions are by no means obvious. The more experienced the tax adviser, the easier it is to identify and ask the right questions. For the beginner, asking the right question is often the most difficult part of tax research. Even the most seasoned tax veteran can easily overlook a very important question. For this reason, successful tax practitioners make it a general practice to require an internal review of all tax research before stating an opinion to anyone outside the firm. This precaution often is extended to even include the preparation of a written record of all oral responses made to informal inquiries. The probability of overlooking either an important tax question or a part of the law is simply too great to permit any less thorough procedure.

The difficulty experienced in properly identifying and stating the pertinent tax questions is largely attributable to the high degree of interdependence that exists between the facts, questions, and law. If the tax adviser fails to determine all of the pertinent facts, the chance of overlooking a critical question is greatly increased. Similarly, even if the tax adviser has determined all of the critical facts, the failure to consider a critical part of the law may also lead to the overlooking of a critical question. Finally, even if the tax adviser knows all of the facts and all of the law pertinent to a case, he or she still may overlook an obvious question simply because of human error.

Errors in stating questions are often related to either (1) failure to think originally or creatively about tax problems or (2) failure to pay sufficient attention to detail. A veteran tax adviser will seldom fail to heed detail. On the other hand, precisely because of long years of experience, a tax adviser may be prone to overlook new and different ways of viewing recurrent problems.[1] In some instances, therefore, it is desirable to have the most complex tax situations reviewed by inexperienced as well as experienced personnel. The former individuals might ask the obvious question that otherwise would be overlooked, but only the latter individuals can fully appreciate the significance of even the obvious question once it has been asked. Frequently, one good tax question raises two or more related questions, and before long, the tax result depends on a network of closely related but separate questions.

Initial Statement of the Question

The resolution of a tax problem often evolves through several stages of development. In many instances, the initial statement of the question may be only remotely related to the questions that turn out to be critical to its solution. The greater the technical competence of the researcher, the fewer steps in the evolution of an answer.

The technical competence of tax researchers is, in all likelihood,

---

[1] For example, in *Allen* (see chapter 2) it would have been very easy to overlook the first of the two alternative arguments considered, that is, what exactly was Allen being paid for in the bonus? If it was for not rendering a service, a different result might apply. Admittedly, the argument was not successful in that particular case, but it was pertinent and could have been important.

normally distributed on a continuum ranging from little or no competence to very great expertise. Any attempt to separate these individuals into discrete groups is obviously unrealistic. Nevertheless, for purposes of discussing the difficulties encountered in identifying tax questions, tax advisers could be categorized into one of three groups; namely, those with "minimal" technical competence, those with "intermediate" technical competence, and those with "extensive" technical competence relative to the *subject at hand*. Technical competence in one area of taxation does not guarantee equal competence in other areas. Individuals who have an extensive technical knowledge in one aspect of taxation must move with a beginner's caution when approaching another area of the law. Although the problems are often similar, the applicable rules are sometimes quite different. As was stated earlier, a final tax result depends upon three variables: facts, law, and an administrative (and/or judicial) process. Just as the facts of one case may differ from another, so also may the law.

Minimal Technical Competence

A tax adviser with minimal technical competence usually can state tax questions in only the broadest of terms. After reviewing the facts, the beginner typically is prepared to ask such general questions as the following:

1. Is gross income recognized "in these circumstances"?
   a. If so, how much income must be recognized?
   b. If so, is that income ordinary or capital?
2. Can a deduction be claimed "in these circumstances"?
   a. If so, how much can be deducted?
   b. If so, in which year can the deduction be claimed?
   c. If not, can the tax basis of an asset be increased?
3. What is the tax basis of a specific asset?

In any real situation, of course, the actual facts of the case must be substituted for the phrase "in these circumstances" in the hypothetical questions posed above. For example, in the first question suggested above, the facts might justify a question like this: "Can an individual shareholder of a corporation whose stock is completely redeemed by a cash distribution from that corporation recognize a capital gain on the sale of his or her stock?" Observe that even the initial statement of a tax question should be very carefully phrased to include what appears to be all of the important facts of the situation.

Because beginning staff members typically enter the tax departments of accounting firms with minimal technical competence, usually they are prepared to ask only broad, general questions. If properly phrased, however, the broad questions posed by the new staffperson are ultimately the same questions that the more knowledgeable tax adviser seeks to answer. The more senior adviser tends, however, to phrase initial questions in somewhat different terms.

Intermediate Technical Competence

The tax adviser with an intermediate level of technical competence often can review a situation and state the pertinent questions in terms of specific statutory authority. For example, the question already considered for the beginning adviser might be verbalized by a person with more experience in words like this: "Can an individual shareholder whose stock is completely redeemed by a cash distribution from a corporation waive the family constructive ownership rules of section 318 in order to recognize a capital gain on the sale of his or her stock under section 302, even though the remaining outstanding stock is owned by his or her children and the individual continues to do consulting work for the corporation?"

A comparison of the same two hypothetical questions, as phrased by the person with minimal competence versus that phrased by the person with an intermediate level of competence, reveals several interesting differences.

First, the more experienced person generally understands the statutory basis of authority applicable to the tax questions. Or, to put this same difference in another way, the more experienced person: (1) knows that most tax questions have a statutory base and (2) knows which code sections are applicable to the facts under consideration.

Second, the tax adviser with intermediate technical competence often phrases questions in such a way that they imply the answer to a more general question, subject only to the determination of the applicability of one or more special provisions to the facts under consideration. For example, the phrasing of the question suggested earlier for the person with intermediate-level skills may really imply something like this: "The distribution of cash by a corporation to a shareholder in his or her capacity as a shareholder will result in dividend income under the general rule of section 301 unless the distribution qualifies for sale or exchange treatment under either section 302 or 303."[2] Note that questions phrased by persons with greater technical competence frequently suggest where the answers can be located. If a researcher knows which code sections are applicable to a given fact situation, the task of locating pertinent authority is greatly simplified.

Third, the more competent tax adviser is apt to include more facts in any statement of the question than is the beginning adviser. Thus, for example, the adviser recognizes the importance of determining the ownership of the remaining outstanding stock by adding the phrase "even though the remaining outstanding stock is owned by his or her children." Furthermore, the adviser recognizes that continuing to work for the corporation even as an independent contractor may also be critical. This tendency to add more facts to the statement of the question is the result of experience. The inclusion of additional information to the statement of the question indicates that the more experienced person recognizes some of the apparently innocent facts that can so critically modify a tax result.

In daily tax practice, a person with minimal technical tax competence acquires a great deal of knowledge by seeking answers to the specific questions posed by more competent colleagues. This saves valuable and expensive time by directing the beginner to look in the right places. Without this assistance, the beginner must spend many hours just locating the general authority that is pertinent to a question.[3] We might note, however, that the beginner

---

[2] This statement assumes that the corporation has sufficient earnings and profits to cover the distribution. If the transaction is treated as a dividend, an individual shareholder reports the entire distribution as ordinary income. A corporate shareholder may be eligible for a dividend received deduction. If the transaction is treated as a sale, the amount of the distribution is reduced by the basis of the stock redeemed to arrive at the amount of capital gain or loss. Furthermore, capital gains may be offset by capital losses. Thus, the purpose of section 302 is to distinguish between distributions that are to be taxed as dividends and distributions that are to be taxed as capital gains realized on the sale of stock.

[3] The various methods of locating authority are described in chapter 4.

typically prepares working papers detailing the research steps undertaken to answer the questions posed by supervisors. These working papers allow the supervisor to review the adequacy of the staffperson's conclusions as well as leave a permanent record of the facts and the authorities that were considered in solving any given tax problem. These records may prove to be invaluable should the IRS later question the way the tax adviser handled a particular tax problem.

Extensive Technical Competence

The tax adviser with an extensive level of technical competence in a given area can often review a situation and state the pertinent question in a still more refined manner. For example, the tax expert may ask questions like this: "Does the reasoning used in *Estate of Lennard* allow the section 302(c)(2) waiver of family attribution in this case, thus allowing sale or exchange treatment? Or, does *Lynch* apply in this case to prevent the waiver of family attribution under section 302(c)(2), thus causing dividend treatment?" By stating a question in this way, the expert implies not only the general statutory authority for an answer, but also specific interpretative authority that would in all likelihood apply to the facts under consideration. The expert often needs only to determine the most recent events to resolve a tax question. Unless something new has happened, this phrasing of the question suggests that a very specific answer can be found to the general, but unstated, question.

Thus, the expert's question—"Does the reasoning used in *Estate of Lennard* allow the section 302(c)(2) waiver of family attribution in this case, thus allowing sale or exchange treatment?"—may in reality be the same question that the beginner phrased this way: "Can an individual shareholder of a corporation whose stock is completely redeemed by a cash distribution from that corporation recognize a capital gain on the sale of his or her stock?" The former question implies that the answer to the latter question may be found in judicial or administrative interpretations of the statute. The phrasing of the expert's question recognizes, however, that there may be ample reason why specific interpretative authority would not apply. For example, the facts of the two cases may differ in some material way—perhaps the taxpayer lives in a different judicial circuit from the *Lynch* or *Estate of Lennard* decisions—or perhaps these decisions have been otherwise modified by a regulation, ruling, or subsequent judicial decision. If one knows his or her way around a tax library, it obviously will require even less time to answer the question posed by the expert than it will to answer the question posed by the adviser with intermediate competency. Unfortunately, however, not all tax questions are so easily stated or resolved, even by the expert.

Restatement of the Initial Question After Some Research

In some circumstances, even an expert must move cautiously from facts to questions to authority and then back to more facts, more questions, and more authority before resolving a tax problem. The search for authority to resolve an initial question sometimes leads to the realization that facts previously deemed unimportant are critical to the resolution of the problem. In that event, the tax adviser returns to the fact determination procedure before looking any further for answers. At other times the initial search suggests considering other tax rules rather than isolating more facts. Sometimes it suggests the need to consider both additional facts as well as additional rules. Before reaching the administrative or judicial process, the tax adviser has only two raw materials with which to work: facts and rules. Therefore, the tax adviser must learn how to identify and phrase pertinent questions by examining facts in light of rules. That microscopic examination is what reveals the need for further facts and/or rules. The tax research process is not complete until all of the facts have been fully examined in light of all of the rules and all pertinent questions have been resolved to the extent possible.

This "research procedure" is illustrated conceptually in figure 3.1.

The spiral line shows how the researcher proceeds from an initial statement of the facts (F_1), to an initial statement of the questions (Q_1), to an initial search for authority (A_1). If the initial authority suggests new and different questions (Q_2), as it often does, the researcher continues by making additional fact determinations (F_2) and/or by considering additional authority (A_2). The procedure continues over and over until all the facts are known, all

Figure 3.1

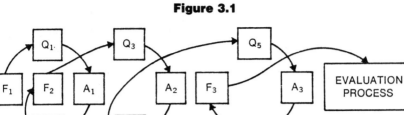

the authorities are considered, and all the questions are answered—at least tentatively. At this juncture, the tax adviser evaluates the facts and authorities just identified and reaches a conclusion.

Dangers Inherent in Statements of Questions

The danger of overlooking pertinent alternatives is greatly increased if tax questions are stated too narrowly. This danger is particularly acute for the more experienced tax adviser because, as noted earlier, he or she generally knows where to begin looking. Once the search for pertinent authority is restricted to a particular segment of the code, for all practical purposes all other alternatives may be eliminated.

This danger has been vividly demonstrated to the authors on several occasions. While teaching a university course in tax research methodology, it is necessary to design sample cases that lead students to make important discoveries of their own. A large number of the sample cases are drawn from live problems suggested by various tax practitioners. In more cases than we care to admit, possibly the best solutions have been those never considered by either the authors or by those who initially suggested the problems to us. Beginning students, unhampered by predilection and blessed by natural curiosity and intelligence, have managed on more than one occasion to view the problem in an entirely different light. This is mentioned in order to stress the importance of imagination and creativity in tax research and planning. As was noted in chapter 2, the "thinking step," the point at which the practitioner spends time considering facts, alternatives, and options, is an indispensable segment of the research process.

A second danger inherent in the statement of the question is the tendency to phrase the question using conclusions rather than elementary facts. The important distinction between conclusions and facts was noted in the prior chapter. The use of conclusions in stating questions is hazardous because conclusions tend to prejudice the result by subtly influencing the way one searches for pertinent authority. If, for example, one begins to search for authority on the proper way to handle a particular expenditure for tax purposes, the question posed might be: Should the expenditure of funds for "this-and-that" be capitalized? The answer probably will be affirmative. On the other hand, if the same question is rephrased in terms something like: Can the expenditure of funds for "this-and-that" be deducted? Once again, the answer will probably be affirmative. Obviously, if the facts are the same (that is, if the "this-and-that" in the two questions are identical), both answers cannot be correct. The explanation for the conflicting results probably can be traced to the place where the researcher looks for authority. The prior question tends to lead the researcher to decisions in which section 263 is held to be of primary importance, whereas the latter question leads to decisions in which section 162 is of greater importance.[4] Ideally, the index of reference volumes would include citations to both decisions in both places, but the cost of duplication quickly becomes prohibitive, and the human element in any classification system is less than perfect. Consequently, the statement of the question may assume unusual importance in asking a leading question. To the maximum extent possible, tax questions should be phrased neutrally and without conclusions to permit the researcher greater freedom in finding the best possible authority for resolving the question.

---

[4] Section 263 reads in part as follows: "No deduction shall be allowed for—(1) Any amount paid out for new buildings or for permanent improvements or betterments made to increase the value of any property or estate." Section 162 reads in part as follows: "There shall be allowed as a deduction all the ordinary and necessary expenses paid or incurred during the taxable year in carrying on any trade or business. . . ." Obviously, reasonable persons can and do differ in their application of these rules to specific fact situations.

A Comprehensive Example

The remainder of this chapter is a detailed review of a comprehensive example that demonstrates the elusive nature of tax questions. In the process of developing this example, we shall attempt to illustrate the way in which facts, rules, and questions are inextricably interrelated in tax problems. In following this example the reader should not be concerned with the problem of locating pertinent authority. The next chapter will explain how the reader might find that same authority if he or she is working alone on this problem. To begin, let us assume the following statement of facts.

> On February 10, of the current year, Ima Hitchcock, a long-time client of your CPA firm, sold one-half of her equity interest in General Paper Corporation (hereafter, GPC) for $325,000 cash. Ms. Hitchcock has owned 60,000 shares (or 20 percent) of the outstanding common stock of GPC since its incorporation in 1951. During the past twenty years, she has been active in GPC management. Following this sale of stock, however, she plans to retire from active business life. Her records clearly reveal that her tax basis in the 30,000 shares sold is only $25,000 (one-half of her original purchase price).

Given no additional facts, both the beginner and the seasoned tax adviser would be likely to conclude that Ms. Hitchcock should report a $300,000 long-term capital gain in in the current year because of her sale of the GPC stock. The case appears to be wholly straightforward and without complication as long as no one asks any questions or volunteers any additional information. Although few persons would ask for it in this case, the statutory authority for the suggested conclusion rests upon sections 1001, 1012, 1221, 1222, and 1223. Section 1221 establishes the fact that the stock is a capital asset; sections 1222 and 1223 determine the long-term status of the capital gain realized; section 1012 specifies the cost basis of the shares sold; section 1001 defines the gain realized as the difference between the $325,000 received and the $25,000 cost basis surrendered and requires the entire $300,000 realized gain be recognized. If, however, someone happened to ask who purchased Ms. Hitchcock's shares, problems could quickly arise.

Diagraming the Facts

Before this example is considered in more detail, a simple stick figure diagram of the transaction may be made. In the authors' opinion, every tax adviser should become accustomed to preparing such simple diagrams of the essential facts of any case before asking any questions or searching for any authority. In addition to diagraming the transaction itself, the practitioner should diagram a simple portrayal of the fact situation as it existed both before and after the transaction under examination. Each person can create his or her own set of symbols for any problem. This illustration, however, uses only a stick figure to represent an individual taxpayer (Ima Hitchcock) and a square to represent a corporate taxpayer (General Paper Corporation).

Figure 3.2

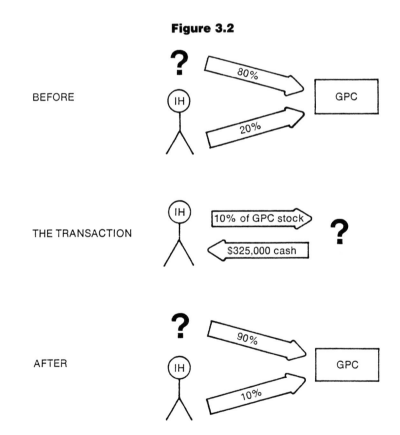

First Questions Call for Additional Facts

As is evident in the diagram, the first two critical questions appear
to be: (1) Who owns the other 80 percent of GPC stock? and (2) Who
purchased the shares from Ms. Hitchcock? The answers to these
two questions obviously call for the determination of more facts,
not for additional authority.

Suppose the CPA knows from prior work with this client that
GPC is a closely owned corporation; that is, it has been equally
owned by five local residents (including Ms. Hitchcock) since its
incorporation in 1951. However, the CPA needs to know who
purchased the stock. Under these circumstances, we can easily
imagine a conversation between Ms. Hitchcock and her CPA as
follows:

CPA:	Who purchased your stock in GPC, Ms. Hitchcock?
Mrs. H:	Ghost Publishing, Incorporated.
CPA:	That's a name I haven't heard before. Is it a local firm?
Ms. H:	Yes, it's my grandson's corporation.

From there, this conversation would proceed to establish the facts
that Ghost Publishing, Incorporated (hereafter, GPI) is indeed a
small but very profitable corporation whose stock is entirely owned by Ms. Hitchcock's favorite grandson, Alvred Hitchcock. GPI
decided to purchase the GPC stock both to guarantee its own
supply of paper and because Alvred was convinced that GPC was a
sound financial investment.

Before we proceed to examine possible authority, we should
stop to observe two apparently innocent facts that have vital importance to the resolution of this tax problem: (1) The GPC shares
were purchased from Ms. Hitchcock by GPI, and (2) GPI is owned
by Ms. Hitchcock's grandson. Unless these two facts are discovered, and their importance fully appreciated, this problem could
not proceed any further. We might also pause briefly to re-diagram
both our transaction and the after-the-transaction situation to
accommodate the new facts that we have just determined. Once
again, this diagram serves to highlight the potential problems that
lie ahead of us.

Figure 3.3

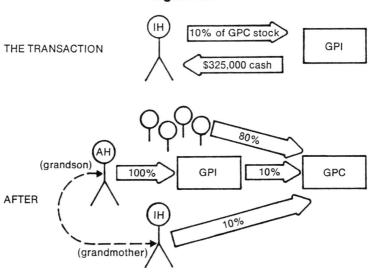

The discovery of these additional facts may begin to separate the beginner from the more experienced tax adviser. The beginner quite possibly would not modify the prior conclusion concerning Ms. Hitchcock's need to report a $300,000 long-term capital gain. An experienced researcher, however, would realize the danger implicit in sales between related parties and would want to determine whether this transaction should be treated in some other way because of the potential relationships involved. The tax adviser with extensive technical competence in the taxation of corporations and corporate shareholder relations might realize this is a potential section 304 transaction and would turn directly to that section to determine the next appropriate question: "Does section 304 apply to Ms. Hitchcock's sale of 30,000 shares of GPC stock to GPI?"

The Authority

Understanding section 304 may be difficult. However, a basic understanding of at least some of this provision is critical in determining which facts and issues in this transaction must be examined. The purpose of section 304 is to ensure that certain sales of stock in one corporation to a related corporation do not avoid the section 302 tests. As mentioned previously, the section 302 tests are used to make the distinction between distributions that are to be taxed as dividends and distributions that are to be taxed as capital gains.[5] Section 304 reads, in part, as follows:[6]

SEC. 304. REDEMPTION THROUGH USE OF RELATED
    CORPORATIONS.

(a) Treatment of Certain Stock Purchases.—

(1) Acquisition by related corporation (other than subsidiary).—
For purposes of sections 302 and 303, if—
(A) one or more persons are in control of each of two corporations, and
(B) in return for property, one of the corporations acquires stock in the other corporation from the person (or persons) so in control, then (unless paragraph (2) applies) such property shall be treated as a distribution in redemption of the stock of the corporation acquiring such stock. . . .

(2) Acquisition by subsidiary.—For purposes of sections 302 and 303, if—
(A) in return for property, one corporation acquires from a shareholder of another corporation stock in such other corporation, and
(B) the issuing corporation controls the acquiring corporation, then such property shall be treated as a distribution in redemption of the stock of the issuing corporation.

(b) Special Rules for Application of Subsection (a).—

(1) Rule for determinations under section 302(b).—In the case of any acquisition of stock to which subsection (a) of this section applies, determinations as to whether the acquisition is, by reason of section 302(b), to be treated as a distribution in part or full payment in exchange for the stock shall be made by reference to the stock of the issuing corporation. . . .

(c) Control.—

(1) In general.—For purposes of this section, control means the

---

[5] See note 2, supra.
[6] Since section 304 is a difficult provision, only those parts that are important for our illustrations are reproduced here.

ownership of stock possessing at least 50 percent of the total combined voting power of all classes of stock entitled to vote, or at least 50 percent of the total value of shares of all classes of stock. . . .

(3) Constructive Ownership.—(A) In general.—Section 318(a) (relating to constructive ownership of stock) shall apply for purposes of determining control under this section.

Although the beginner might require assistance in interpreting and applying this code section to the facts of Ms. Hitchcock's sale, every beginner must learn how to read and understand the language of the code if he or she is ever to succeed as a tax adviser.[7]

Learning how to understand the code is most certainly a time-consuming process. After a careful reading of section 304, however, even a beginner will realize that certain words and phrases deserve special attention. For example, understanding whether section 304 applies to this transaction necessarily requires (1) an understanding of sections 302 and 303, (2) the ability to identify an acquisition of stock in a controlled corporation by another controlled corporation (for example, an acquisition by a related corporation that is not a subsidiary) and an acquisition of stock of a corporation that controls the corporation acquiring the stock (such as, an acquisition of a parent corporation's stock by a subsidiary corporation), and (3) an understanding of the way in which the constructive ownership rules of section 318 are applied in determining control. For both the beginner and the experienced tax adviser, these issues constitute the next pertinent set of questions.

Additional Questions

Stated in the order in which they must be answered, these questions are as follows:

---

[7] Certainly the beginner might take comfort in knowing that even such a distinguished jurist as Learned Hand found this to be a formidable assignment. He once said: "In my own case the words of such an act as the Income Tax, for example, merely dance before my eyes in a meaningless procession: cross-reference to cross-reference, exception upon exception—couched in abstract terms that offer no handles to seize hold of—leave in my mind only a confused sense of some vitally important, but successfully concealed, purport, which it is my duty to extract, but which is within my power, if at all, only after the most inordinate expenditure of time." (Learned Hand, "Thomas Walter Swan," *Yale Law Journal* 57 [December 1947]: 169.)

1. Both before and after the sale of 30,000 shares of GPC common stock to GPI, what shares does Ms. Hitchcock own, directly and indirectly, for purposes of section 304, giving full consideration to the constructive ownership rules of section 318?

2. Does section 304 apply to this sale of stock? That is, can the sale of 30,000 shares of GPC stock to GPI by Ms. Hitchcock be considered, for purposes of section 304, as either (*a*) an acquisition by a related (but not subsidiary) corporation or (*b*) an acquisition by a subsidiary corporation?

3. If the answer to either question in (2), above, is affirmative, what is the tax effect of section 302 and/or 303 on this disposition of stock?

To solve these three questions we must turn to the constructive ownership rules found in section 318.

More Authority

Fortunately, section 318 does not, at least at the outset, appear to be as confusing as section 304. Section 318 reads in part as follows:[8]

SEC. 318. CONSTRUCTIVE OWNERSHIP OF STOCK.

(a) General Rule.—For purposes of those provisions of this subchapter to which the rules contained in this section are expressly made applicable—

    (1) Members of family.—
        (A) In general.—An individual shall be considered as owning the stock owned, directly or indirectly, by or for—
            (i) his spouse (other than a spouse who is legally separated from the individual under a decree of divorce or separate maintenance), and
            (ii) his children, grandchildren, and parents.

    (2) Attribution from partnership, estates, trusts, and corporations.—

            • • • •

---

[8] Here, again, only the pertinent parts of section 318 are reproduced.

(C) From corporations.—If 50 percent or more in value of the stock in a corporation is owned, directly or indirectly, by or for any person, such person shall be considered as owning the stock owned, directly or indirectly, by or for such corporation, in that proportion which the value of the stock which such person so owns bears to the value of all the stock in such corporation.

(3) Attribution to partnerships, estates, trusts, and corporations.—

• • • •

(C) To corporations.—If 50 percent or more in value of the stock in a corporation is owned, directly or indirectly, by or for any person, such corporation shall be considered as owning the stock owned, directly or indirectly, by or for such person.

• • • •

(5) Operating rules.—
(A) In general.—Except as provided in subparagraphs (B) and (C), stock constructively owned by a person by reason of the application of paragraph (1), (2), (3), or (4), shall, for purposes of applying paragraphs (1), (2), (3), and (4), be considered as actually owned by such person.

More Questions and More Facts

A careful reading of section 318 suggests the need to determine some additional facts before proceeding toward a solution. More specifically, we must know exactly who it is that owns the other 80 percent of GPC. Earlier it was stated that GPC was "equally owned by five local residents." After reading the quoted portion of section 318, it should be obvious that we must ask if any of the other four GPC owners are related to Ms. Hitchcock within any of the family relationships described in section 318(a)(1). At the same time, we probably should make certain that none of the other four original owners has sold any of the original stock in GPC. If they have, we also must determine the relationship, if any, between those purchasers and Ms. Hitchcock. Let us assume that two of the other four owners of GPC are Ms. Hitchcock's sons and that all of the other four original owners continue to own all of their shares in GPC. Having determined this, we can now reach our first tentative conclusions.

First Tentative Conclusions

Specifically, we are now prepared to answer the first of the three questions suggested on page 70. "Both before and after the sale of 30,000 shares of GPC common stock to GPI, what shares does Ms. Hitchcock own, directly and indirectly, for purposes of section 304, giving full consideration to the constructive ownership rules of section 318?" Before the sale, Ms. Hitchcock is deemed to own 60 percent of GPC (20 percent actually and 40 percent constructively), since pursuant to section 318(a)(1)(A)(ii), she is deemed to own the stock of GPC that her two sons own. Furthermore, Ms. Hitchcock is deemed to own 100 percent of GPI (all constructively) because under the same authority, she is deemed to own the stock her grandson owns. After the sale, Ms. Hitchcock is still deemed to own 100 percent of GPI because of her grandson's ownership in that corporation. For the beginner, Ms. Hitchcock's ownership in GPC after the sale may be unexpected. First, pursuant to section 318(a)(2)(C), Alvred is deemed to own the 30,000 shares of GPC that GPI purchased. Furthermore, as mentioned previously, Ms. Hitchcock is treated as owning the stock owned by her grandson. Pursuant to section 318(a)(5)(A), this includes the stock that Alvred is deemed to own.[9] This means, of course, that Ms. Hitchcock is, for purposes of section 304, deemed to own that which she just sold. Thus, she owns 60 percent of GPC (10 percent actually, 40 percent constructively through her two sons, and 10 percent constructively through GPI and her grandson). In summary, Ms.

---

[9] The only exception to this is stated in the operating rules of section 318(a)(5)(B), which reads as follows: "Stock constructively owned by an individual by reason of the application of paragraph (1) [that is, by family attribution] shall not be considered as owned by him for purposes of again applying paragraph (1) in order to make another the constructive owner of such stock." Since Alvred's indirect ownership of GPC shares comes about by application of paragraph (2)(C) of section 318 and not by application of paragraph (1), section 318(a)(1)(A)(ii) requires that Ms. Ima Hitchcock also include in her indirect ownership any shares that GPI owns.

Hitchcock is treated as owning 60 percent of GPC and 100 percent of GPI both before and after the sale of her stock.[10]

Having made this determination, we can now also answer the second of the three questions posed earlier: "Does section 304 apply to this sale of stock?" In other words, is the purchase of the 30,000 shares by GPI either an acquisition by a related, but nonsubsidiary corporation (that is, does Ms. Hitchcock control both GPC and GPI), or an acquisition by a subsidiary corporation (that is, is GPI controlled by GPC?). The answer to this question depends upon the term "control."

Pursuant to section 304(c)(1), control is defined as the ownership of at least 50 percent of the stock of a corporation, taking into account the constructive ownership rules of section 318. Since, under section 318, Ms. Hitchcock is deemed to own 60 percent of GPC and 100 percent of GPI, she is in control of both corporations. Thus, the purchase of stock by GPI is the acquisition of stock in a controlled corporation by another controlled corporation and section 304(a)(1) applies to the transaction.[11]

The careful reader will have observed that, even at this point, we have not yet determined the correct tax treatment of Ms. Hitchcock's stock disposition. Before we can make that determination, we must ask still more questions.

More Questions, More Authority

Code section 304(a)(1) simply provides that Ms. Hitchcock's sale should be treated as a distribution in redemption of stock, and it

---

[10] Incidentally, the revised diagram of the facts pictured in figure 3.3 actually suggests this conclusion with much less confusion than do all of the words of the code. Perhaps one picture can be worth a thousand words. Note that simply following the dotted lines of that diagram back from Alvred to Ms. Hitchcock shows that the conclusion just reached is not really so farfetched afterall.

[11] Taken literally, this transaction is also the acquisition of parent stock by a subsidiary corporation since, using the constructive ownership rules, GPC controls GPI. However, for reasons that go well beyond this illustration, a section 304 parent-subsidiary transaction occurs only if the stock of the subsidiary is owned by the parent, either actually, or constructively in a direct chain of ownership. For a discussion of this issue, see Bittker and Eustice, *Federal Taxation of Corporations and Shareholders, Fifth Edition*, p. 9–58. See also Stewart and Randall, "A Proposed Solution to the Statutory Overlap of Sections 304(a)(1) and 304(a)(2)," *The Journal of Corporate Taxation*, 125 (1982).

suggests that we look to two additional code sections to see what that means. Our next question, then, must be: "If Ms. Hitchcock's disposition of GPC stock is to be treated as a stock redemption under section 302 and/or 303, what, if anything, do those sections say about the tax treatment of the transaction?"

On further searching we could quickly discover that section 303 deals only with distributions in redemption of stock to pay death taxes. Clearly, the facts of our problem do not suggest anything about Ms. Hitchcock's making this disposition to pay death taxes. Thus, we may safely conclude that section 303 is not applicable to our solution. We turn, therefore, to section 302, which reads, in pertinent part, as follows:

SEC. 302. DISTRIBUTIONS IN REDEMPTION OF STOCK.

(a) General Rule.—If a corporation redeems its stock (within the meaning of section 317(b)), and if paragraph (1), (2), (3), or (4) of subsection (b) applies, such redemption shall be treated as a distribution in part or full payment in exchange for the stock.

(b) Redemptions Treated as Exchanges.—

(1) Redemptions not equivalent to dividends.—Subsection (a) shall apply if the redemption is not essentially equivalent to a dividend.

(2) Substantially disproportionate redemption of stock.—
(A) In general.—Subsection (a) shall apply if the distribution is substantially disproportionate with respect to the shareholder.
(B) Limitation.—This paragraph shall not apply unless immediately after the redemption the shareholder owns less than 50 percent of the total combined voting power of all classes of stock entitled to vote.
(C) Definitions.—For purposes of this paragraph, the distribution is substantially disproportionate if—
(i) the ratio which the voting stock of the corporation owned by the shareholder immediately after the redemption bears to all the voting stock of the corporation at such time,
is less than 80 percent of—
(ii) the ratio which the voting stock of the corporation owned by the shareholder immediately before the redemption bears to all of the voting stock of the corporation at such time.

For purposes of this paragraph, no distribution shall be treated as substantially disproportionate unless the shareholder's ownership of the common stock of the corporation (whether voting or nonvoting) after and before redemption also meets the 80 percent requirement of the preceding sentence.

(3) Termination of shareholder's interest.—Subsection (a) shall apply if the redemption is in complete redemption of all of the stock of the corporation owned by the shareholder.

(4) Redemption from a noncorporate shareholder in partial liquidation.—Subsection (a) shall apply to a distribution if such distribution is—(A) in redemption of stock held by a shareholder who is not a corporation, and (B) in partial liquidation of the distributing corporation.

• • • •

(c) Constructive Ownership of Stock.—

(1) In general.—Except as provided in paragraph (2) of this subsection, section 318(a) shall apply in determining the ownership of stock for purposes of this section.

• • • •

(d) Redemptions Treated as Distributions of Property.—Except as otherwise provided in this subchapter, if a corporation redeems its stock (within the meaning of section 317(b)), and if subsection (a) of this section does not apply, such redemption shall be treated as a distribution of property to which section 301 applies.

Obviously, this new and relatively lengthy code section simply brings more new questions to mind. The careful reader should observe that section 302(a) provides a general rule that a redemption will be treated as *"a distribution in part or full payment in exchange for the stock"* if the conditions of any one of four paragraphs are satisfied [emphasis added]. This means that if the conditions of any one of the four subsections can be satisfied, a taxpayer from whom stock is redeemed can treat the disposition as a sale. In most instances this would result in a capital gain computed by subtracting the basis of the stock redeemed from the amount received. The general rules of subsection (a) say nothing, however, about the proper tax treatment of the redemption proceeds if those conditions cannot be satisfied. That possibility is treated in subsection (d), which says, "Such redemption shall be treated as *a distribution of property to which section 301 applies*" [emphasis added]. On further investigation, we discover that section 301 generally provides dividend treatment for properties distributed by a corporation to its shareholder. This means, of course, that the redeemed shareholder would have to report the entire amount of the distribution as ordinary income rather than computing a capital gain on the sale of stock.

If we continued to examine the facts of our illustrative problem in detail against all of the rules of section 302, we would have to proceed through another relatively complex set of code provisions not unlike those we have just examined in some detail. Because this procedure is no longer new, and because we really are interested only in demonstrating the complex relationship that exists between facts, authorities, and tax questions, we shall discontinue our detailed step-by-step approach and state the remainder of this analysis in more general terms. We can begin such a summary treatment of our problem as follows:

1. *Question:* Is Ms. Hitchcock's disposition a redemption within the meaning of section 317(b), as required by section 302(a)?

   Authority: Section 317(b) reads as follows:

   > Redemption of stock.—For purposes of this part, stock shall be treated as redeemed by a corporation if the corporation acquires its stock from a shareholder in exchange for property, whether or not the stock so acquired is cancelled, retired, or held as treasury stock.

   Conclusion: The intended meaning of this section is not obvious. It seems to suggest that what the acquiring corporation does with shares it acquires from its shareholders will in no way effect the classification of the stock acquisition as a stock redemption. Furthermore, the section seems initially not to apply to our case because it refers to a corporation acquiring *its* stock from a shareholder. A more general reflection on how this section is made applicable to related corporations through section 304 suggests, however, that these words must be stretched to include the stock of a related corporation if the purpose of section 304 is not to be circumvented. Hence, we would likely conclude that Ms.

Hitchcock's disposition probably is a redemption within the meaning of section 317(b).

2. *Question:* Is Ms. Hitchcock's sale (redemption) of 30,000 shares of GPC stock to GPI a redemption that falls within the meaning of any one of the exceptions of section 302(b)(1) through (b)(4)?

Authority: Read again section 302(b)(1) through (b)(4) as quoted previously.

Conclusions (in reverse order):

a. Upon further investigation of the facts, it is found that GPC is not involved in a partial liquidation. Thus, section 302(b)(4) is not applicable.

b. Clearly, the exception of section 302(b)(3) is not applicable. Ms. Hitchcock continues to own directly 30,000 shares of GPC stock even after her sale of 30,000 shares to GPI.

c. Clearly, the exception of section 302(b)(2) is not applicable. Considering her indirect ownership as well as her direct ownership, Ms. Hitchcock owns after the sale exactly what she owned before the sale. (Note that section 302(c) requires that the attribution rules of section 318 be applied to stock redemptions.)

The Final Question

Without having carefully examined each of the intermediate questions and authorities suggested above, the reader might have some trouble in stating the final question. If you took the time to do so, however, it would seem that Ms. Hitchcock's final question might be stated thus: "Is Ms. Hitchcock's sale of 30,000 shares of GPC to GPI properly treated as a 'redemption not essentially equivalent to a dividend' as that phrase is used in section 302(b)(1)?" The implied conclusion stems importantly from (1) the requirement in section 304 (with assistance from section 318) that Ms. Hitchcock's apparent sale be treated not as a sale at all but as a redemption of a corporation's stock, and (2) the requirement in section 302 that a stock redemption be treated as a dividend unless one of the four exceptions in section 302(b) is satisfied.

Any detailed assessment of the authority that is pertinent to an interpretation of section 302(b)(1) would lead us well into the objective of chapter 5 of this tax study. Consequently, we shall not undertake that assessment here. We shall note, in passing, some general observations that would become pertinent to a resolution of the problem were we actually to undertake a detailed assessment. First, the Treasury regulations indicate that the application of section 302(b)(1) depends upon the facts and circumstances in each case.[12] Second, in the Treasury regulations the only example of a stock redemption qualifying for exchange treatment under section 302(b)(1) is as follows: "For example, if a shareholder owns only nonvoting stock of a corporation which is not section 306 stock and which is limited and preferred as to dividends and in liquidation, and one-half of such stock is redeemed, the distribution will ordinarily meet the requirements of paragraph (1) of section 302(b) but will not meet the requirements of paragraphs (2), (3), or (4) of such section."[13] This example obviously lends no support to the case at hand since the facts of Ms. Hitchcock's ownership are radically different from those described in this regulation. Third, in *Davis*[14], the Supreme Court held that the business purpose of a transaction is irrelevant in determining dividend equivalence. In summary, the authority for granting Ms. Hitchcock sale (that is, capital gain) treatment by operation of the exception stated in section 302(b)(1) appears to be relatively weak. And if the exception of section 302(b)(1) does not apply, Ms. Hitchcock must report $325,000 dividend income by operation of section 302(d).[15]

Summary

The foregoing example demonstrates the critical role of facts, the interdependency of facts and rules, and the elusive nature of pertinent tax questions. If all the facts are discovered and all the rules are known and understood, apparently simple transactions

---

[12] Treas. Reg. Sec. 1.302-2(b).

[13] Treas. Reg. Sec. 1.302-2(a).

[14] *U.S. v. Davis*, 397 U.S. 301, 70-1 USTC ¶9289 (1970).

[15] Our conclusion assumes a sufficiency of earnings and profits as required by section 316, which defines the word *dividend*. In actual practice, of course, this would constitute another critical fact determination.

have a way of creating relatively complex tax problems in all too many situations. The tax adviser must ask the right questions, not because he or she desires to convert a simple situation into a complex problem and a larger fee, but because the correct reporting of a tax result depends so directly upon asking those questions. Questions often evolve from fact determination to rule application. For example, in our illustration the first critical questions were (1) Who purchased the shares? and (2) Who owned the purchaser? Certainly those are fact questions. Nevertheless, unless a person has some appreciation of the applicable rules, it would be highly unlikely for that person to continue to ask the right questions. After the facts are determined, the critical questions concerned the application of rules to known facts; for example, (1) Does section 304 apply to Ms. Hitchcock's sale of 30,000 shares of GPC to GPI? (2) Does section 318 apply to make this transaction a section 304 brother-sister transaction? and (3) Does the exception of section 302(b)(1) apply to this same disposition? Each question appears to be more esoteric than the preceding one. Yet, to an important degree every question depends upon the tax adviser's knowledge of the authority that is applicable to the given fact situation.

4

... reasons are as two graines of wheate,
hid in two bushels of chaffe;
you shall seeke all day ere you finde them...

WILLIAM SHAKESPEARE

Locating Appropriate Authority

In chapters 2 and 3 we discussed the importance of facts and the methodology employed to delineate questions that must be answered to solve tax problems successfully. To determine a technically correct answer to a tax question, the tax adviser may consult statutory, administrative, judicial, and, in some instances, editorial authority. This process consists of two distinct phases: (1) the tax adviser must locate the appropriate authority, and (2) he or she must assess the importance of that authority, augment it if it is found to be incomplete, and, on occasion, choose between conflicting authorities. The following pages will identify the various kinds of tax authorities and ways to locate them, and chapter 5 will concentrate on the assessment of authorities. The basic types of tax law include: legislative or statutory authority, administrative authority, and judicial law. Additionally, editorial interpretation, while not authoritative tax law per se, serves a valuable role in locating and assessing the law.

The Tax-Legislation Process

Our present income taxing system began with the Tariff Act of October 3, 1913. Since then, numerous revenue acts have been enacted into law. Due to their number and increasing complexity, existing revenue acts were codified in 1939 into a single document called the Internal Revenue Code. The Internal Revenue Code of 1939 was revised and simplified again in the Internal Revenue Code of 1954. In 1986, the TRA '86 created the Internal Revenue Code of 1986, which revised the 1954 Internal Revenue Code. During the periods 1939 to 1954, 1954 to 1986, and 1986 to the present, all revenue acts enacted into law simply amend the 1939, the 1954, and the 1986 Internal Revenue Codes, respectively.

By virtue of Article I, section 7, of the U.S. Constitution, all revenue bills must originate in the House of Representatives and cannot be sent to the Senate until the House has completed action on the bill. After introduction, most of the actual work on a revenue bill takes place in the House Ways and Means Committee. In the case of major bills, public hearings are scheduled. The first and most prominent witness during these hearings usually is the secretary of the Treasury, representing the executive branch of government. Upon conclusion of the hearings, the committee goes into executive session, and, after tentative conclusions have been reached, prepares the House Ways and Means Committee report. This report includes the proposed bill drafted in legislative language, an assessment of its effect on revenue, and a general explanation of the provisions in the bill. The report, prepared by the staff of the House Ways and Means Committee, details the reasons for the committee's actions, and, therefore, constitutes an important reference source for the courts, the Internal Revenue Service, and practitioners in determining legislative intent in connection with each section of the bill. Upon completion of the committee report, the bill is reported to the floor of the House for action. Prior to 1975, revenue legislation usually was considered "privileged" business and, as such, had priority over other matters on the floor. In the past, the approval of the Rules Committee usually was sought before a bill was placed on the floor. This procedure was followed so that a tax bill could be debated under the "closed rule"; thus, amendments from the floor were forbidden unless the Ways and Means Committee approved them. Recent revenue legislation has been debated under a "modified closed rule," which allows for a limited set of amendments to be approved for a floor vote by the Ways and Means Committee.

After approval by the House, a tax bill is sent to the Senate, where it is immediately referred to the Finance Committee. If it is a major bill, the Senate Finance Committee schedules its own hearings and prepares its own committee report. This report, prepared by the staff of the Senate Finance Committee, also constitutes part of the legislative history of a tax act. Debate on the floor of the Senate proceeds with few restraints; consequently, Senate amendments to a revenue bill are commonplace. Obviously, the Senate Finance Committee report will not disclose the intent of Congress on the amended portion of a bill. For those portions it becomes necessary to consult the *Congressional Record* to understand the reasons for the amendment.

If the House and Senate pass different versions of the same bill, further congressional action is necessary. After the House adopts a motion to disagree with the Senate version of a revenue bill, a conference committee is appointed to iron out the differences. Like the House Ways and Means Committee and the Senate Finance Committee, the conference committee may prepare its own committee report, concentrating on the areas of disagreement. This report also becomes part of the legislative history. Statements made on the floor of either chamber prior to the final vote on the conference report are entered in the *Congressional Record*. These statements often shed light on congressional intent for the amended sections. In addition to the committee reports, the staff of the Joint Committee on Taxation prepares its own explanation of major tax statutes.[1] These explanations are typically written after the new bill has been enacted into law. Many tax advisers find these explanations very useful. Technically, the *Blue Book* is not part of the legislative history of a tax act. However, it does constitute substantial authority for purposes of avoiding the penalty imposed by section 6662 for the substantial understatement of

---

[1] Sometimes this explanation by the staff of the Joint Committee on Taxation is referred to as the *Blue Book*.

income tax.[2] After approval of the conference bill by both the House and the Senate, the bill is sent to the President to be signed.[3]

To illustrate how a tax adviser might utilize his or her knowledge of the foregoing process, let us refer to the TRA '86, which was signed by the President as Public Law 99-514 on October 22, 1986, amending the Internal Revenue Code of 1954. One of the major changes introduced by the Act involved section 382 which deals with limiting net operating loss carryforwards of a loss corporation following a change of ownership. In general, one of the functions of this section is to limit the deductibility of net operating losses in any year ending after the ownership change to an amount that is equal to the value of the corporation before the ownership change, multiplied by the long-term tax-exempt rate.

Section 382(e) states that the value of the loss corporation is the value of the stock of the corporation (including nonvoting limited preferred stock) immediately before the ownership change. Furthermore, any redemption or other corporate contraction that occurs in connection with the ownership change is to be taken into account in determining this value. Finally, section 382(k)(5) states that the term *value*, when used in this section means *fair* market value.

The determination of fair market value, of course, can be subject to various interpretations; yet, no further guidance is given in the statute. Section 382(m) does authorize the Secretary of the Treasury to issue regulations as necessary to carry out the purposes of the section. To date, no regulations addressing the definition of fair market value have been issued. Thus, a taxpayer, faced with the question of what constitutes fair market value for this purpose, might consult the committee reports accompanying the TRA 86.

The Conference Committee report states that the intent of the committee was that the price at which the stock changes hands in an arm's-length transaction would be evidence, but not conclusive evidence, of the value of the stock. Through an example, the report expresses the concern that the price paid for a block of stock which carries with it effective control of the corporation might not be an

---

[2] Treas. Reg. Sec. 1.6662-4(d)(3)(iii).

[3] For a more complete discussion of the legislative process, see Joseph A. Pechman, *Federal Tax Policy*, 5th ed. (Washington, D.C.: The Brookings Institution, 1987).

appropriate measure of the value of all the corporation's stock.[4] Although this report does not answer all questions that may arise dealing with this issue, it does, at least, provide some additional guidance to what is given in the statute itself.

Accessing Public Documents

Committee reports can be obtained in a number of ways. The official report of each committee (House Ways and Means, Senate Finance, and Conference) is published by the Government Printing Office (GPO). These reports are available in the government documents section of any library that has been designated as an official depository. Committee reports appear in the *Cumulative Bulletin*. They can also be found in the *U.S. Code Congressional and Administrative News* (USCCAN), published by West Publishing Company. The *Blue Books* of major tax acts appear in the *Cumulative Bulletin*. In addition, major revenue acts—such as the Tax Reform Act of 1986, the Revenue Act of 1987, and the Technical and Miscellaneous Revenue Act of 1988—are published with partial or full texts of the accompanying committee reports by various publishing companies (for example, Commerce Clearing House, Inc.). The editors of the Rabkin and Johnson tax service (*Federal Income, Gift and Estate Taxation*) also typically extract important segments of committee reports and intersperse them among the code sections contained in the "Code" volumes of the service.

At times, it becomes necessary to trace the history of a particular 1954 code section to the 1939 code or to previous revenue acts. In Code Volume I of the tax service, *Standard Federal Tax Reports*, published by Commerce Clearing House (CCH), the researcher will find helpful cross reference tables that have been prepared as aids in comparing the provisions of the Internal Revenue Code of 1954 with provisions of the Internal Revenue Code of 1939. A cross-reference table between the Internal Revenue Codes of 1986 and 1954 is not provided since the Internal Revenue Code of 1986 kept the numbering system and organization of the 1954 Internal Revenue Code. Tables cross-referencing the acts that have supplemented the 1954 and 1986 Codes are also provided.

Barton's *Federal Tax Laws Correlated* (FTLC), a multivolume

---

[4] U.S. Congress, Conference Report, 99th Congress, 2d sess., 1986, H. Rept. 3838, p. II-137.

reference service, is a useful tool in guiding the researcher from the 1954 code to the 1939 code and prior acts. Barton's FTLC gives the researcher citations to the official committee reports, the USCCAN, and *Cumulative Bulletin* where applicable segments of committee reports can be found. Another source for references to committee reports is *Seidman's Legislative History of Federal Income Tax and Excess Profits Tax Laws*. This three-volume work contains the legislative history of tax statutes enacted from 1861 to 1953, including the original text of revenue acts and 1939 code sections, with excerpts from applicable committee reports. Yet another source of recent legislative history of the code is Tax Management's *Primary Sources*, consisting of five series. Series I is a multivolume legislative history of the Internal Revenue Code from the TRA '69 through 1975. Series II is a multivolume legislative history of the Internal Revenue Code from the Tax Reform Act of 1976 through 1977. Series III is a multivolume series covering the history from the Revenue Act of 1978 through the Miscellaneous Revenue Act of 1980. The multivolume Series IV includes the legislative history from the Economic Recovery Tax Act of 1981 up to the Tax Reform Act of 1986. Finally, Series V covers the legislative history of selected sections of the Internal Revenue Code as affected by the TRA '86 and subsequent law.[5]

Well-informed tax advisers should stay abreast of congressional activities involving tax statutes in order to determine the potential positive and negative tax effects such developments may harbor with respect to their clients. One effective means of keeping in touch with such daily congressional tax activities is through *Tax Notes*, a weekly newsletter published by Tax Analysts, Arlington, Virginia. For a more comprehensive listing of tax newsletters, see Exhibit 4.14, pages 134 and 135 of this chapter.

The Internal Revenue Code

All federal statutes passed by Congress are compiled and published in the *United States Code*. Title 26 of the *United States Code*

---

[5] Walter E. Barton and Carroll W. Browning, *Federal Tax Laws Correlated* (Boston: Warren, Gorham & Lamont, Inc., 1969); J.S. Seidman, *Seidman's Legislative History of Federal Income Tax Laws, 1851–1938 and Seidman's Legislative History of Federal Income and Excess Profits Tax Laws 1939–1953* (New York: Prentice Hall, 1959); Tax Management, *Primary Sources* (Washington, D.C.: Bureau of National Affairs, 1987).

contains the statutes that authorize the Treasury Department, specifically the Internal Revenue Service, to collect taxes for the federal government. The present code is commonly known as the Internal Revenue Code of 1986. Prior to 1986, statutory authority for the collection of taxes rested with the Internal Revenue Code of 1954. Although the Internal Revenue Code is amended almost annually, the designation 1986 remains fixed with the present Internal Revenue Code.

The Internal Revenue Code of 1986 is divided into the following segments:

Subtitles	*Chapters*
A. Income taxes	1–6
B. Estate and Gift Taxes	11–14
C. Employment Taxes	21–25
D. Miscellaneous Excise Taxes	31–47
E. Alcohol, Tobacco, and Certain Other Excise Taxes	51–54
F. Procedure and Administration	61–80
G. The Joint Committee on Taxation	91–92
H. Financing of Presidential Election Campaigns	95–96
I. Trust Fund Code	98
J. Coal Industry Health Benefits	99

The bulk of the income tax provisions is found in chapter 1 of subtitle A. Chapter 1 is divided into twenty-two subchapters, A through V. (Effectively, however, chapter 1 currently consists of only twenty subchapters, since subchapters R and U have been repealed.) These subchapter designations are often used by tax practitioners as part of their everyday vocabulary to identify general areas of income taxation. Some of the most frequently used designations are as follows:

Subchapter	
C	Corporate distributions and adjustments
F	Exempt organizations
J	Estates, trusts, beneficiaries, and decedents
K	Partners and partnerships

(continued)

Subchapter

N   Taxation of multinational corporations

S   Tax status election of small business operations

Section numbers are additional subdivisions of the Internal Revenue Code and run consecutively through the entire code. For example, subchapter A, which deals with the determination of an entity's tax liability, includes section numbers 1 through 59A. To the extent that section numbers are unassigned, the arrangement is suitable for future expansion of the code. The reader should also note that section numbers give a clue to which general income tax topic is involved. For example, code section numbers in the 300 series indicate that the section will deal with the topic of corporate distributions and adjustments (subchapter C of chapter 1). Each section is further broken down into categories (see exhibit 4.1).

The Internal Revenue Code is published annually in paperback editions by various publishing companies, including Commerce Clearing House, Inc. (CCH), Research Institute of America (RIA), Clark Boardman Callaghan (publishers of *Mertens Law of Federal Taxation*), and Matthew Bender & Co. (publishers of *Rabkin and Johnson's Federal Income, Gift and Estate Taxation*). The code is also published in most multivolume tax services, either separately in a looseleaf volume or serially in several volumes. In the latter case, the volume includes editorial comments arranged on a topical and/or section number basis.

Administrative Interpretations

Within the executive branch, the Treasury Department has the responsibility of implementing the tax statutes passed by Congress. This function is specifically carried out by the Internal Revenue Service division of the Treasury Department. The duties of the Internal Revenue Service (IRS) are two-fold: first, the statutes must be interpreted according to the intent of Congress, and second, the statutes must be enforced.

The interpretive duties of the Treasury and IRS range from the general to the specific. Treasury regulations are written in broad, general terms to explain the provisions of the Internal Revenue

Exhibit 4.1

[Sec. 318]

SEC. 318. CONSTRUCTIVE OWNERSHIP OF STOCK.

[Sec. 318(a)]

(a) GENERAL RULE.—For purposes of those provisions of this subchapter to which the rules contained in this section are expressly made applicable—

(1) MEMBERS OF FAMILY.—

(A) IN GENERAL.—An individual shall be considered as owning the stock owned, directly or indirectly, by or for—

(i) his spouse (other than a spouse who is legally separated from the individual under a decree of divorce or separate maintenance), and

(ii) his children, grandchildren, and parents.

(B) EFFECT OF ADOPTION.—For purposes of subparagraph (A) (ii), a legally adopted child of an individual shall be treated as a child of such individual by blood.

(2) ATTRIBUTION FROM PARTNERSHIPS, ESTATES, TRUSTS, AND CORPORATIONS.—

(A) FROM PARTNERSHIPS AND ESTATES.—Stock owned, directly or indirectly, by or for a partnership or estate shall be considered as owned proportionately by its partners or beneficiaries.

(B) FROM TRUSTS.—

(i) Stock owned, directly or indirectly, by or for a trust (other than an employees' trust described in section 401(a) which is exempt from tax under section 501(a)) shall be considered as owned by its beneficiaries in proportion to the actuarial interest of such beneficiaries in such trust.

(ii) Stock owned, directly or indirectly, by or for any portion of a trust of which a person is considered the owner under subpart E of part I of subchapter J (relating to grantors and others treated as substantial owners) shall be considered as owned by such person.

(C) FROM CORPORATIONS.—If 50 percent or more in value of the stock in a corporation is owned, directly or indirectly, by or for any person, such person shall be considered as owning the stock owned, directly or indirectly, by or for such corporation, in that proportion which the value of the stock which such person so owns bears to the value of all the stock in such corporation.

Section 318

Subsection (a)

Paragraph (2)

Subparagraph (B)

Clause (ii)

Code. Revenue rulings, on the other hand, interpret the code only with respect to specific facts and are inapplicable to fact situations that deviate from those stated in a particular revenue ruling.

Treasury Regulations

Section 7805 of the Internal Revenue Code gives the secretary of the Treasury or his delegate a general power to prescribe necessary rules and regulations to administer the tax laws as passed by Congress. In addition to section 7805, specific reference is made throughout the code to the effect that the secretary or his delegate shall prescribe such regulations as may be necessary to carry out the purpose of a specific chapter or section.

Treasury regulations may be divided into regulations that are almost statutory and those that are interpretive. Examples of "statutory regulations" are those promulgated under section 1502 dealing with consolidated tax returns. Because of the complexity of the subject, Congress failed to legislate in detail in the area of consolidated tax returns and delegated this responsibility to the secretary of the Treasury or his delegate. Apparently, in 1954, Congress had second thoughts concerning the delegation of legislative power to the secretary. Had the 1954 code been enacted in the form in which it passed the House of Representatives, the consolidated return regulations actually would have been written into the statute. The Senate Finance Committee disagreed, however, and in the conference committee the view of the Senate prevailed.[6] Due to the complexity and detail involved in the consolidated return regulations, Congress apparently felt that revisions and amendments should be left under the purview of the Treasury.

Taxpayers electing to file consolidated returns must execute a consent form in which they agree to be bound by the provisions of the regulations.[7] Presumably, such an agreement leaves almost no appeal from the provisions of the consolidated return regulations

---

[6] U.S., Congress, Senate, Committee on Finance, 83d Cong., 2d sess., 1954, S. Rept. 1622, p. 120.

[7] Treas. Reg. Sec. 1.1502-75.

and, in that sense, gives them a position more nearly "statutory" than the interpretive regulations.

The purpose of the interpretive regulations is to clarify the language of the code as passed by Congress. At times, the wording of the regulations is almost identical to the language of the code or the accompanying committee report and is of little assistance. In recent years, however, the Treasury has made frequent attempts to add helpful examples to the regulations. In effect, even the interpretive regulations may come to have the force of law. However, technically, if they contradict the intent of Congress, they can be overturned by the courts.[8] Nevertheless, the odds are very much against the taxpayer or his or her representative who tries to win a case against the Internal Revenue Service solely by attempting to declare a specific Treasury regulation to be in conflict with the code or the intent of Congress. For a more complete discussion on the status of Treasury regulations, see chapter 5.

Regulations must be issued in proposed form before they are published in final form. Proposed regulations for a new or existing part of the code may begin with the formation of a special task force that may include representatives of the IRS, the American Bar Association, the American Institute of Certified Public Accountants, and other knowledgeable individuals. This was the case with the regulations under section 1502. Usually, however, regulations are prepared solely by members of the Treasury Department. Interested parties generally are given at least thirty days from the date the proposed regulations appear in the *Federal Register* to submit objections or suggestions.[9] Depending upon the controversy surrounding a proposed regulation, it will, after the given time period, be either withdrawn and issued in permanent form or amended and reissued as a new proposed regulation.

Temporary regulations are periodically issued to provide prompt guidance in an area where the tax law has changed. These

---

[8] See, for example, *W.W. Marett*, 325 F.2d 28 (CA-5, 1963).

[9] According to the Technical and Miscellaneous Revenue Act of 1988, (adding Code Sec. 7805(f)), the Secretary of the Treasury is required to submit all proposed regulations to the Administrator of the Small Business Administration for comment. The administrator will have four weeks from the date of submission to respond.

regulations, even though not subject to the same review and comment procedures, have the same force of law as final regulations. In the past, temporary regulations could remain in effect for an indefinite period. However, currently, the period of time temporary regulations may remain effective is limited to three years. In addition, a temporary regulation that is issued must also be issued as a proposed regulation.[10] In summary, the tax adviser should know that temporary regulations are in full force from the day they are issued; proposed regulations are merely issued for comment and review purposes.

Permanent regulations are initially published as official Treasury Decisions (T.D.) and appear in the *Federal Register*. They subsequently are reprinted by the Government Printing Office in codified form and are officially cited as Title 26 of the *Code of Federal Regulations* (26 C.F.R. . . . .). Various publishing companies periodically publish paperback editions of the Treasury regulations.

The identifying number of a specific part of the regulations can be divided into three segments, as follows:

Treas. Reg. Sec. 1.1245-2(a)(3)(ii)

Segment   I   II   III

Segment I indicates that the regulation deals either with a specific tax or with a procedural rule. Title 26 of the *Code of Federal Regulations* uses the following designations as the identification numbers for what we call "segment I" of a correct citation of a Treasury regulation:

Part 1	Income Tax
Part 20	Estate Tax
Part 25	Gift Tax
Part 31	Employment Tax
Parts 48 or 49	Excise Taxes
Part 301	Administrative and Procedural
Part 601	Statement of Procedural Rules

---

[10] Section 7805(e).

Segment II simply coincides with the specific code section that the regulation interprets. Thus, in the above example, one can determine that the regulation cited (1) deals with the income tax (because of the prefix 1) and (2) refers specifically to section 1245 of the Internal Revenue Code. Segment III represents the sequence of the regulation and a breakdown of its content. Thus, segment III in the example refers to paragraph (a), subparagraph (3), subdivision (ii) of the second regulation under section 1245. Generally, there is no direct correlation between the sequence designation of the Internal Revenue Code and the organization of a Treasury regulation. For instance, code section 1245(c) discusses "Adjustment to Basis," while the interpretive discussion of the same topic is found in Treas. Reg. Sec. 1.1245-5.

Frequently, there is a considerable delay between the time a particular section is added to the code and the time when the Treasury issues proposed, temporary, or permanent regulations. As mentioned previously, if this is the case, taxpayers must rely on the committee reports in order to obtain any guidance the reports may contain.

Occasionally, when a major change of a particular code section has been enacted and the secretary of the Treasury subsequently issues new regulations, two sets of regulations will appear covering the same code section for a time. The regulations currently published under section 170, on charitable contributions, are a case in point. Due to the major revisions in the TRA '69, new regulations were issued in 1972 to govern section 170. New regulations are distinguishable from those applicable to tax years prior to 1970 through addition of a capital letter A. That is, Treas. Reg. Sec. 1.170A-1 applies to years after 1969; Treas. Reg. Sec. 1.170-1, to years before 1970. Conversely, pre-1966 section 1502 regulations, still published by CCH in their paperback volumes, are identified with the capital letter A. The post-1965 regulations are without the identifying notation. To identify current and noncurrent regulations, the researcher must be aware of this procedure.

Revenue Rulings

Another interpretive tool used by the Internal Revenue Service to apply tax laws to specific situations is the revenue ruling. A revenue ruling is an official interpretation by the IRS of the internal revenue laws, related statutes, tax treaties, and regulations.[11] Revenue rulings are often the result of rulings to taxpayers, technical advice to district offices, court decisions, and so on.[12] Care is taken to protect the identity of the actual taxpayer making the initial request to comply with statutory provisions prohibiting the disclosure of information obtained from the public.

Initially, revenue rulings are published in the weekly *Internal Revenue Bulletin*. The same rulings later appear in the permanently bound *Cumulative Bulletin*, a semiannual publication of the Government Printing Office. A typical citation for a revenue ruling would appear in the following forms:

Rev. Rul. 92-34, 1992-18 I.R.B. 11

or

Rev. Rul. 92-34, 1992-1 C.B. 433

The first citation refers to the 34th revenue ruling published in 1992 in the eighteenth weekly *Internal Revenue Bulletin*, page 11. The second citation refers to the same revenue ruling; however, in this instance, its source is the first volume of the 1992 *Cumulative Bulletin*, page 433.

Prior to 1953, rulings by the Internal Revenue Service appeared under various titles, such as appeals and review memorandas (A.R.M.), internal revenue mimeographs (I.R.-Mim.), and tax board memoranda (T.B.M.), to name just a few. While some of these rulings still have potential value, in Revenue Procedure 67-6, 1967-1 C.B. 576, the IRS announced a continuing review program of rulings.[13] If the IRS revokes or modifies a prior revenue ruling, open tax years can be retroactively affected for all taxpayers other than the taxpayer who initially requested the ruling. The modification will affect the latter party only if a misstatement or omission of material facts was involved. In researching a problem, the tax practitioner should consult a current status table to avoid the embarrassment of relying on a ruling that has been revoked or modified. The current rulings volume (* RULINGS) of *Mertens Law of Federal Income Taxation* is particularly helpful for this task. The

---

[11] Treas. Reg. Sec. 601.201(a)(1).
[12] Rev. Proc. 89-14, 1989-1 C.B. 814.
[13] Supplemented by Rev. Rul. 67-112, 1967-1 C.B. 381.

CCH *Standard Federal Tax Reporter*, in the M-Z Citator, also contains a Finding List, which lists the current status of revenue rulings, and an Obsolete Rulings Table. The *Federal Tax Coordinator, 2d* published by the Research Institute of America (RIA) features a main table of revenue rulings and procedures that are still valid. In addition, this tax service includes a separate table listing obsolete, revoked, and superseded rulings and procedures.

According to Revenue Procedure 89-14,[14] published revenue rulings have less force than Treasury regulations because they are intended to cover only specific fact situations. Consequently, published rulings provide valid precedent only if a second taxpayer's facts are substantially identical. In dealing with revenue agents and other Internal Revenue Service personnel, however, one might remember that regulations, revenue rulings, and acquiesced Tax Court decisions constitute the official policy of the service. Thus, an agent is often more easily persuaded by a revenue ruling than by a district court or even a circuit court decision.

Letter Rulings

Private letter rulings are issued directly to taxpayers who formally request advice about the tax consequences applicable to a specific business transaction. Such ruling requests have been employed frequently by taxpayers to assure themselves of a preplanned tax result before they consummate a transaction and as a subsequent aid in the preparation of the tax return. The Internal Revenue Service may refuse a ruling request. When a ruling is given, it is understood that the ruling is limited in application to the taxpayer making the request. Although IRS personnel will not rely on or use private rulings as precedents in the disposition of other cases, a private ruling is substantial authority for purposes of the penalty assessed for the substantial understatement of income tax.[15]

The Internal Revenue Service has no legal obligation to make advanced rulings on prospective transactions. Nevertheless, their policy is to offer guidance when requested, except for certain

---

[14] Rev. Proc. 89-14, 1989-1C.B. 814, para. 7.01(4).
[15] See the "Introduction" section of any Internal Revenue Bulletin, as well as Treas. Reg. Sec. 1.6662-4(d)(3)(iii).

sensitive areas of the law. Each year the IRS issues revenue procedures that list areas in which the IRS will not rule.[16]

During the 1970s, the continuation of private rulings was placed in serious jeopardy. Through legal action brought by various taxpayers against the Internal Revenue Service under the Freedom of Information Act (FOIA), the IRS was ordered to release unpublished rulings.[17] Some experts thought that the release of such rulings to the general public would diminish their usefulness because confidential information relating to important prospective business deals could be jeopardized.

The TRA '76 inserted section 6110 into the Internal Revenue Code, allowing the public disclosure of IRS written determinations issued after October 31, 1976. Under this provision private rulings and other written determinations are generally open to public inspection once material has been "sanitized" to remove means of identifying the taxpayer requesting the information.

CCH publishes a looseleaf service that contains letter rulings issued by the IRS. In addition, letter rulings can be found on computer retrieval systems, such as TAXRIA, LEXIS, WESTLAW, and CCH ACCESS Online. Although such rulings cannot be used as precedent, they help taxpayers and their advisers to determine current IRS thought on a particular topic. Publication of rulings has apparently not slowed requests significantly because the IRS continues to issue thousands of these rulings annually.

Revenue Procedures

A Revenue procedure is a statement of procedure that affects the rights or duties of taxpayers or other members of the public under the code, or information that "should be a matter of public knowledge," although not necessarily affecting the rights and duties of the public.[18] Like revenue rulings, revenue procedures have less force and effect than Treasury regulations. However, revenue procedures should be binding on the service and may be relied upon by taxpayers. The depreciation guidelines announced in

---

[16] See, for example, Rev. Proc. 93-3, 1993-1 I.R.B. 71.

[17] *Tax Analysts and Advocates*, 505 F.2d 350 (D.C. Cir. 1974); also *Fruehauf Corp.*, 369 F.Supp. 108 (D. Mich. 1974), aff'd 6th Cir. 6/9/75.

[18] Treas. Reg. Sec. 601.601(d)(2)(i)(b); Rev. Proc. 89-14, 1989-1 C.B. 814.

Revenue Procedure 87-56 are an example of a frequently used revenue procedure.[19]

Publication and identification methods for revenue procedures are identical to those used for revenue rulings. That is, they are initially published in the *Internal Revenue Bulletin* and subsequently in the *Cumulative Bulletin* and are numbered in the sequence of their appearance. Only the prefix "Rev. Proc." is different.

Notices and Announcements

When expeditious guidance concerning an item of the tax law is needed, the IRS publishes notices in the Internal Revenue Bulletin. These notices are intended to be relied on by taxpayers to the same extent as a revenue ruling or revenue procedure.[20]

Information of general interest can also appear in the form of an announcement. These have, in the past, been used to summarize new tax law or to publicize procedural matters. Just as with notices, announcements may be relied upon by taxpayers.[21]

Technical Advice Memoranda, General Counsel Memoranda, and Determination Letters

The technical advice memorandum (TAM), a special after-the-fact ruling, may be requested from the technical staff of the Internal Revenue Service. For example, if a disagreement arises in the course of an audit between the taxpayer or the taxpayer's representative and the revenue agent, either side may request formal technical advice on the issue(s) through the district director. If the advice is favorable to the taxpayer, IRS personnel usually will comply with the ruling. In some instances, such technical advice also has been used as the basis for the issuance of a revenue ruling. TAMs are also published as private letter rulings.

General counsel memoranda (GCM) are legal memoranda that are prepared by the IRS Chief Counsel's Office. They analyze and review proposed revenue rulings, private letter rulings, and technical advice memoranda. GCMs issued after March 12, 1981 consti-

---

[19] Rev. Proc. 87-56, 1987-2 C.B. 674.
[20] Rev. Rul. 90-91, 1990-2 C.B. 262.
[21] Ibid.

tute substantial authority for purposes of the penalty assessed for the substantial understatement of income tax.[22]

At times, a taxpayer may ask the local IRS district office for the IRS's position on a particular transaction that has already been completed. If this occurs, the IRS's response is contained in a determination letter. A determination letter is issued only when a determination can be made on the basis of clearly established rules in the statute or regulations.[23]

Technical Information and News Releases

Until March 30, 1976, technical information releases (T.I.R.s) were used by the Internal Revenue Service to disseminate important technical information on specific issues. T.I.R.s were not published in the *Internal Revenue Bulletin* but were distributed via a practitioners mailing list. In addition, the major tax services published the T.I.R.s in their current-matters volume. If the IRS decided that a T.I.R. had enough general application, it was reissued as a revenue procedure. In such an instance, of course, the T.I.R. appeared in the *Internal Revenue Bulletin* and subsequently in the *Cumulative Bulletin*. A technical information release usually included a statement indicating the extent to which the practitioner could rely on the announcement.

The information formerly contained in T.I.R.s is now published in news releases (I.R.-News Releases), which are distributed only to the press. The reason for discontinuing the T.I.R.s, according to the IRS, was simply a matter of cost; the mailing list for T.I.R.s had grown too large. I.R.s are found in the CCH *Standard Federal Tax Reporter* via the Finding List in the M-Z Citator and in RIA *United States Tax Reporter* via the Finding List in the index volume.

Judicial Interpretations

In situations in which statutory authority alone does not provide a clear solution for a particular problem, taxpayers or their advisers

---

[22] Treas. Reg. Sec. 1.6662-4(d)(3)(iii).
[23] Rev. Proc. 93-1, 1993-1 I.R.B. 10.

must consult judicial as well as administrative authority in forming an opinion. Judicial interpretations provide varying degrees of precedent, depending upon the nature of the conflict and the jurisdictional authority of the court that rendered the opinion.

While a vast majority of all disagreements with the Internal Revenue Service are settled on the administrative level, unsettled disputes may be litigated in one of three courts of original jurisdiction: the U.S. Tax Court, a U.S. district court, or the U.S. Court of Federal Claims. Appeals from these courts are heard by various courts of appeals. Twelve of these courts of appeals (eleven numbered and one for the District of Columbia) hear cases based upon the geographical residence of the taxpayer. The Thirteenth Court of Appeals (the court of appeals for the federal circuit) hears cases that are appealed from the U.S. Court of Federal Claims. Appeals from any circuit court of appeals may be directed to the U.S. Supreme Court by requesting a writ of *certiorari*.

After receiving a request for *certiorari* from either the government or the taxpayer, the Supreme Court decides whether or not it should review a case. *Certiorari* is most commonly granted in situations in which a conflict already exists between two or more circuit courts of appeals. Sometimes, the Supreme Court will grant *certiorari* without a prior conflict if it thinks a case has special significance. The judicial alternatives available to a taxpayer are depicted in figure 4.1. In order to understand fully the weight of a court decision, and the degree to which it sets precedent, an elementary understanding of the jurisdiction of each court is essential.

United States Tax Court

The U.S. Tax Court consists of nineteen judges, separate and distinct from the Treasury Department, appointed by the President for fifteen-year terms. The Chief Judge of the Tax Court may also appoint special trial judges. These special trial judges are primarily used to help alleviate the heavy case load of the appointed tax court judges. The decisions that these special judges render, however, are just as authoritative as other tax court decisions. Although the principal office of the Tax Court is located in Washington, D.C., the court conducts hearings in most large cities

Figure 4.1

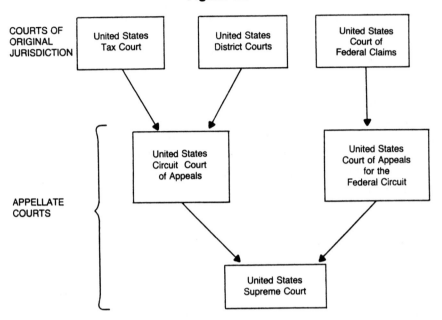

in the United States. The Tax Court is organized by divisions, which usually consist of only one judge, although they may consist of more than one. Proceedings before the Tax Court may be conducted with or without a trial; if sufficient facts are stipulated, the assigned judge may render an opinion without a formal trial.

After hearing a case, the assigned judge will submit the findings of fact and an opinion, in writing, to the chief judge, who then decides whether or not the case should be reviewed by the full court. Should the chief judge decide that a full review is not necessary, the original decision will stand and be entered either as a "regular" or a "memorandum" decision. Regular decisions are published by the Government Printing Office.

Prior to 1943, the Tax Court was known as the Board of Tax Appeals, the decisions of which were published in forty-seven volumes covering the period from 1924 to 1942. These volumes are cited as the *United States Board of Tax Appeals Reports* (B.T.A.). For example, 39 B.T.A. 13 refers to the thirty-ninth volume of the *Board of Tax Appeals Reports*, page 13. In the latter part of 1942, Congress changed the name of the court to the Tax Court of the United

States. Finally, on January 1, 1970, the court received its present name: The United States Tax Court. The proceedings of the Tax Court of the United States (October 22, 1942–December 31, 1969) were published as *The Tax Court of the United States Reports* (T.C.); the proceedings of the United States Tax Court (January 1, 1970– present) are published as the *United States Tax Court Reports* (T.C.). Thus, the citations of the two courts are the same (T.C.). An example of the first would be 12 T.C. 101; an example of the latter would be 83 T.C. 309. Bound volumes of the Tax Court reports are published only by the U.S. Government Printing Office.

Tax Court memorandum decisions are reproduced by the government in mimeograph form only. However, Commerce Clearing House (CCH) publishes memorandum decisions in their *Tax Court Memorandum Decisions* (T.C.M.) series, and Research Institute of America (RIA) makes them available as the *RIA TC Memorandum Decisions* (RIA TC Memo).[24] In recent years, the Tax Court has handed down more memorandum opinions than regular opinions. Memorandum opinions usually involve conclusions that, in the opinion of the chief judge, have been well established and require only a delineation of the facts. Nevertheless, memorandum decisions do have precedential value.

If, in the opinion of the chief judge, a case contains an unusual point of law or one on which considerable disagreement exists among the judges of the Tax Court, the chief judge may assign the case to the full court. After each judge has had an opportunity to study the case, the court meets for an expression of opinions and a vote. In such instances, it is possible that one or more majority and minority opinions will be prepared and that the trial judge—possibly the only one to have actually heard the proceedings—could write the minority opinion. The majority opinion is entered as the final decision of the Tax Court.

---

[24] In 1991, Thomson Professional Publishing acquired a line of tax products that had previously been published by the Prentice Hall Information Services Division and, since 1989, by Maxwell Macmillan. The materials were transferred by Thomson to its Research Institute of America (RIA) publishing division. RIA changed the name of some publications (for example, *Federal Taxes, 2nd* became *United States Tax Reporter*). Other products (including, *Citator, Citator 2nd Series, American Federal Tax Reports (AFTR)*, and *(AFTR, 2nd)*) kept their names. Thus, older editions of some of these products such as the *RIA TC Memorandum Decisions* will have either the Prentice Hall or Maxwell Macmillan name on the spine.

As a general rule, the Tax Court's jurisdiction rests with the determination of *deficiencies* in income, excess profits, self-employment, estate, or gift taxes. The Tax Court also has jurisdiction over declaratory judgments with respect to qualification of retirement plans[25] and over any penalty imposed for failure to pay the amount of tax shown on a tax return.[26] Claims for refund must be tried in either a district court or the U.S. Court of Federal Claims. Thus, in order to bring suit in the Tax Court of the United States, a taxpayer must have received a notice of deficiency, the so-called ninety-day letter or ticket to the Tax Court, and, subsequently, have refused or failed to pay the deficiency.

Some Tax Court transcripts disclose that a "decision has been entered under Rule 155" (prior to 1974, known as Rule 50). This notation signifies that the court has reached a conclusion regarding the facts and issues of the case but leaves the computational aspects of the decision to the opposing parties. Both parties will subsequently submit to the court their versions of the refund or deficiency computation. If both parties agree on the computation, no further argument is necessary. In the event of disagreement, the court will reach its decision on the basis of the data presented by each party. Unfortunately, data submitted or arguments heard under Rule 155 are usually not a part of the trial transcript.

Under section 7463, special trial procedures are available for disputes involving $10,000 or less.[27] A taxpayer may request trial before the Small Tax Case Division by executing Form 2 of the Tax Court and paying a filing fee of $60.[28] Even this fee may be waived if, in the opinion of the court, the petitioner is unable to make the payment. Hearings are not before judges but before commissioners appointed by the Chief Judge of the Tax Court. Legal counsel is not required, and taxpayers may represent themselves. Trial procedures are conducted on an informal basis with the filing of briefs permitted but not required. Only an informal record of the trial proceedings is prepared, and every decision is final, making an appeal from a decision of the Small Tax Case Division of the Tax

---

[25] Section 7476.

[26] Section 6214(a).

[27] The $10,000 limitation includes the initial tax contested, potential additional amounts, and penalties, but excludes interest. Section 7463(e).

[28] Section 7451.

Court impossible. Decisions of this division may not be cited as precedent in other cases.

Acquiescence Policy. In some instances, the commissioner of internal revenue will publicly "acquiesce" or "nonacquiesce" to a *regular* Tax Court decision in which the Court has disallowed a deficiency asserted by the Commissioner. The acquiescence or nonacquiescence relates only to the issues decided against the Government. This policy does not encompass Tax Court memorandum decisions or decisions of other courts. In announcing an acquiescence, the commissioner publicly declares agreement with a conclusion reached by the Tax Court. This does not necessarily mean that the commissioner agrees with the *reasoning* used by the court in reaching the conclusion, but only that in the future, unless otherwise announced, the Internal Revenue Service will dispose of similar disputes in a manner consistent with that established in the acquiesced case. In those situations in which the Tax Court has ruled against the government, the commissioner may wish to express nonacquiescence to inform taxpayers that similar disputes will continue to be contested in the future.

Acquiescence and nonacquiescence are announced in the first weekly *Internal Revenue Bulletin* for July and January and are republished in the semiannual *Cumulative Bulletin*. In addition, citators of the major tax services indicate whether the commissioner has acquiesced or refused to acquiesce in a particular decision, giving specific reference to the *Cumulative Bulletin* in which the commissioner's announcement can be found. If the tax adviser plans to rely on a specific acquiesced case, it is important that he or she check the original announcement, because it is possible that only a partial acquiescence exists. For example, a single Tax Court case may involve multiple issues, and the commissioner may acquiesce in only one of those issues. An interesting example of this is found in *The Friedlander Corporation*, 25 T.C. 70 (1955), in which the Tax Court considered three issues. The commissioner remained silent on the first issue, expressed nonacquiescence to the second, and acquiesced to the third.[29]

The commissioner's acquiescence may also be withdrawn with

---

[29] Cumulative List of Announcements Relating to Decisions of the Tax Court, 1972-2 C.B. 2.

retroactive effect. For example, in *Caulkins*, 1 T.C. 656 (1943), the commissioner initially published a nonacquiescence but later changed this to acquiescence when the court of appeals sustained the Tax Court.[30] Eleven years later, another commissioner reinstated the initial nonacquiescence.[31] A taxpayer who claimed reliance on *Caulkins* before the acquiescence was retroactively withdrawn found no relief when, in *Dixon*, the Supreme Court upheld the commissioner's right to do so.[32]

United States District Court

The federal judicial system is divided into thirteen judicial circuits, as illustrated in figure 4.2. Eleven of the circuits are numbered; the twelfth covers Washington, D.C. and the thirteenth is the Court of Appeals for the Federal Circuit, which is the court of appeals for the U.S. Court of Federal Claims. Each of the first twelve circuits is further divided into districts. At least one district judge is assigned to each federal district. Depending upon need, however, two or more federal district judges may hear cases in any district. Taxpayers may bring suit in a federal district court only after they have paid a tax, either with the return or as a deficiency assessment, and have processed a request for refund.[33] A U.S. district court is the only court in which a taxpayer can request a jury trial in a tax dispute. Published proceedings of the federal district courts can usually be found in the *Federal Supplement* reporter series, published by West Publishing Company. However, some district court opinions (like Tax Court memorandum decisions) are apparently never officially published in a primary source such as the *Federal Supplement*, and a researcher must consult a secondary source, such as *United States Tax Cases* (CCH) or *American Federal Tax Reports* (RIA) for the text of a district court decision.

United States Court of Federal Claims

The U.S. Court of Federal Claims (called the U.S. Claims Court before October 29, 1992) was created by Congress in 1982, replacing the old Court of Claims. The U.S. Court of Federal Claims

---

[30] See 1943-1 C.B. 28 and 1944-1 C.B. 5.
[31] Rev. Rul. 55-136, 1955-1 C.B. 7.
[32] W. *Palmer Dixon*, 381 U.S. 68 (1965).
[33] Section 7422.

Figure 4.2

UNITED STATES COURTS OF APPEALS
INCLUDING HEADQUARTERS OF EACH CIRCUIT

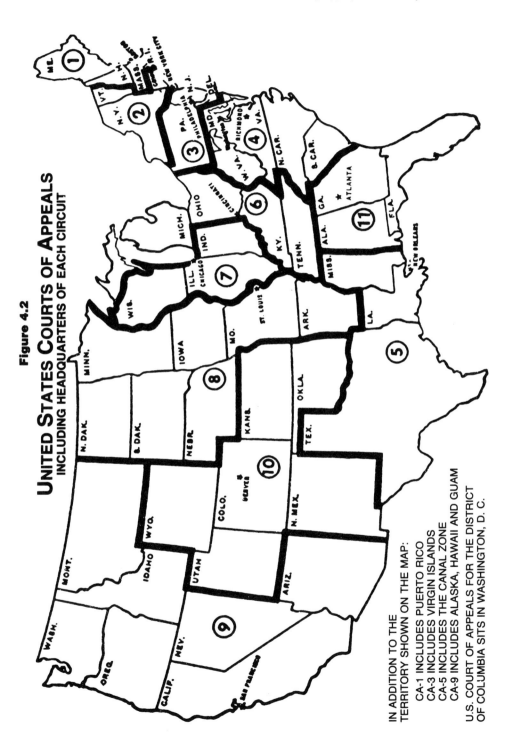

IN ADDITION TO THE
TERRITORY SHOWN ON THE MAP:

    CA-1 INCLUDES PUERTO RICO
    CA-3 INCLUDES VIRGIN ISLANDS
    CA-5 INCLUDES THE CANAL ZONE
    CA-9 INCLUDES ALASKA, HAWAII AND GUAM

U.S. COURT OF APPEALS FOR THE DISTRICT
OF COLUMBIA SITS IN WASHINGTON, D. C.

handles claims against the U.S. Government. Although this court is headquartered in Washington, D.C., it may hold court at such times and in such places as it may fix by rule of the court. The prerequisites for filing suit in the U.S. Court of Federal Claims are identical with those applicable to a district court; that is, the petitioners must have paid a tax and subsequently filed a request for refund that the commissioner rejected. The proceedings of the U.S. Court of Federal Claims can be found in the *Federal Claim Reporter* (Fed. Cl.) published by West Publishing Company. The proceedings of the Claims Court (the name of the U.S. Court of Federal Claims prior to October 29, 1992) can be found in the *United States Claims Court Reporter* (Cl. Ct.) series also published by West Publishing Company. The proceedings of the Court of Claims (the predecessor to the U.S. Claims Court) can be found in the *Court of Claims Reporter* series published by the U.S. Government Printing Office (GPO). In addition, West's *Federal Reporter 2d* series includes all Court of Claims cases between 1929 and 1932 and after 1959. From 1932 to 1960 the Court of Claims cases were published in West's *Federal Supplement* series. They are also published in CCH's *U.S. Tax Cases* (USTC) and RIA's *American Federal Tax Report* (AFTR and AFTR 2d).

United States Circuit Courts of Appeals

In addition to the U. S. Court of Appeals for the Federal Circuit and the District of Columbia Circuit, the states and U.S. territories are geographically partitioned into judicial circuits numbered from one through eleven (see figure 4.2).[34] Decisions of the Tax Court and a district court may be appealed by either the taxpayer or the government to the circuit court in which the taxpayer resides. Decisions from the U.S. Court of Federal Claims are appealed to the U.S. Court of Appeals for the Federal Circuit. Hearings before a circuit court are conducted by a panel of three judges. However, the Federal Circuit may have panels larger than three and less than twelve.

Depending on need and policies within each particular circuit, federal district judges may be asked to serve on a panel during a session. Upon request by any circuit judge, the full circuit court (that is, all the judges in that circuit) may review the decision of a trial panel. The proceedings of the circuit courts are published by

---

[34] The U.S. Court of Appeals for the Federal Circuit was created by P.L. 97–164, effective October 1, 1982.

West Publishing Company in the *Federal Reporter* (1st and 2d series), by CCH in USTC, and by RIA in AFTR and AFTR 2d.

United States Supreme Court

Final appeals from a circuit court of appeals rest with the Supreme Court. As previously explained, appeal requires a writ of *certiorari*, which the Supreme Court may or may not grant. Supreme Court decisions are of special importance because they constitute the final judicial authority in tax matters. The Supreme Court decisions can be found in any one of the following publications: *United States Supreme Court Reports* (US), the Government Printing Office; *Supreme Court Reports* (S.Ct.), West Publishing Company; *United States Reports, Lawyer's Edition* (LEd), Lawyer's Cooperative Publishing Company; *United States Tax Cases* (USTC), Commerce Clearing House; and *American Federal Tax Reports* (AFTR and AFTR 2d), Research Institute of America. They are also published in the *Cumulative Bulletin*.

Special Tax Reporter Series

All *tax* decisions rendered by the Supreme Court, the circuit courts of appeals, the Claims Court, federal district courts, and some state courts are separately published by CCH in the *United States Tax Cases* (USTC) series and by RIA in the *American Federal Tax Reports* (AFTR and AFTR 2d) series. These two special judicial reporter series provide a tax practitioner with two major advantages: first, by collecting *only* tax cases in one reporter series, it is economically possible for most tax practitioners to acquire at least one complete set of all judicial authority dealing with tax problems; second, the space required to store one complete tax reporter series is minimal when compared with the many volumes that would otherwise be necessary (tax cases would be mixed among other civil and criminal proceedings).

Tax Court decisions, which comprise a separate volume, are not included in either the USTC or AFTR series. In addition to the Tax Court reporter series published annually by the Government Printing Office, however, both CCH and RIA provide a current looseleaf service that offers all regular and memorandum Tax Court decisions on a timely basis. If these looseleaf volumes are retained, it is unnecessary to purchase the government (T.C.) series to obtain a complete set. Most practitioners, however, make that purchase anyway in order to obtain bound volumes of the

Exhibit 4.2
Summary of Primary and Secondary Citations

	Primary		Secondary	
	Publisher	Standard Citation	Publisher	Standard Citation
Supreme Court[a]	U.S. Government Printing Office	Harris v. Comm., 340 U.S. 106 (1950)	The Lawyers' Co-Operative Publishing Company	Harris v. Comm., 95 L.Ed. 111
	West Publishing Company	Harris v. Comm., 71 S. Ct. 181 (1950)	Research Institute of America	Harris v. Comm., 39 AFTR 1002
			Commerce Clearing House	Harris v. Comm., 1950-2 USTC ¶10,786
Circuit Courts of Appeal[b]	West Publishing Company	Salome Jr. v. U.S., 395 F.2d 990 (5th Cir. 1968)	Research Institute of America	Salome Jr. v. U.S., 22 AFTR, 2d 5039
			Commerce Clearing House	Salome Jr. v. U.S., 1968-2 USTC ¶9440
District Courts	West Publishing Company	Whittington v. Jones, 96 F. Supp. 967 (W.D. Okla. 1951)	Research Institute of America	Whittington v. Jones, 40 AFTR 553
			Commerce Clearing House	Whittington v. Jones, 1951-1 USTC ¶9302
Court of Claims[c]	West Publishing Company	Scott v. U.S., 354 F.2d 292 (Ct. Cl. 1965)	Research Institute of America	Scott v. U.S., 16 AFTR, 2d 6087
	U.S. Government Printing Office	Scott v. U.S., 173 Ct. Cl. 650 (1965)	Commerce Clearing House	Scott v. U.S., 1966-1 USTC ¶9169
Claims Court[d]	West Publishing Company	Raphan v. U.S., 3 Cl. Ct. 457 (1983)	Research Institute of America	Raphan v. U.S., 52 AFTR 2d 83-5987 (Cl. Ct. 1983)
			Commerce Clearing House	Raphan v. U.S., 83-2 USTC ¶9613 (Cl. Ct. 1983)

Board of Tax Appeals	U.S. Government Printing Office	*Charles F. Long*, 12 B.T.A. 488 (1928)
Board of Tax Appeals (memorandum decisions)	Research Institute of America	*Frank L. Owen*, 40 B.T.A. 1377, Dock 87811 (Memo), June 6, 1939, 1939 P-H ¶6530
Tax Court	U.S. Government Printing Office	*Mae F. Meurel*, 20 T.C. 614 (1953)
	Research Institute of America	
	Commerce Clearing House[e]	
Tax Court (memorandum decisions)	Research Institute of America	*Kenneth D. Malamed*, 1993 RIA TC Memo ¶93,001.
	Commerce Clearing House	*Stephen L. & Doris M. Morrow*, T.C.M. 1967-1222

[a] The *Supreme Court Reporter* (West) is considered primary authority prior to publication of the official report by the GPO.

[b] Includes, since 1982, the new U.S. Court of Appeals for the Federal Circuit.

[c] Primray citations to cases decided on the Court of Claims are to either the West publications or the GPO's *Court of Claims Reporter*.

[d] In 1982, the predecessor Court of Claims was merged into the new U.S. Court of Appeals for the Federal District. In its place, the Claims Court was created. The proceedings of the Claims Court can be found in the *United States Claims Court Reporter* (Cl. Ct.) series, published by West Publishing Company. Also, in 1992, the name of the Claims Court was changed to the United States Court of Federal Claims. The proceedings of the U.S. Court of Federal Claims are published by West Publishing Company in the *Federal Claims Reporter*.

[e] Both RIA and CCH publish "advance sheets" on all Tax Court decisions. Even though they are never *bound*, if a person collected and retained all of the looseleaf (advance sheets), he or she would, in effect, have the T.C. reports.

regular Tax Court decisions. As noted earlier, unlike the government, both CCH and RIA publish bound volumes of the Tax Court memorandum decisions.

Although the duplication of a single judicial proceeding in several court reporter series has advantages, that same duplication creates the problem of multiple citations. The extent of the present duplication is shown in exhibits 4.2 and 4.3. In preparing external tax communications, a writer can never be certain of which reporter series is most readily available to the reader; therefore, it is difficult to know which series should be cited. In order to standardize citation presentation, most formal publications have accepted the practice of presenting at least an initial reference to the "official" or "standard" reporter series. If other (secondary) citations are also given, they generally follow the standard citation. Thus, one might properly cite the decision in *Harris* as *Harris v. Commis-*

Exhibit 4.3
Publication Summary of Judicial Decisions

		1900	1905	1910	1915	1920	1925	1930	1935	1940	1945	1950	1955	1960	1965	1970	1975	1980	1985	1990	1993
SUPREME COURT	U.S. Supreme Court Reports																				
	Supreme Court Reporter																				
	U.S. Reports																				
	American Federal Tax Reports																				
	United States Tax Cases (1)			(1913)																	
CIRCUIT COURT OF APPEALS	Federal Reporter (2)																				
	American Federal Tax Reports																				
	United States Tax Cases (1)			(1913)																	
DISTRICT COURTS	Federal Supplement									(1932, end)											
	Federal Supplement							(1932)													
	American Federal Tax Reports																				
	United States Tax Cases (1)			(1913)																	
U.S. COURT OF FEDERAL CLAIMS, COURT OF CLAIMS, AND CLAIMS COURT	Federal Claims Reporter																				(1993)
	U.S. Court of Claims Reports																	(1982)			
	Federal Supplement							(1932)						(1960)							
	Federal Reporter (2)						(1929) (1932)							(1960)							
	American Federal Tax Reports																				
	United States Tax Cases (1)			(1913)																	
	United States Claims Court Reporter																	(1982)			
BOARD OF APPEALS and TAX COURT (regular & memo decisions)	U.S. Board of Tax Appeals Reports						(1924)				(1942)										
	United States Tax Court Reports (3)									(1942)											
	Tax Court Memorandum Decisions (RIA)						(1928)														
	Tax Court Memorandum Decisions (CCH)									(1942)											

(1) From 1913 to 1933, only opinions of genuine precedent value are included from the circuit courts of appeal, district courts, and Court of Claims.
(2) Since 1925, the *Federal Reporter* is published as the *Federal Reporter 2d Series.*
(3) Prior to 1970, this publication was known as *Tax Court of the United States Reports.*

sioner, 340 U.S. 106 (1950), 39 AFTR 1002, 50-2 USTC ¶10,786. Obviously, additional secondary references could be added to the two in the above illustration.

The Citator

The tax researcher who must consider judicial authority has a most useful tool at his or her disposal in a citator, which is simply a compilation of cross-references to judicial decisions. Following the initial entry of each judicial proceeding in an alphabetical sequence, a citator includes later cross-references to additional citations—that is, to other cases—that in some way contain a reference to the initial entry. To illustrate, assume that only five judicial decisions have ever been rendered (those being *Able, Baker, Charlie, Daley*, and *Evert*, in chronological order). Assume further that the court in *Baker* made some mention of the *Able* decision; that the court in *Daley* made some reference to the decisions in *Able* and *Charlie*, but not to *Baker*; and that the court in *Evert* made reference only to the decision in *Baker*. Given these assumptions a complete citator could be prepared as follows:

> *Able* (initial citation)
> ...*Baker* (cross-reference to page in *Baker* that "cites" *Able*)
> ...*Daley* (cross-reference to page in *Daley* that "cites" *Able*)
> *Baker* (initial citation)
> ...*Evert* (cross-reference to page in *Evert* that "cites" *Baker*)
> *Charlie* (initial citation)
> ...*Daley* (cross-reference to page in *Daley* that "cites" *Charlie*)
> *Daley* (initial citation)
> *Evert* (initial citation)

Obviously, there are thousands of judicial decisions and many thousands of cross-references. Were there no citators (or other equivalent data retrieval systems), it would be virtually impossible to locate much of the pertinent judicial authority on most tax questions. With citators available, the task is at least feasible. To illustrate, consider the problem of interpreting what the words "ordinary" and "necessary" mean as they are used in code sections 162 and 212. This task was undertaken by the Supreme Court in 1933 in *Welch v. Helvering*, 290 U.S. 111 (1933). Since that 1933 decision, *Welch v. Helvering* has been "cited" in hundreds of subsequent court decisions. A citator greatly facilitates the task of locating any or all of these decisions, which may offer additional perspective on the meaning of the words "ordinary" and "necessary," because it identifies a reasonable set of cases to examine further. In most instances, of course, the list of cases suggested by a citator is much smaller.

Using the Citator. To demonstrate the methodology applied in searching for pertinent judicial decisions, assume that a tax researcher has somehow identified a potentially important case with a primary citation. If that practitioner has only the USTC or AFTR reporter series available, an "equivalent" secondary citation must first be found before the decision he or she is interested in reviewing can be read. If the AFTR series is available, the practitioner should begin with the *RIA Citator*; if the USTC series is available, the practitioner should begin with the *CCH Citator*. Each citator will give the secondary citation for its own reporter series only. The case "names" (technically called *style*) are arranged in alphabetical sequence in both citators. However, the *RIA Citator* consists of five separate volumes, plus cumulative supplements, each covering a specific time period. The *CCH Citator* consists of only two volumes arranged alphabetically. Thus, in working with RIA materials, tax researchers may have to consult more than one volume *if* they want to locate all of the subsequent decisions that have cited the initial entry. The number of volumes to be consulted will depend on the year the initial case was heard. If a case was first tried sometime between 1863 and 1941, the researcher using the RIA series must consult all three volumes of the AFTR series, volumes 1 and 2 of the AFTR 2d series, and the cumulative supplements for current citations. On the other hand, if the case being examined was first tried sometime between 1948 and 1954, the researcher would consult only volume 3 of the AFTR series, volumes 1 and 2 of the AFTR 2d series, and the cumulative supplements. Exhibit 4.4 compares the *CCH Citator* with the *RIA Citator*.

Any meaningful comparison of these two citator services goes beyond the apparent convenience factor of working with two CCH

Exhibit 4.4
Key to Citator Services

	1863–1941	1941–1948	1948–1954	1954–1977	1978–1989	Since 1989
Research Institute of America	1st Series vol. 1	1st Series vol. 2	1st Series vol. 3	2d Series vol. 1	2d Series vol. 2	Cumulative Supplements
Commerce Clearing House			Two looseleaf volumes covering all dates.			

volumes as opposed to multiple RIA volumes because the usefulness of either citator becomes a function of what the researcher wants to find. Should he or she desire to obtain a brief judicial history of a case, the *CCH Citator* is a handy research tool. For example, assume that the researcher wants to trace the history of *Germantown Trust Co.* This case came to the researcher's attention in a tax periodical where it was cited as 309 U.S. 304 (1940). A simple check in the two-volume *CCH Citator*, which is arranged in alphabetical order, discloses that *Germantown Trust Co.* was originally tried by the Board of Tax Appeals in 1938 and entered as a memorandum decision; this decision was reversed by the Third Circuit Court of Appeals and in turn was reversed by the Supreme Court (see exhibit 4.5). In addition, the *CCH Citator* discloses that *Germantown Trust Co.* has subsequently been cited in over thirty additional cases, most recently in 1992. All of this information may or may not be pertinent to the researcher's tax problem. Of course, the *CCH Citator* gives the cross-reference of the case in the USTC series. Finally, the citator includes paragraph references where the case is discussed in CCH's looseleaf reference service, entitled *Standard Federal Tax Reporter* (discussed later in this chapter).

To gather this same information through the use of the *RIA Citator*, the researcher would proceed along the following lines (see exhibits 4.6 through 4.11). The original citation, *Germantown Trust Co.*, 309 U.S. 304 (1940), discloses the decision year; thus, the researcher turns to volume 1 of the *RIA Citator* (1863–1941) to learn that the Board of Tax Appeals was the court of original jurisdiction, which tried the case twice. Furthermore, the *RIA Citator* shows that the B.T.A. decision was reversed by the Third Circuit Court of Appeals and that the text of the Supreme Court decision may be found at 23 AFTR 1084. Whether that decision sustained or re-

(continued on page 121)

Exhibit 4.5
CCH Citator Page

GER   **93,488** ————CCH————

Gerli & Co., Inc.—continued
El Paso Co., CtCls, 81-2 USTC ¶ 9528
Gerling International Ins. Co. . . . . ¶ 42,932.11,
42,981.10
● **CA-3**—(rev'g and rem'g TC), 88-1 USTC ¶ 9158;
839 F2d 131
Gerling International Ins. Co., TC, Dec. 48,247, 98
TC —, No. 44
Home Group, Inc., CA-2, 89-1 USTC ¶ 9329, 875 F2d
377
● **TC**—Dec. 43,392; 87 TC 679; 679 No. 41
Gerling International Ins. Co., TC, Dec. 48,247, 98
TC —, No. 44
Gerling International Ins. Co. . . . . ¶ 8470.578,
20,610.288, 26,387.041
● **TC**—Dec. 48,247; 98 TC —, No. 44
Gerling Int'l Ins. Co. . . . . ¶ 42,964.20, 42,981.10
● **TC**—Dec. 42,952; 86 TC 468
Gerling International Ins. Co., TC, Dec. 48,247, 98
TC —, No. 44
Tidler, TC, Dec. 43,948(M), 53 TCM 934, TC Memo.
1987-268
Gerling International Ins. Co., TC, Dec. 43,392, 87
TC 679
Fisher, TC, Dec. 43,082(M), 51 TCM 1097, TC
Memo. 1986-217
Gerlinger, Geo. T. . . . . ¶ 15,402.90
● **CA-9**—(rem'g BTA), 39-2 USTC ¶ 9773; 106 F2d
997
● **BTA**—Dec. 10,628-C; March 17, 1939
Germac Roofing, Inc. . . . . . ¶ 39,087.55, 40,230.3338,
42,288.207
● **DC-Pa**—87-1 USTC ¶ 9222
Germain, Homer H.
. . . . ¶ 2350.242, 8500.14, 42,994.72
● **TC**—Dec. 18,831(M); 11 TCM 226
Germain, John . ¶ 3100.065, 20,611.051, 39,917.38,
40,551G.77
● **TC**—Dec. 40,059(M); 45 TCM 1374; TC Memo.
1983-220
Germain, John M. . . . . ¶ 40,843.02
● **DC-Mich**—84-2 USTC ¶ 9713
German Est., Estelle E. . . . . (Estate Tax)
● **ClsCt**—85-1 USTC ¶ 13,610; Cls Ct
German Hungarian Home Co. . . . . ¶ 22,607.0365
● **BTA**—BTA memorandum opinion, Dec. 12,592-K;
July 24, 1942
German, Leatrice . . . . ¶ 8582.7205
● **TC**—Dec. 43,270(M); 52 TCM 170; TC Memo.
1986-370
German, Max . . . . ¶ 25,427.90
● **TC**—Dec. 13,378; 2 TC 474; A. 1943 CB 9
Evans, CA-7, 71-2 USTC ¶ 9597, 447 F2d 547
Stanback, CA-4, 59-2 USTC ¶ 9759, 271 F2d 514
Paul, TC, Dec. 22,560(M), 16 TCM 752, TC Memo.
1957-170
Stein, TC, Dec. 17,561, 14 TC 494
Wenig, TC, Dec. 16,198(M), 6 TCM 1340
Scherr, TC, Dec. 16,063(M), 6 TCM 1067
Shwayder, TC, Dec. 15,717(M), 6 TCM 362
Weizer, TC, Dec. 15,710(M), 6 TCM 337
Awrey Est., Dec. 14,595, 5 TC 222
Thorrez, TC, Dec. 14,560, 5 TC 60
Brennen, TC, Dec. 14,515, 4 TC 1260
Van Tongeren, TC, Dec. 14,480(M), 4 TCM 353
Hirsch, TC, Dec. 14,309(M), 4 TCM 4
Croft, TC, Dec. 14,177(M), 3 TCM 1064
Loftus, TC, Dec. 14,137(M), 3 TCM 974
German Society of Maryland, Inc. . . . . . ¶ 35,507.40
● **TC**—Dec. 40,050; 80 TC 741
Shunk Assn., Inc., DC--Ohio, 85-2 USTC ¶ 9830
Mannheimer Charitable Trust, TC, Dec. 45,828, 93
TC 35
Germantown Trust Co. (See McLean Will, Sarah B.)
Germantown Trust Co. v. Lederer . . . . . ¶ 42,288.56
● **CA-3**—263 Fed 672
Haar, DC, 1927 CCH ¶ 7172, 1927 CCHFCV page
7595, 1927 CT ¶ 4380, 19 F2d 399
Germantown Trust Co., Trustee . . . . ¶ 39,925.42,
43,175.991
● **SCt**—(rev'g CA-3), 40-1 USTC ¶ 9263; 309 US 304;
60 SCt 566; Ct D 1446; 1940-1 CB 178
Buelow, CA-7, 92-2 USTC ¶ 50,518
Mason, DC--Ga, 92-2 USTC ¶ 50,403
Deleet Merchandising Corp., SCt, 84-1 USTC ¶ 9150,
104 SCt 756
Badaracco, Sr., SCt, 84-1 USTC ¶ 9150, 464 US 386,
104 SCt 756, Ct D 2024, 1984-1 CB 254
Automobile Club of Mich., SCt, 57-1 USTC ¶ 9593,
353 US 180, 77 SCt 707, Ct D 1807, 1957-1 CB
513
Lane-Wells Co., SCt, 44-1 USTC ¶ 9195, 321 US 219,
64 SCt 511, Ct D 1602, 1944 CB 539
Siben, CA-2, 91-1 USTC ¶ 50,215, 930 F2d 1034

Germantown Trust Co., Trustee—continued
Neptune Mutual Association, Ltd. of Bermuda, CA-
FC, 88-2 USTC ¶ 16,469, 862 F2d 1546
Moore, CA-7, 80-2 USTC ¶ 9627, 627 F2d 830
Durovic, CA-7, 73-2 USTC ¶ 9728, 487 F2d 36
McGillick Foundation, CA-3, 60-2 USTC ¶ 9481, 278
F2d 643
Chilhowee Mills, Inc., CA-DC, 45-2 USTC ¶ 9462, 152
F2d 137
Cross, BC-DC, 91-2 USTC ¶ 50,318
D'Avanza, Jr., DC--Fla, 89-2 USTC ¶ 9503, 101 BR
787
Harrison, DC--NY, 72-2 USTC ¶ 9573
Michaud, DC--Pa, 70-2 USTC ¶ 9658, 317 FSupp
1002
Dubuque Packing Co., DC--Iowa, 55-1 USTC ¶ 9120,
126 FSupp 796
Henk, SCt, 60-1 USTC ¶ 9325, 101 NW2d 415
Synanon Church, TC, Dec. 45,749(M), 57 TCM 602,
TC Memo. 1989-270
Rutland, TC, Dec. 44,372, 89 TC 1137
Beard, TC, Dec. 41,237, 82 TC 766
Shapland, TC, Dec. 36,224(M), 38 TCM 1172, TC
Memo. 1979-300
Durovic, TC, Dec. 30,204, 54 TC 1364
West Coast Ice Co., TC, Dec. 28,812, 49 TC 345
California Thoroughbred Breeders Ass'n, TC, Dec.
28,225, 47 TC 335
Stevens Bros., Foundation, Inc., TC, Dec. 25,708,
39 TC 93
Houston, TC, Dec. 25,571, 38 TC 486
McKinley Corp. of Ohio, TC, Dec. 25,057, 36 TC
1182
Caswal Corp., TC, Dec. 24,270(M), 19 TCM 757, TC
Memo. 1960-143
McGillick Co., TC, Dec. 23,144, 30 TC 1130
Rose, TC, Dec. 21,166, 24 TC 755
Danz, TC, Dec. 19,013, 18 TC 454
Mandis, TC, Dec. 17,737(M), 9 TCM 520
Tarbox Corp., TC, Dec. 14,920, 6 TC 35
Chilhowee Mills, Inc., TC, Dec. 14,312, 4 TC 558
Wilson, Dec. 13,612, 2 TC 1059
Sunnyside Land Co., TC, Dec. 13,334(M), 2 TCM
347
Masterson, TC, Dec. 12,913, 1 TC 315
Porto Rico Coal Co., BTA, Dec. 11,777, 44 BTA 221
Rev. Rul 74-203, 1974-1 CB 330
● **CA-3**—(reversing BTA), 39-2 USTC ¶ 9617; 106
F2d 139
● **BTA**—Dec. 10,423-A; August 24, 1938
Germon, Louis J. . . . . ¶ 20,611.10, 36,471.90,
40,558.205
● **TC**—Dec. 21,839(M); 15 TCM 795; TC Memo.
1956-159
Gernert, Steve G. (See Taylor Oil & Gas Co.)
Gernhardt-Strohmaier Co., Inc. . . . . (Expired Excess
Profits Tax)
● **DC-Calif**—49-1 USTC ¶ 5933; 84 FSupp 51
Gernie, Mary v. Moe . . . . ¶ 41,520.1891
● **DC-NY**—60-1 USTC ¶ 9350
Gernon, Helen J. (See Dixon, W. Palmer)
Gerosa, Anthony v. Burnet . . . . ¶ 41,520.177,
41,520.296
● **CA-2**—(dis'g BTA), Apr. 4, 1933
● **BTA**—Dec. 6630; 21 BTA 1234
Gerow, Daniel T., Coll of Int. Rev. (Fla.)
Listed under taxpayer's name
Gerrard, John M. v. Campbell . . . . . . ¶ 40,230.3338
● **DC-Ill**—49-1 USTC ¶ 9144; 81 FSupp 752
Gerrard, Josephine M. . . . . . . ¶ 39,480.07, 39,480.17
● **DC-Calif**—87-2 USTC ¶ 9647; 656 FSupp 570
Jones v. Cavazos, CA-11, 89-2 USTC ¶ 9661, 889 F2d
1043
Gerres, Thomas E.
. . . . ¶ 3100.085, 8474.265, 12,177.70
● **TC**—Dec. 43,522(M); 52 TCM 1119; TC Memo.
1986-573
Gerrish, Edward S. . . . . ¶ 6094.90
● **TC**—Dec. 19,709(M); 12 TCM 594
Gerrish, Harry A. . . . . ¶ 5508.145, 38,549.21,
38,554.494
● **TC**—Dec. 18,493(M); 10 TCM 778
Intervest Enterprises, Inc., TC, Dec. 31,569, 59 TC
91
Gerrish, Samuel D. . . . . ¶ 28,649.90, 45,190.25
● **TC**—Dec. 40,641(M); 47 TCM 503; TC Memo.
1983-720
Gersh, Max . . . . ¶ 40,558.50, 42,787B.052
● **CA-2**—(dism'g taxpayer's appeal), 1985
● **TC**—Dec. 41,526(M); 48 TCM 1260; TC Memo.
1984-522
Gershkowitz, Herbert . . . . ¶ 5802.34, 7010.007,
7010.06, 25,383.032, 25,424.415, 25,826.04
● **TC**—Dec. 43,857; 88 TC 984

Exhibit 4.6
RIA Citator—Volume 1 for AFTR Series

Germantown «   821 822   » Germantown

Gerhardt, Phillip L.—continued
  a Gerhardt; Comm. v, **92 F(2d) 999,
    20 AFTR 370 (CCA 2)**
GERLACH-BARKLOW CO., 16 BTA 201
  2 Canton Cotton Mills, 26 BTA 339
  f-2 Walton Cotton Mills Co., 26 BTA 353
GERLACH; COMM. v, 68 F(2d) 996, 13 AF
    TR 634
  sr Gerlach, Theodore R., 27 BTA 565
GERLACH, THEODORE R., 27 BTA 565
    (NA) XII-1 CB 17
  r Gerlach; Comm. v, 68 F(2d) 996, 13
    AFTR 634
  1 Myers, George R., 42 BTA 644
GERLINGER v COMM., 106 F(2d) 997, 23
    AFTR 830, 1939 P.-H. ¶ 5.697 (CCA 9,
    Nov 13, 1939)
  Remanding, Gerlinger, George T., 39
    BTA 1241, Dock 90117 (Memo), Mar
    17, 1939, 1939 P.-H. ¶ 6.293
  Swindells, William & Irene G., 44 BTA
    340
GERLINGER, GEORGE T., 39 BTA 1241,
    Dock 90117 (Memo), Mar 17, 1939,
    1939 P.-H. ¶ 6.293
  Remanded, Gerlinger v Comm., 106
    F(2d) 997, 23 AFTR 830, 1939 P.-H.
    ¶ 5.697 (CCA 9)
GERMANTOWN BRAID CO., 3 BTA 1336
    (A) VI-1 CB 2
  1 Kile & Morgan Co. v Comm., 41 F(2d)
    926, 8 AFTR 11028
  1 Eby Shoe Co. v U. S., 44 F(2d) 277,
    9 AFTR 328, 70 Ct Cl 554
  1 M. S. C. Holding Corp., 7 BTA 222
  1 Suffolk Lumber Co., 18 BTA 729
GERMANTOWN TRUST CO. BOND IN-
    VEST. FUND, 38 BTA 1531, Dock
    89166 (Memo), Aug 24, 1938, 1938
    P.-H. ¶ 6.439
  r Germantown Trust Co.; Comm. v,
    106 F(2d) 139, 23 AFTR 319, 1939 P.-H.
    ¶ 5.529 (CCA 3)
  s Germantown Trust Co. v Comm., 309
    US 304, 60 S Ct 566, 84 L Ed 770,
    23 AFTR 1084, 1940-1 CB 178, 1940
    P.-H. ¶ 62,023
  s Germantown Trust Co. Bond Invest.
    Fund, 40 BTA 1380, Dock 89166
    (Memo), Sept 5, 1939, 1939 P.-H.
    ¶ 6.744
GERMANTOWN TRUST CO. BOND IN-
    VEST. FUND, 40 BTA 1380, Dock
    89166 (Memo), Sept 5, 1939, 1939
    P.-H. ¶ 6.744
  s Germantown Trust Co. v Comm., 309
    US 304, 60 S Ct 566, 84 L Ed 770,
    23 AFTR 1084, 1940-1 CB 178, 1940
    P.-H. ¶ 62,023
  s Germantown Trust Co. Bond Invest.
    Fund, 38 BTA 1531, Dock 89166
    (Memo), Aug 24, 1938, 1938 P.-H.
    ¶ 6.439
GERMANTOWN TRUST CO. v COMM., 309
    US 304, 60 S Ct 566, 84 L Ed 770,
    23 AFTR 1084, 1940-1 CB 178, 1940
    P.-H. ¶ 62,023 (Feb 26, 1940)
  sr Germantown Trust Co.; Comm. v,
    106 F(2d) 139, 23 AFTR 319, 1939 P.-H.
    ¶ 5.529 (CCA 3)
  s Germantown Trust Co. Bond Invest.
    Fund, 38 BTA 1531, Dock 89166
    (Memo), Aug 24, 1938, 1938 P.-H.
    ¶ 6.439
  s Germantown Trust Co. Bond Invest.
    Fund, 40 BTA 1380, Dock 89166
    (Memo), Sept 5, 1939, 1939 P.-H.
    ¶ 6.744
  f-1—Marshall Heirs v Comm., 111 F(2d)
    936, 25 AFTR 8, 1940 P.-H. page 62,853
    (CCA 3)
  g-1 Lane-Wells Co., 43 BTA 479
  n-1 Lane-Wells Co., 43 BTA 481
  g-1 Porto Rico Coal Co., 44 BTA 227
  f-1 Walter, Caroline S., Trust Under
    Schedule B, Stipulation of Settle-
    ment, — BTA —, Dock 102074, 1941
    (P.-H.) BTA Memo. Dec. page 41,579

Germantown Tr. Co. v Comm.—continued
  3 Alkire Invest. Co. v Nicholas, 114
    F(2d) 610, 1940 P.-H. page 63,279
    (CCA 10)
  g-3 Lane-Wells Co., 43 BTA 480
  n-3 Lane-Wells Co., 43 BTA 481
  3—Huron River Syndicate, 44 BTA 864
GERMANTOWN TRUST CO.; COMM. v,
    106 F(2d) 139, 23 AFTR 319, 1939 P.-H.
    ¶ 5.529 (CCA 3, July 14, 1939)
  r Germantown Trust Co. v Comm., 309
    US 304, 60 S Ct 566, 84 L Ed 770,
    23 AFTR 1084, 1940-1 CB 178, 1940
    P.-H. ¶ 62,023
  sr Germantown Trust Co. Bond Invest.
    Fund, 38 BTA 1531, Dock 89166
    (Memo), Aug 24, 1938, 1938 P.-H.
    ¶ 6.439
  s—Germantown Trust Co. Bond Invest.
    Fund, 40 BTA 1380, Dock 89166 (Memo),
    Sept 5, 1939, 1939 P.-H. ¶ 6.744
  q-6—Marshall Heirs v Comm., 111 F(2d)
    936, 25 AFTR 8, 1940 P.-H. page 62,853
    (CCA 3)
GERMANTOWN TRUST CO. v HELVER-
    ING, 309 US 304
  1—Botts, Carrie M., Est. of, 42 BTA 983
GERMANTOWN TRUST CO. v LEDERER,
    263 Fed 672, 4 AFTR 4246
  1 Fidelity & Deposit Co. of Md. v U.
    S., 259 US 302, 42 S Ct 514, 66 L
    Ed 952, 3 AFTR 3175. I-2 CB 351
  1 Fidelity Title & Trust Co. v U. S.,
    259 US 308, 42 S Ct 516, 66 L Ed
    955, 3 AFTR 3177, I-2 CB 346
  f-1 Lederer v Real Estate Title Ins. &
    Trust Co., 295 Fed 673, 4 AFTR
    3775
  1 Malley v Old Colony Trust Co., 299
    Fed 526, 4 AFTR 4421
  2 Malley v Old Colony Trust Co., 299
    Fed 529, 4 AFTR 4424
  3 Mayes v U. S. Trust Co., 280 Fed 27,
    4 AFTR 4358
  3 Malley v Walter Baker & Co., 281
    Fed 47, 2 AFTR 1698, I-2 CB 305
  f-3 Hampton & L. F. Ry. Co. v Noel, 300
    Fed 440, 4 AFTR 4459, III-2 CB
    136
  3 U. S. v Reitmeyer, 11 F(2d) 649, 5
    AFTR 5906
  3 Wood & Ewer Co. v Ham, 14 F(2d)
    995, 6 AFTR 6314
  g-3 U. S. v Haar, 19 F(2d) 402, 6 AFTR
    6731
  3 Rieck v Heiner, 25 F(2d) 454, 6 AF
    TR 7541, VII-1 CB 201
  f-3 Trust No. B. I. 35, etc.; U. S. v, 107
    F(2d) 24, 23 AFTR 852, 1939 P.-H. page
    5.1392 (CCA 9)
  3—Fidelity & Casualty Co. of N. Y.; U. S.
    v, 115 F(2d) 478, 25 AFTR 1017, 1940 P.-H.
    page 63,664 (CCA 3)
GERMANTOWN TRUST CO., TRUSTEE
    (GERMANTOWN TRUST CO.
    BOND INVEST. FUND), — BTA
    —, Dock 89166 (Memo), Aug 14, 1938,
    1938 P.-H. ¶ 6.439 (See Germantown
    Trust Co. Bond Investment Fund)
GERMANTOWN TRUST CO., TRUSTEE
    (GERMANTOWN TRUST CO.,
    BOND INVEST. FUND), 40 BTA
    1380, Dock 89166 (Memo), Sept 5,
    1939, 1939 P.-H. ¶ 6.744 (See Ger-
    mantown Trust Co. Bond Invest.
    Fund)
GERMANTOWN TRUST CO., TRUSTEE
    (GERMANTOWN TRUST CO.
    BOND INVEST. FUND) v COMM.,
    309 US 304, 60 S Ct 566, 84 L Ed 770,
    23 AFTR 1084, 1940-1 CB 178, 1940
    P.-H. ¶ 62,023 (See Germantown
    Trust Co. v Comm.)
GERMANTOWN TRUST CO., TRUSTEE
    (GERMANTOWN TRUST CO.
    BOND INVEST. FUND); COMM.
    v, 106 F(2d) 139, 23 AFTR 319 (See
    Germantown Trust Co.; Comm. v)

Exhibit 4.7
RIA Citator—Volume 2 for AFTR Series

Germantown «   » Germantown

Gerhardt; Helvering v—continued
g-7—Shamberg, Est. of; Comm. v, 144
F(2d) 1003, 32 AFTR 1300, 1944 P.-H. page
63,155 (CCA 2)
f-7—Murphy, Matthew H., 46 BTA 1062
7—Clock, John G., 46 BTA 1069
7—Curtis, James F., 3 TC 650
f-7—Baker, William E. & Martha D., 4 TC
312
GERLINGER, GEORGE T., — BTA —, Dock
90117, Mar 17, 1939, 1939 (P.-H.) BTA
Memo. Dec. ¶ 39,115 [1939 P.-H. ¶ 6.293]
GERMAN HUNGARIAN HOME CO., 47 BTA
1043, Dock 108524, July 24, 1942, 1942
(P.-H.) BTA Memo. Dec. ¶ 42,427 [1942
P.-H. ¶ 64,845]
GERMAN, MAX, 2 TC 474, 1943 P.-H. ¶ 64,-
778 (A) 1943 CB 9, 1943 P.-H. ¶ 66,319
1—Webster, H. D., 4 TC 1173
1—Webster, H. D., 4 TC 1174
1—Brennen, George K., 4 TC 1265
n-1—Brennen, George K., 4 TC 1271B
1—Thorrez, Camiel, 5 TC 72
n-1—Parker, Francis A., 5 TC 986
1—Canfield, Claire L., 7 TC 141
1—Loftus, Peter F., — TC —, 1944 (P.-H.)
TC Memo. Dec. page 44—1085
g-1—Croft, George A., — TC —, 1944
(P.-H.) TC Memo. Dec. page 44—1180
1—Viber Co., Ltd., — TC —, 1944 (P.-H.)
TC Memo. Dec. page 44—1187
g-1—Awrey, Fletcher E., Est. of, 5 TC
238
g-1—Hirsch, William J., — TC —, 1945
(P.-H.) TC Memo. Dec. page 45—4
1—Van Tongeren, Chester, — TC —, 1945
(P.-H.) TC Memo. Dec. page 45—392
1—Scherr, Isaac, — TC —, 1947 (P.-H.)
TC Memo. Dec. page 47—948
g-1—Wenig, Irving, — TC —, 1947 (P.-H.)
TC Memo. Dec. page 47—1145

GERMANTOWN TRUST CO. BOND IN-
VESTMENT FUND, — BTA —, Dock
89166, Aug 24, 1938, 1938 (P.-H.) BTA
Memo. Dec. ¶ 38,297 [1938 P.-H. ¶ 6.439]
iv—Roosevelt & Son Investment Fund, 34
BTA 38

GERMANTOWN, TRUST CO. BOND IN-
VEST. FUND, — BTA —, Dock 89166,
Sept 5, 1939, 1939 (P.-H.) BTA Memo.
Dec. ¶ 39,414 [1939 P.-H. ¶ 6.744]

GERMANTOWN TRUST CO. v COMM.,
309 US 304, 23 AFTR 1084
f-1—Chilhowee Mills, Inc. v Comm., 152
F(2d) 138, 34 AFTR 555, 1945 P.-H. page
73.331 (D of C App)
1—Fletcher Trust Co., Trustees & Trans-
ferees, 1 TC 803
1—Wilson, Henry, Est. of, 2 TC 1080
1—Conrad & Co., Inc., 9 TC 227
1—Sunnyside Land Co., Inc., — TC —,
1943 (P.-H.) TC Memo. Dec. page 43—
991
g-1—Weizer, William, — TC —, 1947
(P.-H.) TC Memo. Dec. page 47—307
1—Shwayder, Ben, — TC —, 1947 (P.-H.)
TC Memo. Dec. page 47—317
g-2—Masterson, Anna Aliza, 1 TC 324
g-2—Chilhowee Mills, Inc. (Dissolved), 4
TC 562
g-3—Lane-Wells Co.; Comm. v, 321 US
222, 64 S Ct 513, 88 L Ed 686, 31 AFTR 972,
1944 CB 541, 1944 P.-H. page 62.029
g-3—Chilhowee Mills, Inc. (Dissolved), 4
TC 562
f-3—Lane-Wells Co. v Comm., 134 F(2d)
978, 30 AFTR 1356, 1943 P.-H. page 62,658
(CCA 9)
f-3—Morrison Cafeterias Consol., Inc. v
U. S., 42 F Supp 76, 95 Ct Cl 156, 28 AFTR
696, 1941 P.-H. page 63,885
3—Fletcher Trust Co., Trustees & Trans-
ferees, 1 TC 803
g-3—Masterson, Anna Aliza, 1 TC 324
g-3—Tarbox Corp., 6 TC 37
3—Sunnyside Land Co., Inc., — TC —,
1943 (P.-H. TC Memo. Dec. page 43—
991

Germantown Trust Co. v Comm.—continued
3—Bacon, Edward R. Co., — TC —, 1945
(P.-H.) TC Memo. Dec. page 45—982
GERMANTOWN TRUST CO., EXEC.
(EST. OF GREENWOOD, JOHN K.),
— BTA —, 1935 (P.-H.) BTA Memo. Dec.
¶ 35,352
GERMANTOWN TRUST CO. v LED-
ERER, 263 Fed 672, 4 AFTR 4246
3—Van Hooser & Co. v Glenn, 50 F Supp
284, 31 AFTR 297, 1943 P.-H. page 62,625
(DC Ky)
GERMANTOWN TRUST CO., TRUSTEE
(GERMANTOWN TRUST CO. BOND
INVESTMENT FUND), — BTA —, Dock
89166, Aug 24, 1938, 1938 (P.-H.) BTA
Memo. Dec. ¶ 38,297 [1938 P.-H. ¶ 6.439]
(See Germantown Trust Co. Bond In-
vestment Fund)
GERMANTOWN TRUST CO., TRUSTEE
(GERMANTOWN TRUST CO. BOND
INVEST. FUND), — BTA —, Dock 89166,
Sept 5, 1939, 1939 (P.-H.) BTA Memo.
Dec. ¶ 39,414 [1939 P.-H. ¶ 6.744] (See
Germantown Trust Co. Bond Invest.
Fund)
GERSTEN, ALBERT & LUCILLE,
GRANTORS, — TC —, Dock 6116, June
24, 1947, 1947 (P.-H.) TC Memo. Dec.
¶ 47,166 [1947 P.-H. ¶ 74,520] (See Homes
Beautiful, Inc.)

GERSTLE; COMM. v, 95 F(2d) 587, 20 AFTR
1136
g-1—Helm & Smith Syndicate v Comm.,
136 F(2d) 441, 31 AFTR 178, 1943 P.-H.
page 63,022 (CCA 9)
g-1—Homecrest Tract; U.S. v, 160 F(2d)
153, 35 AFTR 973, 1947 P.-H. page 72,476
(CCA 9)
g-1—Bloomfield Ranch v Comm., 167 F(2d)
590, — AFTR —, 1948 P.-H. page 72,694
(CCA 9)
1—Lake, Harry B., — BTA —, 1940 (P.-H.)
BTA Memo. Dec. page 40—159
1—Schulze, Theodore, & Co., Inc., — BTA
—, 1940 (P.-H.) BTA Memo. Dec. page
40—159
g-1—Helm & Smith Syndicate, — BTA —,
1942 (P.-H.) BTA Memo. Dec. page 42,938
1—Russell, Waldo B. & Marion F., — TC
—, 1944 (P.-H.) TC Memo. Dec. page
44—606
f-1—Enright, W. F., — TC —, 1945 (P.-H.)
TC Memo. Dec. page 45—1248
g-1—Bloomfield Ranch, — TC —, 1947
(P.-H.) TC Memo. Dec. 47—71
1—Boots, Edmund R., — TC —, 1947
(P.-H.) TC Memo. Dec. page 47—628

GESSNER, HERMAN, 32 BTA 1258
1—Webster, H. D., 4 TC 1174
1—Brennen, George K., 4 TC 1266
g-1—Nelson, Albert, 6 TC 771
1—Greene, Paul G., 7 TC 152
1—Morley, Walter G., 8 TC 918
1—Godson, E. M., — TC —, 1946 (P.-H.)
TC Memo. Dec. page 46—621
g-1—Shwayder, Ben, — TC —, 1947 (P.-H.)
TC Memo. Dec. page 47—315

GETSINGER, R. C., 5 TC 242, 1945 P.-H.
¶ 74,501 (See Fox, Clarence L.)
App (T) Dec 10, 1945 (CCA 6)
d—Getsinger, R. C. v Comm., — F(2d) —,
1946 P.-H. ¶ 71,116 (CCA 6)

GETSINGER, R. C. v COMM., — F(2d) —,
1946 P.-H. ¶ 71,116 (CCA 6) (See Fox v
Comm.)

GETZ, ESTELLE C., 45 BTA 228, 1941 P.-H.
¶ 64,880 (A) 1942-1 CB 7, 1942 P.-H.
¶ 66.094 (See Meyer, Ben R.)
s—Getz, Estelle C., — BTA —, 1941 (P.-H.)
BTA Memo. Dec. ¶ 41,513

GETZ, ESTELLE C., — BTA —, Dock 72251,
Nov 19, 1941, 1941 (P.-H.) BTA Memo. Dec.
¶ 41,513 [1941 P.-H. ¶ 65.048]
s—Getz, Estelle C., 45 BTA 228

Exhibit 4.8
RIA Citator—Volume 3 for AFTR Series

5884   » Gerhardt — Gessner «

GERHARDT; HELVERING v, 304 US 405, 20 AFTR 1276
e-1—Gunn v Dallman, 171 F(2d) 37, 37 AFTR 597, 1948 P.-H. page 73,203 (CCA 7)
f-1—Ernest, Richard B., — BTA —, 1939 (P.-H.) BTA Memo. Dec. page 39—28
f-1—Dodge, Wallace, — BTA —, 1939 (P.-H.) BTA Memo. Dec. page 39—247
1—Baldwin, Bessie W., — BTA —, 1939 (P.-H.) BTA Memo. Dec. page 39—421
1—Harbaugh, Ross W., — BTA —, 1939 (P.-H.) BTA Memo. Dec. page 39—422
1—McAuliffe, F. M., — BTA —, 1939 (P.-H.) BTA Memo. Dec. page 39—423
1—Martinelli, Jordan L., — BTA —, 1939 (P.-H.) BTA Memo. Dec. page 39—425
1—Sheehy, Frank, — BTA —, 1939 (P.-H.) BTA Memo. Dec. page 39—428
1—Merrithew, Edwin, M. D., — BTA —, 1939 (P.-H.) BTA Memo. Dec. page 39—432
1—O'Connor, Martin P., — BTA —, 1939 (P.-H.) BTA Memo. Dec. page 39—434
1—Owen, Frank L., — BTA —, 1939 (P.-H.) BTA Memo. Dec. page 39—445
f-1—McLaurin, S. L. — BTA —, 1939 (P.-H.) BTA Memo. Dec. page 39—514
4—Wilmette Park District v Campbell, 338 US 419, 70 S Ct 199, 94 L Ed 212, 1950-1 CB 146, 38 AFTR 756, 1949 P.-H. page 72,112

e-4—Gunn v Dallman, 171 F(2d) 37, 37 AFTR 597, 1948 P.-H. page 73,203 (CCA 7)
4—Baldwin, Bessie W., — BTA —, 1939 (P.-H.) BTA Memo. Dec. page 39—421
4—Harbaugh, Ross W., — BTA —, 1939 (P.-H.) BTA Memo. Dec. page 39—422
4—McAuliffe, F. M., — BTA —, 1939 (P.-H.) BTA Memo. Dec. page 39—423
4—Martinelli, Jordan L., — BTA —, 1939 (P.-H.) BTA Memo. Dec. page 39—425
4—Sheehy, Frank, — BTA —, 1939 (P.-H.) BTA Memo. Dec. page 39—428
4—Merrithew, Edwin, M.D., — BTA —, 1939 (P.-H.) BTA Memo. Dec. page 39—432
4—O'Connor, Martin P., — BTA —, 1939 (P.-H.) BTA Memo. Dec. page 39—434
4—Owen, Frank L., — BTA —, 1939 (P.-H.) BTA Memo. Dec. page 39—445
f-4—McLaurin, S. L., — BTA —, 1939 (P.-H.) BTA Memo. Dec. page 39—514
5—Wilmette Park District v Campbell, 338 US 419, 70 S Ct 199, 94 L Ed 212, 1950-1 CB 146, 38 AFTR 756, 1949 P.-H. page 72,112

5—Dodge, Wallace, — BTA —, 1939 (P.-H.) BTA Memo. Dec. page 39—247
5—Baldwin, Bessie W., — BTA —, 1939 (P.-H.) BTA Memo. Dec. page 39—421
5—Harbaugh, Ross W., — BTA —, 1939 (P.-H.) BTA Memo. Dec. page 39—422
5—McAuliffe, F. M., — BTA —, 1939 (P.-H.) BTA Memo. Dec. page 39—423
5—Martinelli, Jordan L., — BTA —, 1939 (P.-H.) BTA Memo. Dec. page 39—425
5—Sheehy, Frank, — BTA —, 1939 (P.-H.) BTA Memo. Dec. page 39—428
5—Merrithew, Edwin, M. D., — BTA —, 1939 (P.-H.) BTA Memo. Dec. page 39—432
5—O'Connor, Martin P., — BTA —, 1939 (P.-H.) BTA Memo. Dec. page 39—434
5—Owen, Frank L., — BTA —, 1939 (P.-H.) BTA Memo. Dec. page 39—445
6—Wilmette Park District v Campbell, 338 US 419, 70 S Ct 199, 94 L Ed 212, 1950-1 CB 146, 38 AFTR 756, 1949 P.-H. page 72,112

f-6—McLaurin, S. L., — BTA —, 1939 (P.-H.) BTA Memo. Dec. page 39—514
7—Dodge, Wallace, — BTA —, 1939 (P.-H.) BTA Memo. Dec. page 39—247
7—Baldwin, Bessie W., — BTA —, 1939 (P.-H.) BTA Memo. Dec. page 39—421
7—Harbaugh, Ross W., — BTA —, 1939 (P.-H.) BTA Memo. Dec. page 39—422
7—McAuliffe, F. M., — BTA —, 1939 (P.-H.) BTA Memo. Dec. page 39—423
7—Martinelli, Jordan L., — BTA —, 1939 (P.-H.) BTA Memo. Dec. page 39—425

Gerhardt; Helvering v—continued
7—Sheehy, Frank, — BTA —, 1939 (P.-H.) BTA Memo. Dec. page 39—428
7—Merrithew, Edwin, M.D., — BTA —, 1939 (P.-H.) BTA Memo. Dec. page 39—432
7—O'Connor, Martin P., — BTA —, 1939 (P.-H.) BTA Memo. Dec. page 39—434
7—Owen, Frank L., — BTA —, 1939 (P.-H.) BTA Memo. Dec. page 39—445

GERICKE, EMMA, — BTA —, 1930 (P.-H.) BTA Memo. Dec. ¶ 30,064 (See Siterlet, Frank J.)
GERICKE, MORRIS, — BTA —, 1930 (P.-H.) BTA Memo. Dec. ¶ 30,064 (See Siterlet, Frank J.)
GERKE, EFFIE M., 1954 (P.-H.) TC Memo. Dec. ¶ 54,136 (See Gerke, H. E.)
GERKE, H. E., 1954 (P.-H.) TC Memo. Dec. ¶ 54,136
GERKE, H. E. & EFFIE M., 1954 (P.-H.) TC Memo. Dec. ¶ 54,136 (See Gerke, H. E.)
GERLACH, HAROLD W., 1954 (P.-H.) TC Memo. Dec. ¶ 54,018 (See Martin, Charles H. & Elizabeth K.)
GERLACH, HAROLD W. & HAZEL, 1954 (P.-H.) TC Memo. Dec. ¶ 54,018 (See Martin, Charles H. & Elizabeth K.)
GERMAIN, HOMER H. & AGNES, 1952 (P.-H.) TC Memo. Dec. ¶ 52,063
GERMAN, MAX, 2 TC 474
g-1—Stein, Herbert, 14 TC 502, 14-1950 P.-H. TC 281
GERMANTOWN TRUST CO. v. COMM., 309 US 304, 23 AFTR 1084
Morrison, Emma H., Trustee, — BTA —, 1940 (P.-H.) BTA Memo. Dec. page 40—684
3—Danz, John, 18 TC 465, 18-1952 P.-H. TC 257
3—C. A. C. Bldg. Site, — BTA —, 1940 (P.-H.) BTA Memo. Dec. page 40—357
f-3—Mandis, Demos. — TC —, 1950 (P.-H.) TC Memo. Dec. page 50—467
GERNHARDT-STROHMAIER CO., INC. v U. S., 84 F Supp 51, 37 AFTR 1541, 1949 P.-H. ¶ 72,438 (DC Calif, April 23, 1949)
GERRARD v CAMPBELL, 81 F Supp 752, 37 AFTR 804, 1949 P.-H. ¶ 72,320 (DC Ill, Jan. 24, 1949)
GERRISH, EDWARD S., 1953 (P.-H.) TC Memo. Dec. ¶ 53,187
GERRISH, HARRY A., 1951 (P.-H.) TC Memo. Dec. ¶ 51,241
GERSON, BEESLEY & HAMPTON, INC. v SHUBERT THEATRE CORP., 7 F Supp 399, 14 AFTR 121 (DC NY)
g-3—Roberts & McInnis v Emery's Motor Coach Lines, Inc., — West Va. Cir Ct, Berkley County —, 42 AFTR 1344, 1950 P.-H. page 73,324
GERSTLE; COMM. v, 95 F(2d) 587, 20 AFTR 1136 (CCA 9)
Koshland, Execx.; U. S. v, 208 F(2d) 640, — AFTR —, 1953 P.-H. page 73,597 (CCA 9)
e—DuPont, Francis V., — BTA —, 1940 (P.-H.) BTA Memo. Dec. page 40—470
g-1—Mendelsohn, Walter, — BTA —, 1939 (P.-H.) BTA Memo. Dec. page 39—242
GERSTLE, MARK L., 33 BTA 830
g-1—Mendelsohn, Walter, — BTA —, 1939 (P.-H.) BTA Memo. Dec. page 39—242
g-1—DuPont, Francis V., — BTA —, 1940 (P.-H.) BTA Memo. Dec. page 40—470
2—Koshland, Execx.; U.S. v, 208 F(2d) 640, — AFTR —, 1953 P.-H. page 73,597 (CCA 9)
GERWICK, BEN C., INC., 1954 (P.-H.) TC Memo. Dec. ¶ 54,100
GESSNER, HERMAN, 32 BTA 1258
1—White, Oren C., 18 TC 386, 18-1952 P.-H. TC 212
1—Culbertson, Ruth, 1953 (P.-H.) TC Memo. Dec. page 53—181

Exhibit 4.9
RIA Citator—Volume 1 for AFTR 2d Series

<table>
<tr><td align="center">GERARD—GERNIE</td><td align="right">1387</td></tr>
</table>

GERARD, SUMNER, JR., EXEC. v COMM., 35
AFTR2d 75-1641, 513 F2d 1232 (USCA 2) (See
Gerard, Sumner, Est. of v Comm.)
GERARDO, ANDREW, 1975 P-H TC Memo ¶ 75,341
remd—Gerardo, Andrew v Comm., 39 AFTR2d 77-1176,
552 F2d 549 (USCA 3)
GERARDO, ANDREW v COMM., 39 AFTR2d 77-1176,
552 F2d 549 (USCA 3, 3-18-77)
No cert (G) 1977 P-H ¶ 61,000
remg—Gerardo, Andrew, 1975 P-H TC Memo ¶ 75,341
f-1—Gordon, Harry v Comm., 40 AFTR2d 77-5728
(USCA 9)
GERBER, BERNARD C. & MARCELLA A., 1974 P-H
TC Memo ¶ 74,065 (See Bormes, Robert E. & Patricia
A.)
GERBER, ERWIN & RUTH B., 32 TC 1199, ¶ 32.115
P-H TC 1959
e-1—Farber v Comm., 11 AFTR2d 517, 312 F2d 736
(USCA 2)
1—Loveman, D. & Son Export Corp., 34 TC 807,
34-1960 P-H TC 589
e-1—Braude, Paul & Anne, 35 TC 1163, 35-1961 P-H
TC 865
g-1—Thomson, Arthur D. & Mary C., 42 TC 832, 42
P-H TC 603
1—Meneguzzo, Barry, 43 TC 825, 43 P-H TC 599
g-1—Alper, Louis, Est. of, 1961 P-H TC Memo 61-1785
1—Huebner, Paul B. & Carol A., 1966 P-H TC Memo
66-462
GERBER, JOHN, CO., 44 BTA 26
2—Weinberger, Herman, 1955 P-H TC Memo 55—221
f-2—Daniels, George & Isabelle, 1957 P-H TC Memo
57—800
f-2—Ginsberg, Charles J., Est. of, 1958 P-H TC Memo
58-416
GERDEL; U.S. v, 103 F Supp 635, 41 AFTR 1022 (DC
Mo)
Waldin; U.S. v, 1 AFTR2d 919, 253 F2d 553 (USCA 3)
g-5—Waldin; U.S. v, 138 F Supp 795, 49 AFTR 614
(DC Pa)
GERHARD, ERWIN v CAREY, 52 AFTR 1617 (DC
Ohio) (See Moll v Carey)
GERHARD, W. RICHARD & DAWNA V., 1970 P-H TC
Memo ¶ 70,262
GERHARDT; HELVERING v, 304 US 405, 20 AFTR
1276
1—Sims v U.S., 3 AFTR2d 968, 359 US 110, 79 S Ct
644, 3 L Ed 2d 610, 1959-1 CB 637
e-1—Sims v U.S., 1 AFTR2d 966, 252 F2d 438, 1959-1
CB 637 (USCA 4)
1—State Road Dept. of the State of Florida; U.S. v, 1
AFTR2d 2274, 255 F2d 518 (USCA 5)
e-1—Wash. Toll Bridge Auth.; U.S. v, 10 AFTR2d 6354,
307 F2d 333 (USCA 9)
e-1—N.Y., City of v U.S., 36 AFTR2d 75-6552, 394 F
Supp 644 (DC NY)
1—Rev. Rul. 55-227, 1955-1 CB 552
2—Washington Toll Bridge Auth.; U.S. v, 7 AFTR2d
1846, 190 F Supp 98 (DC Wash)
n-3—Child, Ruth K., Execx. v U.S., 38 AFTR2d
76-6285, 540 F2d 589 (USCA 2)
3—Wash. Toll Bridge Auth.; U.S. v, 7 AFTR2d 1846,
190 F Supp 98 (DC Wash)
e-5—Wash. Toll Bridge Auth.; U.S. v, 10 AFTR2d 6354,
307 F2d 333 (USCA 9)
e-5—Troy State University, 62 TC 500, 502, 62 P-H TC
304, 305
f-5—Beer, William J. & Dora, 64 TC 880, 64 P-H TC
487
e-6—Wash. Toll Bridge Auth.; U.S. v, 10 AFTR2d 6354,
307 F2d 333 (USCA 9)
6—Holdeen, Jonathan, Est. of, 1975 P-H TC Memo
75-191
7—Sims v U.S., 1 AFTR2d 967, 252 F2d 440 (USCA 4)
GERKE, EFFIE M., 1954 P-H TC Memo ¶ 54,136 (See
Gerke, H. E.)
GERKE, H. E., 1954 P-H TC Memo ¶ 54,136
d—1955 P-H ¶ 71,094 (USCA 5)
GERKE, H. E. & EFFIE M., 1954 P-H TC Memo ¶
54,136 (See Gerke, H. E.)
GERLACH-BARKLOW CO., THE; U.S. v, 48 AFTR
1858 (DC SC) (See Pee Dee Coach Lines, Inc.; U.S. v)

GERLACH, EDITH M., 55 TC 156, ¶ 55.19 P-H TC (A)
1971-2 CB 2
d—1971 P-H ¶ 61,000 (USCA 6)
rc—Gerlach, Norman v U.S., 34 AFTR2d 74-5132, 201
Ct Cl 884
f—Weiner, Walter H., 61 TC 159, 61 P-H TC 95 [See 55
TC 156, 159]
f—Veverka, Ernest L., 1970 P-H TC Memo 70-1638 [See
55 P-H TC 55-115—55-116]
f—Lambros, Michael N., 1971 P-H TC Memo 71-612
[See 55 TC 167]
Pumi-Blok Co., 1972 P-H TC Memo 72-215 [See 55 TC
168-169]
e—Hayutin, Irving J. & Sima B., 1972 P-H TC Memo
72-592 [See 55 TC 165-167]
e-1—Mirsky, Enid P., 56 TC 674, 675, 56 P-H TC 466,
467 [See 55 TC 167]
g-1—Wright, William C. & Ellen W., 62 TC 390, 62 P-H
TC 238
1—Barnett, John H. & Abigail S., 1974 P-H TC Memo
74-25
1—Wilder, Robert E. & June, 1975 P-H TC Memo
75-282
GERLACH, NORMAN v U.S., 34 AFTR2d 74-5132, 201
Ct Cl 884 (4-27-73)
rc—Gerlach, Edith M., 55 TC 156, ¶ 55.19 P-H TC
GERLER, IRA & SELMA L., 26 TC 315, ¶ 26.38 P-H
TC 1956 (See Grahm, Milton L. & Edith L.)
GERMAN, MAX, 2 TC 474
e—Evans v Comm., 28 AFTR2d 71-5469, 447 F2d 552
(USCA 7) [See 2 TC 480]
1—Stanback v Comm., 4 AFTR2d 5795, 271 F2d 517
(USCA 4)
g-1—Paul, George A. & Pearl, 1957 P-H TC Memo 57—
642
e-1—Otte, Everett, Est. of, 1972 P-H TC Memo 72-324
GERMANTOWN TRUST CO. v COMM., 309 US 304,
23 AFTR 1084
True v U.S., 17 AFTR2d 1320, 173 Ct Cl 713, 354 F2d
327
n-1—Automobile Club of Mich. v Comm., 353 US 191,
77 S Ct 713, 1 L Ed 2d 754, 50 AFTR 1973
1—McGillick Foundation v Comm., 5 AFTR2d 1519,
278 F2d 648 (USCA 8)
1—Michaud, In re, 29 AFTR2d 72-893, 458 F2d 957
(USCA 3)
q-1—Durovic, Marko v Comm., 32 AFTR2d 73-5973,
487 F2d 39 (USCA 7)
n-1—Durovic, Marko v Comm., 32 AFTR2d 73-5980,
73-5981, 73-5982, 73-5983 (USCA 7) 487 F2d 49, 50,
51, 53
1—Dubuque Packing Co. v U.S., 126 F Supp 799, 46
AFTR 1800 (DC Iowa)
1—Rose, Jack, 24 TC 769, 24-1955 P-H TC 420
1—McGillick, F. E. Co., 30 TC 1148, 30-1958 P-H TC
661
g-3—West Coast Ice Co., 49 TC 349, 49 P-H TC 245
g-3—Harrison; U.S. v, 30 AFTR2d 72-5369 (DC NY)
3—McKinley Corp. of Ohio, 36 TC 1191, 36-1961 P-H
TC 884
3—Houston, John H., 38 TC 491, 38 P-H TC 383
3—Stevens Bros. Foundation, Inc., 39 TC 129, 39 P-H
TC 96
3—Gen. Mfg. Corp., 44 TC 523, 44 P-H TC 374
3—California Thoroughbred Breeders Association, 47 TC
338, 339, 47 P-H TC 241, 242
g-3—Durovic, Marko, 54 TC 1386, 1387, 54 P-H TC
986, 987
e-3—Caswal Corp., 1960 P-H TC Memo 60-848
g-3—Henk, Admx. v Columbus Auto Supply, Inc., 5
AFTR2d 832, 101 NW2d 415 (S Ct Minn)
f-3—Rev Rul 74-203, 1974-1 CB 330
GERMANTOWN TRUST CO.; COMM v, 106 F2d 139,
23 AFTR 319 (USCA 3)
6—Caswal Corp., 1960 P-H TC Memo 60-848
GERMANTOWN TRUST CO. v LEDERER, 263 Fed
672, 4 AFTR 4246 (USCA 3)
n-3—Past, Exec.; U.S. v, 15 AFTR2d 1427, 347 F2d 15
(USCA 9)
e-3—Ginsberg v U.S., 19 AFTR2d 1553 (DC Calif)
GERMON, LOUIS J., 1956 P-H TC Memo ¶ 56,159
GERNIE v MOE, 5 AFTR2d 983 (DC NY, 2-17-60)

Exhibit 4.10
RIA Citator—Volume 2 for AFTR 2d Series

1041   GERMANTOWN—GERMANTOWN   1042

GERLI—contd.
e—Orrock, William B. & Cherryle S., 1982 PH TC
Memo 82-1232
e—Ebben, Leo G. & Donna W., 1983 PH TC Memo
83-815
g-1—Union Pacific R.R. Co. & Affiliated Companies v
U.S., 57 AFTR2d 86-935, 9 Cl Ct 705
g-1—Sherwood Properties, Inc., 89 TC 672, 89 PH TC
348
**GERLING INTERNAT. INS. CO., 86 TC 468, ¶ 86.31
PH TC**
App (T) 12-24-86 (USCA 3)
rc—Gerling Internat. Ins. Co. v Comm., 61 AFTR2d
88-553, 839 F2d 131 (USCA 3)
rc—Gerling Internat. Ins. Co., 87 TC 679, ¶ 87.41 PH
TC
e—Flying Tigers Oil Co., Inc., 92 TC 1265, 92 PH TC
638 [See 86 TC 478, n. 8]
e—Tidler, Harold S., 1987 PH TC Memo 87-1298 [See
86 TC 477]
e-1—Fisher, Lee B., 1986 PH TC Memo 86-912
**GERLING INTERNAT. INS. CO., 87 TC 679, ¶ 87.41
PH TC**
r—Gerling Internat. Ins. Co. v Comm., 61 AFTR2d
88-553, 839 F2d 131 (USCA 3)
rc—Flying Tigers Oil Co., Inc., 92 TC 1265, 92 PH TC
638
**GERLING INTERNAT. INS. CO. v COMM., 61
AFTR2d 88-553, 839 F2d 131 (USCA 3, 1-29-88)**
sr—Gerling Internat. Ins Co., 87 TC 679, ¶ 87.41 PH TC
rc—Gerling Internat. Ins. Co., 86 TC 468, ¶ 86.31 PH
TC
e—Flying Tigers Oil Co., Inc., 92 TC 1265, 92 PH TC
638
e-1—Home Group, Inc., The, Agent for City Investing
Co. v Comm., 63 AFTR2d 89-1363, 875 F2d 381
(USCA 2)
**GERMAC ROOFING, INC. v U.S., 59 AFTR2d 87-572
(DC Pa, 1-23-87)**
**GERMAC ROOFING & SIDING v U.S., 59 AFTR2d
87-572 (DC Pa)** (See Germac Roofing, Inc. v U.S.)
GERMAIN, JOHN, 1983 PH TC Memo ¶ 83,220
a—Court Order, 8-31-84 (USCA 6)
e—Diehl, Thomas C., 1987 PH TC Memo 87-743 [See
1983 PH TC Memo 83-895]
e-1—Petzoldt, Charles, 92 TC 685, 92 PH TC 346
e-1—Johnson, J. F. Wilmar, 1985 PH TC Memo 85-123
e-1—Graham, Dana L., 1987 PH TC Memo 87-2096
**GERMAIN, JOHN M. v U.S., 54 AFTR2d 84-5584 (DC
Mich, 6-29-84)**
**GERMAN, ESTELLE E., EST. OF v U.S., 55 AFTR2d
85-1577, 7 Cl Ct 641 (3-26-85)**
e—Union Pacific R.R. Co. & Affiliated Companies v
U.S., 61 AFTR2d 88-1203, 847 F2d 1571 (USCA Fed)
[See 55 AFTR2d 85-1581, 7 Cl Ct 645]
Piper, William T., Sr., Est. of v U.S., 55 AFTR2d
85-1601, 8 Cl Ct 249 [See 55 AFTR2d 85-1581]
e-1—Kretchmar, Frank R. v U.S., 57 AFTR2d 86-311, 9
Cl Ct 198
e-1—Paxton, Floyd G., Est. of, 86 TC 815, 86 PH TC
414
GERMAN, LEATRICE, 1986 PH TC Memo ¶ 86,370
a—Court Order, 5-14-87 (USCA 3)
**GERMAN SOCIETY OF MD., INC. 80 TC 741, ¶ 80.35
PH TC**
f-1—Shunk, John Q., Assn., Inc. v U.S., 57 AFTR2d
86-525, 626 F Supp 569 (DC Ohio)
e-1—Mannheimer, Hans S. Charitable Tr., 93 TC 40, 93
PH TC 21
● **GERMANTOWN TRUST CO. v COMM., 309 US 304,
23 AFTR 1084**
e—Franklin, Lindsay D., 1984 PH TC Memo 84-1068
[See 309 US 309, 23 AFTR 1086]
Nicolaisen, Frederick C. & Linda S., 1985 PH TC Memo
85-539 [Cited at 77 TC 1177]
n-1—Badaracco, Ernest, Sr. v Comm., 53 AFTR2d
84-454, 464 US 403, 104 S Ct 766, 78 LEd2d 563
g-1—Standard Office Bldg. Corp. v U.S., 59 AFTR2d
87-1178, 819 F2d 1381 (USCA 7)
k-1—Neptune Mutual Assn., Ltd. of Bermuda, The v
U.S., 63 AFTR2d 89-877, 862 F2d 1555 (USCA Fed)

GERMANTOWN—contd.
1—Grabinski, John M.; U.S. v, 52 AFTR2d 83-5174, 558
F Supp 1331 (DC Minn)
f-1—Neptune Mutual Assn., Ltd., of Bermuda, The v
U.S., 60 AFTR2d 87-6186, 13 Cl Ct 324
f-1—Rutland, Hulan E., 89 TC 1154, 89 PH TC 594
g-1—Shapland, Earl P., 1979 PH TC Memo 79-1127 [See
309 US 310, 23 AFTR 1087]
e-1—Thomsen, Peter K. & Myrna D., 1986 PH TC
Memo 86-460 [Cited at 77 TC 1177]
e-1—Sunderlin, Thomas J., 1986 PH TC Memo 86-638
[Cited at 77 TC 1177]
e-1—Letter Ruling 8045003, 1980 PH 55,687, 55,688
2—Beard, Robert D., 82 TC 779, 82 PH TC 403
e-3—Moore, David N.; U.S. v, 47 AFTR2d 81-518, 627
F2d 835 (USCA 7)
g-3—Atlantic Land & Improvement Co. v U.S., 58
AFTR2d 86-5132, 790 F2d 858 (USCA 11)
g-3—Standard Office Building Corp. v U.S., 59 AFTR2d
87-331, 87-1332, 640 F Supp 555 (DC Ill)
f-3—D'Avanza, Anthony R., Jr., In Re, 64 AFTR2d
89-5611 (Bkt Ct Fla)
e-3—Reiff, Charles C. & Mildred H., 77 TC 1177, 77 PH
TC 628
e-3—Raley, John C., 1982 PH TC Memo 82-2712
e-3—Tracy, Donald G., 1985 PH TC Memo 85-178
g-3—Synanon Church, The, 1989 PH TC Memo 89-1378
**GERMANTOWN TRUST CO. v LEDERER, 263 Fed
672, 4 AFTR 4246 (USCA 3)**
f-3—Durbin, Marshall, Food Corp. v U.S., 43 AFTR2d
79-989 (DC Ala)
**GERRARD, JOSEPHINE M. v CALIF.
EDUCATIONAL LOAN PROGRAM, 60 AFTR2d
87-5582, 656 F Supp 570 (DC Calif)** (See Gerrard,
Josephine M. v U.S. Office of Education)
**GERRARD, JOSEPHINE M. v U.S. OFFICE OF
EDUCATION, 60 AFTR2d 87-5582, 656 F Supp 570
(DC Calif, 3-23-87)**
e—Thomas, Deborah v Bennett, William, 62 AFTR2d
88-5632, 856 F2d 1169 (USCA 8) [See 60 AFTR2d
87-5582, 656 F Supp 574]
f-1—Roberts, Nadine v Bennett, William (Dept. of
Education), 64 AFTR2d 89-5184, 709 F Supp 224 (DC
Ga)
**GERRES, THOMAS E. & BARBARA E., 1986 PH TC
Memo ¶ 86,573**
**GERRISH, SAMUEL D. & GABRIELLE, 1983 PH TC
Memo ¶ 83,720**
GERSH, MAX, 1984 PH TC Memo ¶ 84,522
d—1985 PH 61,000 (USCA 2)
e-1—Wright, John T. & Susan L., 84 TC 639, 84 PH TC
335
GERSHKOWITZ, HERBERT, 88 TC 984, ¶ 88.54 PH TC
e—Young, William & Ruby, 1987 PH TC Memo 87-2041
[See 88 TC 1017—1019]
1—Moore, Virgil W. & Frances R., 1987 PH TC Memo
87-2697
e—Slavin, Melvin A. & Sandra, 1989 PH TC Memo
89-1052 [See 88 TC 1005]
e—McGuffey, Jack D. & Mary J., 1989 PH TC Memo
89-1320 [See 88 TC 1018—1019]
e—Schrott, John D., 1989 PH TC Memo 89-1751 [See 88
TC 1005]
GERSHMAN, HAROLD, 83 TC 217, ¶ 83.14 PH TC (A)
1985-2 CB viii (See Gershman, Harold & Julia, Family
Foundation)
**GERSHMAN, HAROLD & JULIA, FAMILY
FOUNDATION, 83 TC 217, ¶ 83.14 PH TC (A)**
1985-2 CB viii
e—Reis, Bernard J., Est. of, 87 TC 1020, 87 PH TC 520
[See 83 TC 224—225]
GERSON, DANIEL, 1989 PH TC Memo ¶ 89,052
**GERSTACKER, CARL A. & ESTHER S., 1987 PH TC
Memo ¶ 87,321** (See Branch, C. Benson & Anita)
**GERSTACKER, CARL A. & JAYNE H., 49 TC 522,
¶ 49.57 PH TC**
q-1—Levine, Joseph R., Est. of, 1982 PH TC Memo
82-17
q-1—Smith, Thomas M., 1982 PH TC Memo 82-1948
q-1—Levine Ruling 8021004, 1980 PH 55,042
**GERSTACKER v COMM., 24 AFTR2d 69-5389, 414 F2d
448 (USCA 6)**
e-1—Levine, Irving Seth v Comm., 51 AFTR2d 83-352,
695 F2d 61 (USCA 2)

Exhibit 4.11
RIA Citator—1990–1992 Cumulative Supplement
for AFTR 2d Series

GERARDO—GIBSON 181

GERARDO—contd.
l—Petti, Chris, 1990 PH TC Memo 90-1180
e—Rosa, Miguel A., 1990 PH TC Memo 90-589 [See 1975 PH TC Memo 75-1447—75-1448]
e—Chagra, Jamiel & Elizabeth, 1991 TC Memo 91-1850 [See 1975 PH TC Memo 75-1447—75-1448]
GERARDO, ANDREW v COMM., 39 AFTR2d 77-1176, 552 F2d 549 (USCA 3)
e—Brown, Earl A., Jr. v U.S., 65 AFTR2d 90-462, 890 F2d 1347 (USCA 5) [See 39 AFTR2d 77-1180, 552 F2d 555-556]
e—Walton, William L.; U.S. v, 66 AFTR2d 90-5382, 90-5385, 909 F2d 919, 923 (USCA 6) [See 39 AFTR2d 77-1180, 552 F2d 554-565]
e—Erickson, Sidney A. v Comm., 68 AFTR2d 91-5264, 937 F2d 1551 (USCA 10) [See 39 AFTR2d 77-1180, 552 F2d 554]
e—Rosa, Miguel A., 1990 PH TC Memo 90-589 [See 39 AFTR2d 77-1180, 552 F2d 554]
g—Petti, Chris, 1990 PH TC Memo 90-1180 [See 39 AFTR2d 77-1176, 552 F2d 554-555]
e—Stewart, Marietta, 1990 PH TC Memo 90-1213 [See 39 AFTR2d 77-1178, 552 F2d 552]
e—Berry, Edward F. & Dorothy M., 1990 PH TC Memo 90-1871 [See 39 AFTR2d 77-1180, 552 F2d 554]
e-1—Day, Stephen S. & Jeanette L., 1991 TC Memo 91-662
e-1—Chagra, Jamiel & Elizabeth, 1991 TC Memo 91-1850
GERBER & ASSOCIATES, INC., 1987 PH TC Memo ¶ 87,446
e—Hobson Motor Co., Inc., 1990 PH TC Memo 90-1401 [See 1987 PH TC Memo 87-2366]
GERHART, JAMES M. & PHYLLIS, 1991 TC Memo ¶ 91,035
rc—Berry, Cameron E., 1991 TC Memo 91-701, 91-702
GERINGER, HAROLD I. & ELEANORE N., 1991 TC Memo ¶ 91,032
GERKEN, LOUIS C., 1991 TC Memo ¶ 91,017
GERLI & CO., INC. v COMM., 49 AFTR2d 82-569, 668 F2d 691 (USCA 2)
e—Dietz, R.E., Corp. v U.S., 68 AFTR2d 91-5241—91-5242, 939 F2d 5 (USCA 2) [See 49 AFTR2d 82-575, 668 F2d 698]
GERMAN SOCIETY OF MD., INC., 80 TC 741, ¶ 80.35 PH TC
e—Fischer, Kermit, Foundation, 1990 PH TC Memo 90-1417 [See 80 TC 745]
● **GERMANTOWN TRUST CO. v COMM., 309 US 304, 23 AFTR 1084**
f—Letter Ruling 9022002, 1990 PH 86,474 [See 309 US 310, 23 AFTR 1087]
f-1—Siben, Gary L. v Comm., 67 AFTR2d 91-893, 930 F2d 1036 (USCA 2)
GERRARD, JOSEPHINE M. v U.S. OFFICE OF EDUCATION, 60 AFTR2d 87-5582, 656 F Supp 570 (DC Calif)
e-1—Jones, Adeline v Cavazos, Lauro F., 65 AFTR2d 90-378, 889 F2d 1048 (USCA 11)
k-1—Grider, David v Cavazos, Lauro, 66 AFTR2d 90-5635, 911 F2d 1163 (USCA 5)
GERSHKOWITZ, HERBERT, 88 TC 984, ¶ 88.54 PH TC
d—(T app) 5-1-91 (USCA 2)
rc—Newman, Michael, Est. of v Comm., 67 AFTR2d 91-1117, 934 F2d 427 (USCA 2)
rc—Newman, Michael, Est. Of, 1990 PH TC Memo ¶ 90,230
e—Carberry, Timothy F., Est. of, 95 PH TC 73, 95 PH TC 36 [See 88 TC 1017-1019]
e—Williams, Clarence & Samaria, 1990 PH TC Memo 90-1242, 90-1243 [See 88 TC 1005-1006, 1016]
e—Hogan, Joseph M. & Barbara J., 1990 PH TC Memo 90-1387 [See 88 TC 1017-1019]
f—Rev Rul 91-31, 1991-1 CB 19
GERSHMAN, HAROLD & JULIA, FAMILY FOUNDATION, 83 TC 217, ¶ 83.14 PH TC
e—Wood, Dallas C., 95 PH TC 370, 95 PH TC 183 [See 83 TC 225]
GERTZ, ROBERT L. & J. KAY, 64 TC 598, ¶ 64.60 PH TC
e—Pinson, Theo W., III & Joan B., 1990 PH TC Memo 90-1055 [See 64 TC 599-600]

GERTZ—contd.
e—Washburn, A. Lawrence, Jr. & Susanne, 1991 TC Memo 91-951 [See 64 TC 600]
e-1—Euramco Associates, Inc., 1991 TC Memo 91-150
e-1—Mills, Albert Victor, 1991 TC Memo 91-2882
GESSLER, RICHARD F., 1985 PH TC Memo ¶ 85,390
e-1—Hinojos, Everett H. & Christine, 1991 TC Memo 91-1993
GESTRICH, ROBERT T., 74 TC 525, ¶ 74.38 PH TC
e—Crouch, Holmes F. & Irma J., 1990 PH TC Memo 90-1464, 90-1465 [See 74 TC 529]
e—Cady, Richard H. & Sylvia H., 1990 PH TC Memo 90-2272 [See 74 TC 531]
e—Tafolla, Margaret M., 1991 TC Memo 91-2839 [See 74 TC 530-531]
GETTINGS, CHARLES FLOYD, 1988 PH TC Memo ¶ 88,328
e—Moody, Johnny T. & Kathleen, 1991 TC Memo 91-2899 [See 1988 PH TC Memo 88-1626]
GETTY, JEAN RONALD v COMM., 66 AFTR2d 90-5517, 913 F2d 1486 (USCA 9, 9-14-90)
sr—Getty, Jean Ronald & Karin, 91 TC 160, ¶ 91.16 PH TC
GETTY, JEAN RONALD & KARIN, 91 TC 160, ¶ 91.16 PH TC
r—Getty, Jean Ronald v Comm., 66 AFTR2d 90-5517, 913 F2d 1486 (USCA 9)
GEURKINK v U.S., 17 AFTR2d 040, 354 F2d 629 (USCA 7)
e—Levin, Morton, 1990 PH TC Memo 90-1025 [See 17 AFTR2d 042-043, 354 F2d 632]
e-2—Capitol Fed. Svgs. & Loan Assn. & Subsidiary, 96 TC 217, 96 TCR 108
G & G RECORDS INC., 1983 PH TC Memo ¶ 83,343
e—Bokum, Richard D., II & Margaret B., 94 TC 148, 94 PH TC 75 [See 1983 PH TC Memo 83-1384]
GHIDONI, LAWRENCE L. & JOYCELYN B., 1991 TC Memo ¶ 91,284 (See Ghidoni, Lawrence Lee)
GHIDONI, LAWRENCE LEE, 1991 TC Memo ¶ 91,284
GHILZAI, FARID, 1991 TC Memo ¶ 91,136
d—(T app) 9-20-91 (USCA 9)
GIANNINI PACKING CORP., 83 TC 526, ¶ 83.26 PH TC
g—Garnac Grain Co., Inc., 95 TC 30, 95 PH TC 15
g-1—Morrison, Inc. v Comm., 65 AFTR2d 90-544, 891 F2d 862 (USCA 11)
GIBBONS INTERNAT., INC., 89 TC 1156, ¶ 89.81 PH TC
e—Jet Research, Inc., 1990 PH TC Memo 90-2217 [See 89 TC 1163]
GIBBS, J.W., SR., EST. OF, 21 TC 443, ¶ 21.55 PH TC 1954
e—Rosberg, David, 1990 PH TC Memo 90-1569 [See 21 TC 447]
e—Cruz, Ruben & Olga, 1990 PH TC Memo 90-2927 [See 21 TC 447]
GIBBS, LINDA G. v U.S., 67 AFTR2d 91-749, 929 F2d 1119 (USCA 6) (See Burke, Therese A. v U.S.)
GIBBS v TOMLINSON, 17 AFTR2d 1251, 362 F2d 394 (USCA 5)
e—Hunt, Raymond W.F., 1991 TC Memo 91-2770 [See 17 AFTR2d 1252, 362 F2d 397]
GIBLIN v COMM., 277 F2d 692, 48 AFTR 478 (USCA 5)
e-1—Farrington, Ronald L., In re, 65 AFTR2d 90-618 (Bkt Ct Okla)
GIBSON, DAVID A. v U.S., 68 AFTR2d 91-5102, 761 F Supp 685 (DC Calif, 4-4-91)
GIBSON, JOSEPH H. & GLORIA I., 89 TC 1177, ¶ 89.83 PH TC
e—Perry, Stewart, 1990 PH TC Memo 90-1032 [See 89 TC 1182-1183, 1185-1187]
GIBSON PRODUCTS CO. v U.S., 47 AFTR2d 81-863, 637 F2d 1041 (USCA 4)
g—Lebowitz, S. Peter v Comm., 66 AFTR2d 90-5871, 917 F2d 1319 (USCA 2) [See 47 AFTR2d 81-869—81-870, 637 F2d 1049-1051]
e-1—Bokum, Richard D., II & Margaret B., 1990 PH TC Memo 90-94
e-2—Donahue, Denise, 1991 TC Memo 91-887 [cited at 83 TC 549]
g-2—Baker, Willard R. & Martha G., 1991 TC Memo 91-1658

versed the Circuit Court cannot be determined from the citator. Additional cases in which *Germantown Trust Co.* has been cited are listed, but, in order to compile a more complete listing, all citator volumes must be consulted (that is, in addition to volume 1, volumes 2 and 3 of the AFTR series, volumes 1 and 2 of the AFTR 2d series, the 1990–1991 Cumulative Supplement, and the current monthly cumulative supplement). Note that exhibits 4.6 through 4.11 illustrate all volumes except the current monthly cumulative supplement.

It should be apparent that the *CCH Citator* is the more convenient source for locating a particular case in order to determine its original trial court, to trace its history through the appeals courts, and finally to compile a summary of cases in which the decision was subsequently cited. However, in the case of *Germantown*, the multivolume *RIA Citator*, in the aggregate, discloses a larger number of cases in which *Germantown Trust Co.* has been cited than does the two volume *CCH Citator*. Furthermore, the *RIA Citator* features several other advantages not to be found in the *CCH Citator*, which may be of considerable importance to the tax researcher. Most of these advantages will assist the tax adviser in the process of assessing potential tax authority; thus, a detailed discussion of these desirable features will be deferred until the following chapter.

Editorial Interpretations

The sheer bulk and complexity of the tax statutes make it impossible for any individual to understand all of the rules and regulations pertinent to a tax practice. Fortunately, tax practitioners have at their disposal a variety of editorial interpretations, ranging from extensive looseleaf tax services to brief explanations in professional journals and pamphlets. Much of this information is invaluable to an efficient tax practice.

Tax Services

Perhaps the most significant assistance is available through a subscription to one or more major tax services. (See exhibit 4.12 for a list of some available tax services.) Tax services are designed to help locate statutory, administrative, and judicial authority quickly

Exhibit 4.12
Tax Services

Tax Service	Publisher	Cost*	Index and Organization	Content of Complete Set	Supplementation
Bender's Federal Tax Service†	Commerce Clearing House, Inc. 4025 W. Peterson Ave. Chicago, IL 60646	$ 950[1]	Indexed by topic, code section, cases, and rulings. Organized by topic.	18 volumes with additional binders for weekly newsletter, blank tax forms, and booklets. Has topical analysis and IRC, regulations, and weekly newsletter. Emphasis is on typical analysis.	Updated monthly April–Sept; bimonthly Oct–March
Federal Tax Coordinator 2d	Research Institute of America, Inc. 90 Fifth Ave. New York, NY 10011	1,325[2]	Indexed by topic, 35 looseleaf volumes organizing federal income, estate, gift, and excise taxes into 24 broad subject categories. Additional indexing by code section, cases, rulings, regulations. Also available on CD-ROM.	Thousands of individual self-contained analyses covering specific tax situations, including citations to controlling authorities, applicable code sections, regulations, developments, finding aids, and much more. Analytical approach.	Weekly
Mertens' Law of Federal Income Taxation	Clark Boardman Callaghan 155 Pfingston Road Deerfield, IL 60015	1,350	Organized by topic. Index volume provides key words. Tables and Table of Cases volumes provide the Mertens Chapter and section, which discusses needed IRC, rulings, regulations, and cases.	19 Treatise volumes 18 Rulings volumes 2 Volume paperback code Monthly newsmagazine	Monthly
Rabkin and Johnson Federal Income, Gift and Estate Taxation	Matthew Bender & Co. 1275 Broadway Albany, NY 12204	900[3]	Indexed by topic, code section, cases, and rulings. Organized by topic.	17 volumes; first eight deal with tax topics, next seven with IRC and legislative history of code sections. Spotlight on	Monthly permanent supplements.

Standard Federal Tax Reporter	Commerce Clearing House, Inc. 4025 W. Peterson Ave. Chicago, IL 60646	2,195[4]	Indexed by code sections and key words. Organized by code section.	commentary, but references included in body of text rather than as footnotes. 23 looseleaf volumes, including IRC, regulations, rulings, court decisions, editorial analysis and comment, and a citator. Covers income, estate, gift, and excise taxes.	Weekly
Tax Management Portfolio Series	Tax Management, Inc. A subsidiary of the Bureau of National Affairs, Inc. 1250 23rd Street, N.W. Washington, D.C. 20037	2,488[5]	Indexed by topics, code sections, and key words. Bibliography at the end of each portfolio refers to other services and sources.	Series of portfolios dealing with specific problem areas of federal income, estate, gift, trust, and foreign business taxation. Each portfolio includes a detailed analysis, working papers section, and bibliography.	Updated or revised portfolio issued periodically. Biweekly memorandum.
Tax Guides	Research Institute of America Inc. 90 Fifth Avenue New York, NY 10011	325–380[6]	Two looseleaf versions available—*Tax Guide*, organized by topic and *U.S. Tax Guide*, organized by Code Section. Paperback edition of the *U.S. Tax Guide* also available. Each set consists of two volumes.	Complete coverage of federal tax issues and current tax law. Encompasses income, estate and gift, excise and payroll taxes. Coverage of significant cases and rulings. Valuable tax-planning checklists and tax rate schedules and tables. Weekly tax alert newsletters.	Tax Guide (Monthly) US Tax Guide (Weekly)

(continued)

Exhibit 4.12
Tax Services (cont.)

Tax Service	Publisher	Cost*	Index and Organization	Content of Complete Set	Supplementation
United States Tax Reporter	Research Institute of America, Inc. 90 Fifth Ave. New York, NY 10011	$1,240[7]	Master key-word index in volume 1 and Index to Current Matter in volume 11.	18 looseleaf volumes, including IRC, regulations, rulings, court decisions, editorial analysis and comment.	Weekly

*The prices shown are as of 1993 but are subject to change without notice. Interested parties should consult publishers.

†At press time, Commerce Clearing House had acquired from Matthew Bender & Co., but not yet renamed, *Bender's Federal Tax Service.*

[1]The price is for a one-year subscription. The price for two years' service is $1,800.

[2]The price is for a one-year contract. The price for a two-year contract is $1,275.

[3]The price is for one year of monthly service. The price for annual renewal is $725.

[4]The price is for a combination of income, estate and gift, and excise tax service on a one-year contract. The price for a two-year contract is $1,995. Each service may be purchased separately at the following prices:

Income	$1,610 for a one-year contract or	$1,465 per year for a two-year contract
Estate and Gift	$ 445 for a one-year contract or	$ 405 per year for a two-year contract
Excise	$ 320 for a one-year contract or	$ 290 per year for a two-year contract

[5]The price is for a combination of U.S. income, estate and gift, and excise tax services on a two-year contract. Each service may be purchased separately at the following prices:

U.S. Income	$1,534 for a one-year contract or $1,381 per year for a two-year contract Renewal is $1,141	
Estates	$ 703 for a one-year contract or $ 633 for a two-year contract Renewal is $ 598	
Foreign	$1,017 for a one-year contract or $ 915 for a two-year contract Renewal is $ 910	

[6]The price for a one-year subscription to the *Tax Guide* is $350; the price for a two-year subscription is $325. The price for a two-year subscription to the *U.S. Tax Guide* is $380; the price for a two-year subscription is $350.

[7]The price is for a one-year contract. The price for a two-year contract is $1,195. *Citator*, in two bound volumes, is a compilation of court cases from 1954 through 1989 plus monthly and annual cumulative supplements that is available on a one-year contract for $425 and on a two-year contract for $375. The following are also available:

Estate and Gift	$430 for a one-year contract
	$400 per year for a two-year contract
Excise	$360 for a one-year contract
	$315 per year for a two-year contract

and to give helpful editorial interpretations of those primary authorities. The various tax services constantly update the information they provide. Subscribers are regularly informed of changes in the statute or regulations, new court decisions and revenue rulings, and other pertinent matters. It would be embarrassing to a practitioner to plan a tax strategy with an outdated authority. Current subscription tax services are a tremendous time-saving device that the tax practitioner can ill afford to be without.

A practitioner usually begins the research process using the service with which he or she is most familiar. Dependence on one service, however, can become detrimental. Each service is compiled and maintained by editors with divergent approaches to solving the same tax problem. Consequently, each service develops a distinct interpretive personality. While the salesperson representing the publisher may believe that his or her product is adequate by itself, the experienced researcher will discover that, because of their unique features, most tax services really complement each other.

The key to utilizing each tax service effectively lies in the mastery of its index systems. Access to materials in individual services may be gained through code section numbers, topical references, or both.

The individuality of the 1993 indexes of at least two frequently used tax services can be demonstrated by the following situation.

A corporation installed an alarm/security system on the chief executive's home to increase his availability and to prevent kidnapping. A question arises about the deductibility of the cost to the corporation for the system.

If the tax researcher begins the inquiry with the topical index of the RIA *United States Tax Reporter* service, then, under the key word entry *improvements*, the researcher will find the subheading, *security or protection*, with a reference to paragraph 2635.18 (20). Paragraph 2635.18 (20) refers to Letter Ruling 8141011, which ruled that an expenditure for a security system in an executive's home created a capital asset and was not currently deductible.

If the researcher begins with the CCH *Standard Federal Tax Reporter* index, the researcher will find a reference to Letter Ruling 8141011 under two different key words. First, under the key word *alarm system cost*, the researcher is directed to paragraph 13,709.0493 which contains a summarized description of Letter Ruling 8141011 and some other related cases. Similarly, the key word *installation costs,* and the subheading *burglar alarm,* direct the researcher to the same paragraph 13,709.0493. However, should the tax adviser search in the CCH index for the key word *improvements,* he or she will not find a reference to Letter Ruling 8141011. Similarly, a search in the RIA index for the key word *alarm system* will not provide the researcher with any guidance.

The foregoing example is not designed to recommend one particular index and tax service over another. Its purpose is to demonstrate the trial-and-error approach necessary to locate pertinent authority. Furthermore, it also demonstrates the advisability of having more than one tax service available.

In addition to variations in index systems, each tax service is known for specific features that may prove to be helpful, depending on the research problem in question. A summary of cost, organization, and techniques of supplementation used by major tax service publishers can be found in exhibit 4.12, pages 122 through 124.

The following general comments outline some of the features of each service. CCH and RIA publish major tax services annually in looseleaf binders under the titles *Standard Federal Tax Reporter* and *United States Tax Reporter,* respectively. In many ways, these two services are similar. Both publications follow the organization of the Internal Revenue Code. Each major division begins with a preliminary discussion introducing the subject in general terms; subdivisions include exact quotations of the code sections and the related Treasury regulations. In addition, each subdivision contains interpretive explanations by the editorial staff and brief synopses of related court decisions, revenue rulings, and revenue procedures. Each service also features a separate volume containing the most recent developments regarding statutory, administrative, and judicial authority.

Mertens tax service, published by Clark Boardman Collaghan and entitled *Law of Federal Income Taxation* , is organized by topic and, therefore, does not follow the sequence of the code. The separate looseleaf volumes of Mertens service can be divided into five groupings: (1) the treatise volumes, each volume containing scholarly discussions of the various tax topics (statutory, administrative, and judicial authorities are cited in footnote form), (2) volumes containing the Internal Revenue Code, (3) a code commentary, (4) the Treasury regulations, and (5) volumes containing various rulings and procedures. Although the code commentary volumes do not feature complete texts of the committee reports, the editorial summaries do provide historical background and suggest the apparent congressional intent for many sections. The rulings volumes comprise revenue rulings, revenue procedures, and miscellaneous announcements beginning with 1954. These volumes embody an efficient index system that, in addition to showing the current status of revenue rulings, assists in identifying all rulings issued in connection with a particular Internal Revenue Code section. Because of its encyclopedic approach to the subject matter, the Mertens service is especially helpful to the individual with limited knowledge of the topic to be researched. Due to its scholarly excellence, Mertens is, at times, cited in court opinions.

Federal Income, Gift and Estate Taxation, by Jacob Rabkin and Mark H. Johnson (Albany, NY: Matthew Bender), is a looseleaf tax service organized by subject rather than by code section. For example, all material dealing with partnerships is found in one cumulative discussion. The Internal Revenue Code and the Treasury regulations are published in separate volumes. One of the outstanding features of the Rabkin and Johnson service is the availability of the legislative committee reports, which are interspersed in the Internal Revenue Code volumes.

The Research Institute of America (RIA) also publishes *Federal Tax Coordinator 2d*, a compilation of professional tax research. The service is divided by topic into various chapters that are contained in separate looseleaf volumes. The *Federal Tax Coordinator 2d* service also contains other volumes for a topical index, finding tables, practice aids, proposed regulations, and Revenue Rulings. Each division begins with an explanation of all problems in a given area, supported by citations to appropriate authorities. Next follows the text of the applicable code section and Treasury regulation. Explanations of latest developments appear immediately following the verbatim reprints of the code and regulations. Editorial explanations include illustrations, planning points, tax traps, and appropriate recommendations. In addition, the *Federal Tax Coordinator 2d* contains helpful aids, such as the weekly *Internal Revenue Bulletin* and Internal Revenue Service audit manuals.

The Bureau of National Affairs (BNA) publishes a portfolio tax service entitled *Tax Management*. At present the total service consists of several hundred portfolios that range in length from 50 to 250 pages. Each portfolio deals with a specific tax topic. The organization of the material with each portfolio follows a standard pattern. Part A contains a detailed analysis of the subject matter. This analysis is written in narrative form, with extensive footnotes to statutory, administrative, and judicial authority. The format of discussion lends itself to research progressing from general backgrounds through specific problems within the topic under consideration. Part B provides helpful working papers, appropriate forms, and illustrations. Part C includes a bibliography of related resource material.

Previously noted were two special judicial reporter series, namely, the Commerce Clearing House USTC series and the Research Institute of America AFTR series. To some extent, the cases appearing in these series are "selected" by editorial staffs. In addition, the editors prepare headnotes for each case published. Headnotes enumerate the issue(s) contained in each case in brief form and give the court's conclusion. Thus, a researcher may gain a quick understanding of the general subject matter of each case included in either series by simply scanning the headnotes. The researcher must remember, however, that the headnotes are editorial comments and not an integral part of any official opinion.

The decision to subscribe to only one tax service or to several must be made on the basis of how many services a practice can support. However, the tax adviser should keep in mind that, just as two heads are better than one, two or more tax services can increase effectiveness. The real benefit of any tax service lies in the time-saving factor that allows the tax practitioner to quickly find a correct answer to a tax question. However, time constraints in a tax practice make it impossible to consult all available services on every problem. Knowing which service will most efficiently direct research to an acceptable solution comes only with experience.

Books

The economics of a tax practice demand that the researcher find the solutions quickly and without excessive cost to the client. Consequently, a tax adviser cannot afford the luxury of pulling a full-length book from the shelf and spending a day or two pursuing the subject in leisurely fashion. However, some treatises on specific tax topics have attained significant reputations among tax practitioners. A few of the more often cited works are *Federal Income Taxation of Corporations and Shareholders*, fifth edition (Boston: Warren Gorham & Lamont, 1987), by Boris I. Bittker and James E. Eustice; *Partnership Taxation*, fourth edition (Colorado Springs, CO: Shepard's/McGraw-Hill, Inc., 1989), by Arthur B. Willis et al; *Federal Taxation of Partnerships and Partners*, second edition (Boston: Warren Gorham & Lamont, 1990), by William S. McKee, William F. Nelson, and Robert L. Whitmire; and *Federal Income Taxation of Corporations Filing Consolidated Returns* (New York: Matthew Bender, 1975), by Herbert J. Lerner et al.[35] Their special status implies that they contain information discussed and summarized in a fashion not elsewhere available.

Numerous tax institutes and seminars are held annually throughout the United States. At such institutes, tax topics are discussed, and papers are presented that usually deal with significant current issues. Three very popular tax institutes—the New York University Tax Institute, the University of Southern California Tax Institute, and the Tulane Tax Institute—publish their proceedings in annual bound volumes. Because of the emphasis on current and complex topics, tax researchers may benefit from consulting such materials.

Tax Magazines

Various magazines are currently published dealing exclusively with taxation and providing valuable assistance to the tax practitioner. Their formats range from those appealing to the general tax practitioner to those specializing in a particular field of taxation. For example, the *Journal of Taxation*, published by Warren, Gorham & Lamont, features regular departments dealing with corporations, estates, trusts and gifts, exempt institutions, partnerships, and so on. The *Tax Adviser*, published monthly by the American

---

[35] All of these books are updated at least annually through the use of supplements.

Institute of Certified Public Accountants, is another popular tax journal for the general practitioner.

To locate pertinent articles in the periodical tax literature, a researcher may consult the cumulative indexes provided in the various issues. Another way of locating journal material is through *CCH Federal Tax Articles*, a multivolume service including in each volume a topical index, a code section index, and an author's index. Warren Gorham & Lamont also publishes an *Index to Federal Tax Articles*. This service features both a topical and an author index. For a list of some of the available tax magazines that may assist the tax researcher, see exhibit 4.13.

Tax Newsletters

Most tax newsletters are published weekly and are, therefore, excellent sources of the most recent developments. They keep the tax adviser in touch with the dynamics of the tax laws. One very popular source is Tax Analysts' *Tax Notes*. See exhibit 4.14, for a listing of other available publications. Occasionally, in scanning a newsletter, a practitioner will spot an item that has relevance to a client's problem. More often, however, the newsletter simply provides the practitioner with ideas that may be recalled and used in later work.

How many technical publications a tax adviser should purchase is, of course, an individual decision. Many publications duplicate information, and reading all of them would demand too much of a tax adviser's valuable time. The decision must, therefore, be based on the size and nature of the practice. The larger the firm, the more varied the personalities, and the greater the areas of specialization represented, the greater the variety of subscriptions required.

Exhibit 4.13
Tax Magazines

Magazine	Cost*	Issues Per Year	Publisher	Coverage
Estate Planning	$125.00	6	Warren, Gorham & Lamont 210 South St. Boston, MA 02111	Tax and nontax aspects of areas of interest to estate planners.
The Journal of the American Taxation Association	20.00	2	The American Taxation Association c/o The American Accounting Association 5717 Bessie Drive Sarasota, FL 34233	A variety of articles, including those on tax education, policy, and compliance.
The Journal of the Corporate Taxation	130.00	4	Warren, Gorham & Lamont 210 South St. Boston, MA 02111	Corporate tax planning articles by tax practitioners.
The Journal of Real Estate Taxation	130.00	4	Warren, Gorham & Lamont 210 South St. Boston, MA 02111	Tax planning with emphasis on real estate transactions.
Journal of Taxation	160.00	12	Warren, Gorham & Lamont 210 South St. Boston, MA 02111	In-depth analysis of current tax developments by leading tax practitioners.

(continued)

Exhibit 4.13
Tax Magazines (cont.)

Magazine	Cost*	Issues Per Year	Publisher	Coverage
The Monthly Digest of Tax Articles	48.00	12	Newkirk Products, Inc. P.O. Box 15200 Albany. NY 12212-5200	Digest of tax articles published in various professional journals, magazines, and lab reviews.
National Tax Journal	50.00	4	National Tax Association— Tax Institute of America 5310 E. Main St. Columbus, OH 43213	Tax policy orientation; frequent theoretical economic analysis.
Oil and Gas Tax Quarterly	175.00	4	Matthew Bender & Co., Inc. 11 Penn Plaza New York, NY 10001-2006	Specialized coverage of oil and gas taxation topics.
The Practical Accountant	64.95	12	Faulkner & Gray 11 Penn Plaza New York, NY 10001	Selected articles on taxation for the general practitioner.
The Real Estate Review	90.00	4	Warren, Gorham & Lamont 210 South St. Boston, MA 02111	Articles dealing with real estate topics.
The Tax Adviser	94.00	12	American Institute of CPAs 1211 Ave. of Americas New York, NY 10036-8775	Current tax developments, estate planning techniques, tax practice management.
The Tax Executive	90.00	6	Tax Executives Institute, Inc. 1001 Pennsylania Ave. N.W., Suite 320 Washington, D.C. 20004-2505	In-depth articles of particular interest to corporate tax executives written by tax professionals, scholars, and management.
The Tax Lawyer	83.00	4	American Bar Association Section of Taxation 2d Floor, South Lobby, 1800 M St., N.W. Washington, D.C. 20036	In-depth coverage of tax topics for the lawyer in tax practice.

Title	Price	Issues	Publisher	Description
Taxation for Accountants	98.00	12	Warren, Gorham & Lamont, 210 South St., Boston, MA 02111	General coverage of tax topics for the accountant in general tax practice.
Taxation for Lawyers	95.00	6	Warren, Gorham & Lamont, 210 South St., Boston, MA 02111	General coverage of tax topics for the lawyer in general practice.
Taxes—The Tax Magazine	140.00	12	Commerce Clearing House, Inc., 4025 West Peterson Ave., Chicago, IL 60646	Selected articles covering current tax developments. Includes a section dealing tax laws.
Trusts and Estates	75.00	12	Communication Channels, Inc., 6151 Powers Ferry Rd., Atlanta, GA 30339	Specialized emphasis on estate and trust taxation and estate planning.

*Prices are shown as of 1993 and are subject to change without notice. Interested parties should consult publishers.

Exhibit 4.14
Tax Newsletters

Newsletters	Cost*	Issues Per Year	Publisher	Coverage
Accountant's Weekly Report	$ 203.40	52	Bureau of Business Practice 24 Rope Ferry Rd. Waterford, CT 06386	Current developments in federal taxation, new tax rulings, law changes, and recent court decisions.
Bender's Tax Week	250.00	52	Commerce Clearing House 4025 West Peterson Ave. Chicago, IL 60646	Digest and commentary of current tax developments oriented to assist in tax planning.
Daily Tax Report	1,755.00	250	Bureau of National Affairs, Inc. 1231 25th St. N.W. Washington, D.C. 20037	Summary and analysis of developments in taxation and finance for preceding 24 hours.
J.K. Lasser Monthly Tax Service	24.00	12	Paramount Publishing 15 Columbus Circle New York, NY 10023	General coverage of tax developments.
Kiplinger Washington Letter	68.00	52	The Kiplinger Washington Editors 1729 H St., N.W. Washington, D.C. 20006	General coverage of major tax developments.
Non-Profit Legal and Tax Letter	195.00	18	Organization Management Inc. 13231 Pleasantview Lane Fairfax, VA 22033	Current developments in taxation affecting tax-exempt organizations.
Practical Accountant Alert	98.00	24	Faulkner & Gray 11 Penn Plaza New York, NY 10001	Fast-breaking coverage of all the major developments that affect your accounting work.
Real Estate Tax Ideas	105.00	12	Warren, Gorham & Lamont 210 South St. Boston, MA 02111	Tax analysis of real estate transactions for real estate professionals.
Tax Consultant	54.00	12	National Tax Training School Monsey, NY 10952	Emphasis on individual taxation and social security.

Name	Price	Issues	Publisher	Description
Tax Notes	1,249.00	52	Tax Analysts 6830 N. Fairfax Drive Arlington, VA 22213	Tax analysis prepared by a public interest firm.
Tax Notes Highlights and Documents	1,749.00	250	Tax Analysts 6830 N. Fairfax Drive Arlington, VA 22213	Summary and full text of previous day's important tax news
Taxes on Parade	65.00	52	Commerce Clearing House, Inc. 4025 West Peterson Ave. Chicago, IL 60646	Weekly reprint of report sent to tax service subscribers; general coverage of weekly developments.
U.S. Tax Bulletin	180.00	52	Research Institute of America 90 5th Avenue New York, NY 10011	Weekly reprint of bulletin sent to tax service subscribers; general coverage of weekly developments, some planning ideas.
Weekly Alert	109.00	52	Research Institute of America 90 Fifth Ave. New York, NY 10011	Current tax developments written with emphasis on tax planning. Also tax return guides and opportunity checklists.

*Prices are shown as of 1993 and subect to change without notice. Interested parties should consult pulisher for latest prices.

5

... as the articulation of a statute increases, the room for interpretation must contract; but the meaning of a sentence may be more than that of the separate words, as a melody is more than the notes, and no degree of particularity can ever obviate recourse to the setting in which all appear, and which all collectively create.

JUDGE LEARNED HAND

Assessing and Applying Authority

After a tax researcher has located authority that seems pertinent to a given problem, the important task of assessing that material begins. The researcher's aim is to arrive at a course of action that can be confidently communicated to the client along with identification of the risks and costs accompanying it.

Locating appropriate authority for a particular tax problem is only half the battle. The technical jargon of many portions of the Internal Revenue Code and Treasury regulations requires the tax adviser to read and comprehend unusually complex sentences in order to determine congressional intent. Other portions of the code and regulations hinge upon deceptively simple words or phrases whose definitions may be debatable. Furthermore, while available secondary authorities or such interpretive sources as Treasury regulations, revenue rulings, or court decisions may be more comprehensible than are primary statutory authorities, they are less authoritative.

The researcher faces another, more serious hurdle when authorities conflict. The applicable law may be questionable due to conflicts in the language of the statute, between the language of the statute and the intent of Congress, between interpretations of the statute, between the IRS interpretations and various federal courts, and among the courts themselves at various levels of jurisdiction. Finally, a researcher may be unable to locate any authority at all on a particular problem.

In attempting to assess authority and apply it to complex practice problems, the researcher may encounter any one of three fundamentally different situations. The first involves clear, concise tax law that could be applied if the researcher were able to gather additional facts from the client. In another, the adviser may be in possession of clearly established facts but find a conflict in the applicable law. Finally, a researcher may encounter a third situation in which existing tax law is incomplete or inapplicable, requiring that issues be resolved through interpolation from related authorities and application of creative thinking.

The Law Is Clear—The Facts Are Uncertain

Frequently, a tax adviser finds it difficult to reach a conclusion and make a recommendation because of insufficient knowledge of the facts in the case rather than because of confusion in the applicable rules. In many situations, the biggest single problem is gathering sufficient evidence to support the taxpayer's contention that he or she be granted the tax treatment clearly authorized in a specific provision of the Internal Revenue Code.

To illustrate this kind of problem, assume that a client, Mr. Jerry Hill, includes what he describes as a "$16,000 casualty loss" with the information he provides for the filing of his income tax return. A cursory line of questioning by his tax adviser reveals that the loss is claimed for a handwoven Indian wall carpet that the client claims was chewed and clawed to bits by a stray dog. Mr. Hill explains that while on vacation last summer, he left his residence in the care of his housekeeper. Apparently, one day, the housekeeper neglected to close a door securely and a stray dog wandered into the house. Upon the Hills' return from vacation, they were told the following story. Attracted by strange noises, the housekeeper entered the study and found a dog gnawing and tearing on the wall rug. As the housekeeper entered the room, the dog turned and ran growling from the house. Although not certain of it, the housekeeper reported noticing foam around the dog's mouth. Later, a neighbor said that a rabid dog had been seen roaming the neighborhood. The housekeeper, who cared for Hill's own dogs, stated that the dog discovered in the study was not one of Mr. Hill's. Mr. Hill checked with the city dogcatcher concerning the reported sighting of a mad dog. He was, however, unable to confirm any such report with the dogcatcher. He did not check with the police department.

Through a little research, the tax adviser is convinced that in order for Mr. Hill to qualify for a casualty loss deduction under section 165(a) he must satisfy the following specific requirements:

1. The loss must have been sudden and unexpected (*Hugh M. Matheson v. Commissioner*, 54 F.2d 537 (CA-2, 1931)).

2. The loss cannot constitute a mysterious disappearance (*Paul Bakewell, Jr.*, 23 T.C. 803 (1955)).

3. The amount of the loss deduction is limited to the lesser of (*a*) the reduction in fair market value (FMV) of the asset caused by the casualty or (*b*) the adjusted basis of the asset, reduced by (1) an insurance recovery, (2) a $100 floor, and (3) 10 percent of the taxpayer's adjusted gross income (Sec. 165(h) and Treas. Reg. Sec. 1.165-7(b)).

4. The loss cannot be attributable to the taxpayer's own dog (*J.R. Dyer*, 20 T.C.M. 705 (1961)).

At this point, a tax adviser would be faced with two alternatives: accept the client's statement at face value and claim the deduction, or suggest that the client accumulate additional evidence to substantiate the loss if he desires to claim the deduction.[1] An adviser following the former alternative is simply postponing the collection of evidence until a possible audit by the IRS, since the presence of a rather sizable casualty loss on a client's tax return

---

[1] For example, the taxpayer should be able to show the type of casualty and when it occurred, that the loss was the direct result of the casualty, and that the taxpayer was the owner of the property with respect to which a casualty loss deduction is claimed (*Gilbert J. Kraus*, 10 T.C.M. 1071 (1951)).

undoubtedly would increase the risk of an audit. Furthermore, it might be self-defeating to defer the collection of evidence because two or three years from now individuals who could render statements on matters now fresh in their minds may be unavailable, or they may not recall necessary details. Furthermore, helpful police records may be destroyed. Since the taxpayer may be unaware of what is needed to substantiate the loss deduction, he may, in the meantime, dispose of important evidence, such as the ruined rug.

If a tax adviser pursues the second alternative, the client should be presented with a list of instructions, including the suggestion that he accumulate the necessary evidence to support the deduction in the event of an audit or eventual litigation. The list could include—

1. Sworn statements from (a) the housekeeper and (b) the individual who saw the apparently rabid dog in the neighborhood.
2. Appraisal by a qualified expert or experts showing the value of the rug before and after the casualty.
3. Color photographs of the rug before and after the casualty.
4. Instructions to retain the damaged rug as evidence, if possible.
5. Statements from, or correspondence with, insurance agents substantiating the amount of any insurance recovery.
6. Purchase invoice showing proof of ownership and cost.

A client may ignore an adviser's request or he or she may be unable to obtain all of the recommended evidence. Nevertheless, the adviser will have informed the client on a timely basis of the requirements necessary to sustain the right to the claimed deduction.

In tax research work involving situations in which tax laws are clear but the facts of the situation are in question, the tax adviser should establish the facts necessary to reach a conclusion and either accumulate appropriate supporting evidence or suggest that the client do so. Then, in the event of an audit, the tax adviser would only need to persuade a revenue agent to accept the mass of overwhelming evidence and, therefore, reach the desired conclusion.

The Facts Are Clear—The Law Is Questionable

The tax researcher may encounter another kind of problem involving situations in which facts are well established but the law is uncertain. Uncertainty may arise (1) in the language of the statute itself, (2) between the language of the statute and the intent of the statute, or (3) between the interpretations of the statute.

Conflicting Statutes

Although it is rather rare, the facts of a problem can sometimes be analyzed in light of two different provisions of the statute, with each provision furnishing a different tax result. In such cases, the adviser and client should carefully evaluate which alternative to take, realizing the possibility of an IRS challenge.

An example of a possible conflict between statutes may be found in sections 164 and 469. Section 164 states *that "... except as otherwise provided in this section,"* [emphasis added] certain taxes are allowed as a deduction. Property taxes on real estate are included in this list of deductible taxes. Among other things, section 164 continues by imposing certain limitations and special requirements for assessed taxes that tend to increase the value of the property, and the apportionment of real estate taxes between the seller and purchaser of real property. On the other hand, section 469 disallows a deduction for losses incurred in a passive activity. Losses in a passive activity are incurred when the expenses of the activity exceed its income. Since the term *passive activity* includes any rental activity,[2] real estate taxes incurred on the passive activity's property would constitute part of the dissallowed passive activity loss. Section 469(i) does provide an exception to this by allowing a deduction of up to $25,000 per year for rental real estate activities in which the owner actively participated during the year. However, even this deduction is completely phased out for taxpayers who have adjusted gross income over $150,000. Thus, there appears to be a conflict between section 164 which allows a deduction for the real estate taxes and section 469 which in many cases will disallow a deduction. Normally, in situations such as this, the

---

[2] Section 469(c)(2).

statute itself resolves the conflict. For example, in section 164 the statute could have said, "except as otherwise provided in this section, *and in section 469,* a deduction shall be allowed for the following taxes." Or in section 469, the statute could have said, *"notwithstanding section 164,* no deduction shall be allowed for a passive activity loss." Currently, however, such explanatory phrases are not found in either section 164 or section 469.

Conflict Between a Statute and the Intent of a Statute

A tax researcher can sometimes find conflicts between the words of a statute and the accompanying House, Senate, and Conference Committee reports which contain the intent of Congress. In this situation, the tax adviser must know under what circumstances he or she can rely on the committee reports. Furthermore, the adviser and the client should be prepared for a possible IRS challenge.

In *Miller v. Comm.*, 88-1 USTC ¶9139 (CA-10, 1988), the U.S. Court of Appeals for the tenth circuit was faced with a conflict between the statute and the intent (legislative history) of the statute. The facts of the case reveal that the taxpayer, an experienced trader of commodity futures, acquired and disposed of a series of gold futures contracts from 1979 to 1980, thereby sustaining a net economic loss of more than $25,000. The taxpayer wanted to claim a short-term capital loss under Act section 108 of the TRA '84.[3]

Section 108 of the TRA '84[4] stated, in part, that any loss from a disposition of futures shall only be allowed if it is "part of a transaction entered into for profit."[5] The Tax Court, in ruling for the taxpayer, relied on the Conference Report accompanying Act section 108, which indicated that the loss would be deductible "if there is a reasonable prospect of any profit."[6] The appellate court, on the other hand, overturned the Tax Court, holding that the taxpayer was not entitled to a deduction since his primary motive was one of tax avoidance rather than economic profit. The appellate court stated in its opinion that the Tax Court relied too heavily

---

[3] Section 108 of the TRA '84 only deals with straddle transactions that were entered into prior to 1982. The law as it now stands would have disallowed these losses.

[4] Section 108 was later amended by the TRA '86.

[5] Tax Reform Act of 1984, Pub. L. 98-369.

[6] H. R. No. 861, 98th Cong. 2d Sess. at 917, *reprinted in* 1984-3 C.B. (Vol. 2) at 171.

on the Conference Report given the long-standing interpretation of the phrase "transaction entered into for profit."

The appellate court did acknowledge that, in some situations, the plain meaning of a statute may be overridden if it is in apparent conflict with the purpose of the legislation. However, the court further stated that:

> ... When there is a conflict between portions of legislative history and the words of a statute, the words of the statute represent the constitutionally approved method of communication, and it would require 'unequivocal evidence' of legislative purpose as reflected in the legislative history to override the ordinary meaning of the statute.[7]

Generally, the tax adviser should not refer to committee reports in situations where the meaning of the statute is clear.[8] However, in situations where the Code is ambiguous or silent, the legislative history can be of great help.[9] The tax adviser should always remember that the purpose of using legislative history is to solve, not to create, an ambiguity.[10]

Conflicting Interpretations

A tax researcher more frequently encounters conflicting interpretations of tax statutes by various authorities. Conflicts may be found between the Treasury regulations and the courts or between two or more federal courts. In such situations, the tax adviser must consider the alternatives and weigh the risks—including the cost of lengthy administrative battles with the IRS and potential litigation—before recommending a particular conclusion or course of action. Furthermore, the taxpayer must consider the potential imposition of a penalty.[11] While it is the responsibility of the tax

---

[7] *Miller v. Comm.*, 88-1 USTC ¶9139 (CA-10, 1988).

[8] E.g., *U.S. v. Shreveport Grain & Elevator Co.*, 287 U.S. 77 (1932).

[9] The weight of legislative history as authority may also vary according to factors such as whether the legislative history is sufficiently specific, clear and uniform to be a reliable indicator of intent. *Miller v. Comm., supra* note 7.

[10] Sheldon I. Banoff, "Dealing with the 'Authorities': Determining Valid Legal Authority in Advising Clients, Rendering Opinions, Preparing Tax Returns and Avoiding Penalties," *Taxes—The Tax Magazine* (December 1988): 1082–1084.

[11] Among others, see section 6662, which imposes a penalty on a taxpayer for a substantial understatement of the tax liability, and section 6694, which imposes penalties on the tax return preparer for negligent or intentional disregard of rules and regulations.

adviser to discover conflicting interpretations of the statutes and to advise the client of the risks and alternatives, the client should decide which course of action to pursue. Although only the client can decide whether to incur the costs of an administrative or legal confrontation with the IRS, he or she generally relies heavily on the recommendation of the tax adviser in reaching that decision. Other pertinent considerations include the general inconvenience associated with such disputes, the risk of exposure to additional audits, and the possibility of adverse publicity.

Regulations Versus Courts. If a regulation has already been challenged, one of three possible outcomes may exist. First, the IRS may have lost the challenge and either revised or withdrawn the contested regulation. Second, the government may have lost one or more specific tests of the regulation but is still unwilling to concede defeat. Third, the IRS has successfully defended a regulation, and, therefore, further attempts to challenge that regulation probably would not hold much promise.

An example of the first outcome described above is the IRS's acknowledgement that part of the temporary regulations issued under section 453 regarding wraparound installment sales is invalid. In *Professional Equities, Inc.*,[12] the Tax Court held that the 1980 Installment Sales Revision Act did not modify the taxing of gains in wraparound installment sales. Thus, Temp. Reg. Sec. 15A.453-1(b)(3)(ii) was held to be invalid. The Service acknowledged the invalidity of the regulation by announcing its acquiescence in the Tax Court decision.[13]

What the authors have said concerning conflicting authority between Treasury regulations and judicial opinions is, obviously, equally applicable to conflicting authority between judicial opinions and revenue rulings, revenue procedures, and other official IRS pronouncements. While a dispute between the IRS and the courts is still in progress, taxpayers with similar questions become prime targets for litigation if they adopt a position contrary to that pursued by the service. The service is often looking for a "better"

---

[12] 89 T.C. 165 (1987) (reviewed opinion, without dissent).
[13] 1988-2 C.B. 1.

fact case (from its point of view) or for a more favorable circuit in which to litigate. Any time a tax adviser recommends a position contrary to that of the IRS, even if that contrary position is adequately supported by judicial authority, the adviser should explain to the client the potential risks and extra costs implicit in taking that position. As far as revenue agents and appellate conferees are concerned, the IRS position is the law, and they will challenge a departure from this position.

One Court's Interpretation Versus Another's. Disagreements between courts on similar issues can be characterized as "horizontal" and "vertical." Horizontal differences mean conflicting opinions issued by courts at the same level of jurisdiction; vertical differences refer to conflicts between lower and higher courts. Horizontal differences can occur between courts of original jurisdiction (Federal District Courts, the Tax Court, and the Court of Federal Claims), or between the several circuit courts. In such conflicts, the service is under no obligation to follow, on a nationwide basis, the precedent set by any of the courts. Thus, a district court opinion favorable to the taxpayer would technically have precedential value only for a taxpayer residing within the jurisdiction of that district court. Similarly, any circuit court opinion technically has precedential value only within the circuit where the decision originated because one circuit court is not bound to follow the precedent of another circuit court. If appealed, conflicting district court opinions, from district courts within the same circuit, are settled by the appropriate circuit court. The Supreme Court, if it grants *certiorari*, settles conflicts between circuits. Prior to the time that a circuit court or the Supreme Court disposes of such opposing views, the tax adviser and client should be fully aware of the risks involved when relying on a court decision that may subsequently be appealed and overturned.

An interesting example of a disagreement between courts involves employee expenses for transportation of the tools of one's trade. Relying on Rev. Rul. 63-100,[14] which allowed an automobile expense deduction to a musician for the transportation of his musical instrument between his personal residence and his place

---

[14] Rev. Rul. 63-100, 1963-1 C.B. 34 (now revoked by Rev. Rul. 75-380, 1975-2 C.B. 59).

of employment, taxpayer Sullivan deducted his driving expenses because he transported a thirty-two-pound bag of tools to work each day. The Tax Court denied the deduction; however, the second circuit reversed and remanded the case to the Tax Court. On rehearing, the Tax Court allowed more than 25 percent of the total driving expenses claimed by the taxpayer.[15] Subsequently, in *Fausner* and in *Hitt*, two airline pilots, who were required by their employers and by government regulations to carry extensive flight gear, attempted to deduct transportation expenses between their home and the airport. In *Fausner*, the Tax Court felt constrained by the *Sullivan* decision, since Fausner resided in the second circuit, and it allowed the deduction for the 1965 tax year.[16] However, because Hitt resided in the fifth circuit, the Tax Court, ruling on the same day, disregarded *Sullivan* and disallowed the deduction.[17] Fausner's returns for 1966 and 1967 were again challenged by the IRS on the same issue, and Fausner once more petitioned the Tax Court to rule on the matter. Although Fausner had resided in New York during 1966 and 1967, he had moved to Texas in 1968 and was thus petitioning from the fifth circuit in the latter years. In this instance, the Tax Court sustained the service, as it had done previously in *Hitt*.[18] Fausner appealed to the fifth circuit and received an adverse ruling.[19] At this point, a conflict between the second and the fifth circuit courts existed, and the Supreme Court granted *certiorari* on an appeal from *Fausner*.[20] The Supreme Court finally settled the controversy by ruling against the taxpayer.[21]

The foregoing example demonstrates both horizontal and vertical differences in judicial decisions. In horizontal differences, a taxpayer cannot rely on a decision rendered by another court at the same level of jurisdiction, because courts at the same level of jurisdiction are not bound by decisions of other courts at that same level. Vertical differences are harder to explain because lower

---

[15] *Sullivan*, 368 F.2d 1007 (CA-2, 1966) and T.C.M. 1968-711.

[16] *Fausner*, 55 T.C. 620 (1971).

[17] *Hitt*, 55 T.C. 628 (1971)

[18] *Fausner*, P-H T.C.M. ¶71,277.

[19] *Fausner*, 472 F.2d 561 (CA-5, 1973).

[20] Actually, the conflict between the circuits involved another decision, in which the court held for the taxpayer (*Tyne*, 385 F.2d 40 (CA-7, 1967)).

[21] *Fausner*, 413 U.S. 838 (1973).

courts generally are bound by decisions of higher courts. In the case of the Tax Court, however, even vertical differences may exist because the Tax Court has national jurisdiction. The Tax Court considers itself bound by the decisions of the circuit courts of appeals only to the extent that taxpayers reside in the jurisdiction of a circuit that has rendered a decision on that issue. This maxim is frequently referred to as the *Golsen* Rule, since it was first expressed by the Tax Court in *J.E. Golsen*, 54 T.C. 742 (1970).

Since the Tax Court is *not* obligated to accept any circuit court opinion on a nationwide basis, it has ample opportunity to express its displeasure with a circuit court opinion by disregarding it in cases involving taxpayers from other circuits. Such a result can be demonstrated with two cases, in which the Tax Court arrived at opposing conclusions, involving two "50-50" stockholders in the same S corporation where each taxpayer had sued on an identical issue. In both *Doehring* and *Puckett*, the issue to be decided was whether or not the two taxpayers' loan company had lost its subchapter S status.[22] The IRS had previously disallowed the election on the grounds that more than 20 percent of the corporation's gross revenue was derived from interest (passive income).[23] The taxpayers, relying on *House v. Commissioner*, 453 F.2d 982 (CA-5, 1972), argued that the ceiling did not apply to loan companies. The Tax Court ruled against the taxpayer in *Doehring*, stating that *House* did not apply since *Doehring* would be appealed to the eighth circuit. In *Puckett*, however, the Tax Court upheld the taxpayer's contention, although disagreeing with it, since appeal would be to the fifth circuit, in which *House* was controlling. Subsequently, *Doehring* was appealed to the eighth circuit, where the taxpayer prevailed.[24] The sequence of events demonstrates, however, the uncertainty created, at least for a time, for taxpayers and their advisers with similar situations.

One taxpayer tested the commissioner's right to ignore established judicial precedent. In that case, the IRS sent deficiency

---

[22] *K.W. Doehring*, T.C.M. 1974-1035; and *P.E. Puckett*, T.C.M. 1974-1038.

[23] Prior to 1983, S corporations were limited in the amount of passive income they could earn.

[24] *K.W. Doehring*, 527 F.2d 945 (CA-8, 1975). The government also appealed *Puckett*, trying for a reversal of *House*. However, the fifth circuit affirmed the original Tax Court decision (*P.E. Puckett*, 522 F.2d 1385 (CA-5, 1975)).

notices to two taxpayers claiming that certain distributions received from their corporation were dividends. Both stockholders challenged the deficiency assessment in the Tax Court. While taxpayer Divine's suit was pending, the Tax Court ruled against taxpayer Luckman.[25] Upon appeal, however, the seventh circuit reversed the Tax Court.[26] The commissioner pressed on with the same position he had taken in *Luckman* and obtained another favorable ruling from the Tax Court in *Divine*.[27] Taxpayer Divine then appealed to the second circuit court, claiming that when the commissioner is relitigating an issue that he has previously lost and the facts are distinguishable only by virtue of the identity of the taxpayer, the commissioner should be barred from again bringing suit. Although the second circuit court held for taxpayer Divine, it struck down his contention that the commissioner was prevented from bringing suit.[28]

The Facts Are Clear—The Law Is Incomplete

As explained earlier, whenever a statute is silent or imprecise on a particular tax question, tax researchers must consult such other interpretive authorities as Treasury regulations, revenue rulings, or court decisions. In their search for proper interpretation, tax advisers soon discover that finding authority with facts identical to their own will be the exception rather than the rule. In most circumstances, therefore, the ability to distinguish cases or rulings on the basis of facts becomes critical, for many times it is necessary to piece together support for the researchers' positions from several authorities.

An illustration of this third class of common tax problems follows. Assume that a client, an Austrian named Werner Hoppe, presents the following facts. Werner visited his brother Klaus, who had immigrated to the United States six years ago and resides in Dallas, Texas. At the time of the visit, Werner was under contract to an Austrian soccer team and was expected to return to the team

---

[25] *Sid Luckman*, 50 T.C. 619 (1968).
[26] *Luckman*, 418 F.2d 381 (CA-7, 1969).
[27] *Harold S. Divine*, 59 T.C. 152 (1972).
[28] *Divine*, 500 F.2d 1041 (CA-2, 1974).

to begin play for the fall 1993 season. Werner's brother Klaus had fallen in love with American football and had become an enthusiastic fan of the Dallas Cowboys. The Cowboys had recently lost their regular kicker to an injury, and a replacement, picked up on waivers, proved to be less than satisfactory. Knowing of Werner's kicking ability, Klaus was convinced that Werner could help the Cowboys if given an opportunity. Klaus took Werner to a Cowboy workout and introduced him to the kicking coach. As a result, Werner was given a tryout by the Cowboys, who were desperate for a good kicker. Werner's performance was far superior to others at the tryout, and the Cowboys offered him the kicking job. Werner, however, was reluctant to accept the offer because he had planned to return to Austria in a few weeks to continue his soccer career. Considerable encouragement from Klaus and the Cowboy organization seemed to be in vain until the Cowboys, at Klaus's suggestion, offered Werner a $100,000 bonus. At this point, Werner overcame his reluctance and signed a contract, which Klaus cosigned as witness and interpreter. Economically speaking, the regular salary offered by the Cowboys was considerably more attractive than was Werner's salary as a soccer player in Austria. Grateful to his brother for assisting as an interpreter and negotiator, and for encouraging him to stay, Werner instructed the Cowboys to pay $15,000 of the negotiated bonus directly to Klaus. Klaus reported the $15,000 as other income on his 1993 income tax return and paid the appropriate tax. After examining Werner's 1993 tax return, the IRS made a deficiency assessment claiming that the $15,000 paid to Klaus constituted income to Werner and should thus be included in his income under section 61(a)(1). The IRS agent relied at least in part upon the authority of *Richard A. Allen*, 50 T.C. 466 (1968).

After determining the foregoing facts, the tax researcher decides that, according to the language of Treas. Reg. Sec. 1.61-2(a)(1), the total bonus payment should be included in Werner's return. The regulations specify that, in general, wages, salaries, and bonuses are income to the recipient unless excluded by law. After additional research, the tax adviser locates the decision in *Cecil Randolph Hundley, Jr.*, which appears to contain a similar situation.[29] In *Hundley*, to which the commissioner acquiesced, the

---

[29] *Cecil Randolph Hundley, Jr.*, 48 T.C. 339, acq. 1967-2 C.B. 2.

taxpayer included the bonus payments in his income but was allowed a business expense deduction for that portion of the bonus paid to his father. Before relying solely on the authority of *Hundley*, the tax adviser must be certain that the facts of *Hundley* are in effect substantially similar to Werner's situation and that the expense of further negotiations with the IRS is warranted and based on a sound premise. Thus, the tax adviser will carefully compare the *Allen* and *Hundley* cases with the facts presented by Werner Hoppe. In doing this, the adviser might prepare the following list of facts.

Allen	*Hoppe*	*Hundley*
1. Professional baseball player received sizable bonus.	1. Professional football player received sizable bonus.	1. Professional baseball player received sizable bonus.
2. Taxpayer was amateur prior to signing contract.	2. Taxpayer was professional soccer player prior to signing contract.	2. Taxpayer was amateur player before signing contract.
3. Parent and ball-playing minor child signed professional ball contract.	3. Ballplayer alone signed contract, but brother signed as witness and interpreter.	3. Parent and ball-playing minor child signed professional ball contract.
4. Some bonus payments were actually made to mother.	4. Some bonus payments were actually made to brother.	4. Some bonus payments were actually made to father.
5. Mother knew little about baseball.	5. Brother had average knowledge of football.	5. Father was knowledgeable in baseball and taught his son extensively.
6. Mother was passive participant in negotiations for contract and bonus.	6. Brother was an active participant in negotiations for contract and bonus.	6. Father handled most of the negotiations for contract and bonus.
7. No oral agreement existed.	7. No oral agreement existed.	7. Oral agreement existed on how to divide the bonus payments.

Because *Allen* was decided for the government and *Hundley* for the taxpayer, it may be important to distinguish the two cases on the basis of facts. Utilizing a simple diagram technique, we begin with seven facts identified in each case.

Figure 5.1

Next, the researcher should identify those issues that are very similar in both cases and those that are more readily distinguishable.

Figure 5.2

The second diagram shows that facts one through four are "neutral" in that they are nearly identical in both cases, and that the important facts, which perhaps swayed the outcome of the *Hundley* case in favor of the taxpayer, appear to be facts five through seven. Comparing *Hundley* with *Hoppe* produces the following result.

Figure 5.3

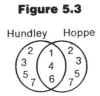

This diagram shows that *Hoppe* and *Hundley* agree in facts one, four, and six only. The following comparison of all three fact situations might provide additional insight for the tax adviser.

Figure 5.4

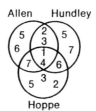

This analysis shows that facts one and four are neutral in all three cases and perhaps should not be considered to have an impact upon the final outcome. Fact two, dealing with the professional status of Hoppe, which can be distinguished from both *Allen* and *Hundley*, might significantly bolster Hoppe's claim for an ordinary and necessary business expense under section 162. Hoppe has already established his business as a professional athlete; fact three, the signing of the contract by Hoppe alone (again distinguished from *Allen* and *Hundley*), seems to support the fact that Klaus was needed in the negotiations as an interpreter, the capacity in which he signed the contract. Facts five and six, which indicate the degree of expertise exhibited by the respective relatives of the ballplayers and the roles played by the relatives in the contract negotiations, seem to be of much greater significance. In Hundley's and Hoppe's cases both relatives took active roles in negotiating final contracts. In *Hundley*, the father was knowledgeable about baseball and contract negotiations. Hoppe's situation is certainly similar. Klaus exhibited an ability to negotiate by recommending that a bonus be offered, and he displayed his expertise as an interpreter. The final fact—number seven—in which *Allen* and *Hoppe* are distinguished from *Hundley*, appears to be a liability to Hoppe's position and weakens his case considerably.

The foregoing analysis demonstrates a situation in which the statute is incomplete and a taxpayer and the adviser must rely on equally incomplete interpretive authority. Careful analysis indicates that previous interpretations appear to apply to some but not all the existing facts. Once a thorough examination of the facts and a review of the applicable authority have been completed, a decision must be made about the course of action. Possible risks must be evaluated and additional expenses must be estimated before the decision to contest the deficiency assessment is made. Consultation with legal counsel concerning litigation hazards will assist the taxpayer in deciding whether to carry the case beyond an administrative appeal and into the courts.

The Facts Are Clear—The Law Is Nonexistent

It is possible that a tax researcher may discover that a problem is not clearly covered by any statutory, administrative, or judicial authority. In such circumstances, the tax adviser has an opportunity to utilize whatever powers of creativity, logical reasoning, and persuasion he or she possesses. Since the revenue agent making an examination likewise will have little authority to substantiate any proposed adjustment, it is up to the tax adviser to present a convincing argument in support of the client's position. However, as stressed throughout this chapter, before the tax adviser proceeds with a course of action, the client should be advised of the possible risks and expenses associated with it. In these circumstances, the client may want to ask the IRS for a letter ruling before a final decision is reached.

We have suggested that in all questionable situations the cost and risk factors be considered before reaching a conclusion. Risk should be interpreted as any possible adverse consequence that might occur as a result of a specific course of action adopted by the taxpayer. One might ask whether the questionable treatment of a particular item on the return will trigger an examination, and whether such an examination is likely to subject other items on the return to scrutiny and a possible proposed adjustment.[30] Furthermore, proposed adjustments on one year's tax return may lead to similar adjustments on a prior year's return. Thus, in addition to developing a strong case against the IRS claims, potential risks must be considered in the final decision process in the treatment of all tax matters. At the same time, one should not forget that the cost of disputing a tax liability is generally deductible but is also subject to the 2 percent of adjusted gross income floor, unless it deals with resolving tax disputes relating to the taxpayer's business as a sole proprietor. For the taxpayer in a high marginal tax

---

[30] A questionable treatment should not be confused with an illegal treatment. The former refers to items supported by adequate authority that lend themselves to honest disagreement between taxpayers and the IRS.

bracket with sufficient miscellaneous itemized deductions, this may be a point in favor of continuing a dispute with the IRS.

Working With the Citator

In addition to its usefulness in locating appropriate authority, the citator can assist in the assessment process. Throughout this chapter we have observed how conflicting interpretations of the code by taxpayers, their tax advisers, the IRS, and the courts result in considerable litigation. In the litigation process, court decisions sometimes are appealed and, subsequently, either affirmed or reversed by the appropriate appellate court. Furthermore, it should be apparent that, while a particular court decision may support a taxpayer's position, subsequent decisions by the same court or by other courts may reverse a previous decision. It is imperative, therefore, that the researcher carefully investigate the judicial history of any decision, as well as other decisions citing that case, before placing much emphasis on it. The citator can assist the researcher in this evaluative process. Verifying the judicial history of a particular case can most easily be accomplished by using the *CCH Citator*. However, identifying the issues involved in cases that cite a particular decision and how they are resolved can only be accomplished through the use of the RIA citator. The *CCH Citator* simply does not include the information necessary to make this determination. To illustrate, let us return to exhibit 4.5, page 114. The entry in the *CCH Citator* for the *Germantown Trust Co.* case discloses that *Germantown* was cited in *Automobile Club of Michigan*, 353 U.S. 180 (1957). Because the latter case was decided by the Supreme Court, it would be important to know which issue was involved and whether or not the Supreme Court upheld its earlier decision in *Germantown Trust Co.* Such information cannot be gleaned from the *CCH Citator*. As shown in exhibit 4.9, page 118, the *RIA Citator* lists information similar to that found in the *CCH Citator*. However, the symbol "n-1" precedes the *Automobile Club* citation, and similar symbols precede other cases in which *Germantown* was cited. The RIA symbol explanation sheet (see exhibit 5.1) discloses that "n" denotes that *Germantown* was cited only in a dissenting opinion. The number "1" in connection with the symbol "n" refers the reader to the corresponding headnote number in the AFTR series, which identifies the issue involved. A further examination of cases in which *Germantown* was cited (exhibit 4.9) indicates that issue "3" is most frequently cited, that, in one instance, *Germantown* was "used favorably" and that, in other instances, it was "distinguished." (See exhibit 5.1 for an explanation of these terms, as well as other interpretive symbols.)

How the *RIA Citator* can assist the researcher can be demonstrated with the decision reached by the Supreme Court in *Wilcox*,

Exhibit 5.1
RIA Citator Symbols

Court Decisions
Judicial History of a Case

a	affirmed by a higher court (Note: When available, the official cite to the affirmance is provided; if the affirmance is by unpublished order or opinion, the date of the decision and the court deciding the case are provided.)
App auth	appeal authorized by the Treasury
App	appeal pending (Note: Later volumes may have to be consulted to determine if the appellate case was decided.)
cert gr	petition for *certiorari* was granted by the U.S. Supreme Court
d	appeal dismissed by the court or withdrawn by the party filing the appeal
(G)	following an appeal notation, this symbol indicates that it was the government filing an appeal
m	the earlier decision has been modified by the higher court, or by a later decision
r	the decision of the lower court has been reversed on appeal
rc	related case arising out of the same taxable event or concerning the same taxpayer
reh den	rehearing has been denied by the same court in which the original case was heard
remd	the case has been remanded for proceedings consistent with the higher court decision
remg	the cited case is remanding the earlier case
reinst	a dismissed appeal has been reinstated by the appellate court and is under consideration again
s	same case or ruling
sa	the cited case is affirming the earlier case
sm	the cited case is modifying the earlier case
sr	the cited case is reversing the earlier case
sx	the cited case is an earlier proceeding in a case for which a petition for *certiorari* was denied
(T)	an appeal was filed from the lower court decision by the taxpayer
vacd	the lower court decision was vacated on appeal or by the original court on remand
vacg	a higher court or the original court on remand has vacated the lower court decision
rev & rem	the decision of the lower court has been reversed and remanded by a higher court on appeal
widrn	the original opinion was withdrawn by the court
x	petition for *certiorari* was denied by the U.S. Supreme Court
•	Supreme Court cases are designated by a bold-faced bullet (•) before the case line for easy location

(continued)

Exhibit 5.1
RIA Citator Symbols (cont.)

Certain notations appear at the end of the cited case line. These notations include:

(A)	the government has acquiesced in the reasoning or the result of the cited case
(NA)	the government has refused to acquiesce or to adopt the reasoning or the result of the cited case, and will challenge the position adopted if future proceedings arise on the same issue
on rem	the case has been remanded by a higher court and the case cited is the resulting decision

Evaluation of Cited Cases

iv	on all fours (both the cited and citing cases are virtually identical)
f	the reasoning of the court in the cited case is followed by the later decision
e	the cited case is used favorably by the citing case court
k	the cited and citing case principles are reconciled
l	the rationale of the cited case is limited to the facts or circumstances surrounding that case (this can occur frequently in situations in which there has been an intervening higher court decision or law change)
n	the cited case was noted in a dissenting opinion
g	the cited and citing cases are distinguished from each other on either facts or law
q	the decision of the cited case is questioned and its validity debated in relation to the citing case at issue
c	the citing case court has adversely commented on the reasoning of the cited case, and has criticized the earlier decision.
o	the later case directly overrules the cited case (use of the evaluation is generally limited to situations in which the court notes that it is specifically overturning the cited case, and that the case will no longer be of any value)
inap	the citing case court has specifically indicated that the cited case does not apply to the situation stated in the citing case.

Note: The evaluations used for the court decisions generally are followed by a number. That number refers to the headnoted issue in the American Federal Tax Reports (AFTR) or Tax Court decision to which the cited case relates. If the case is not directly on point with any headnote, a bracketed notation at the end of the citing case line directs the researcher to the page in the cited case on which the issue appears.

327 U.S. 404 (1946). In this decision the Supreme Court held that embezzled money does not constitute taxable income to the embezzler. The Supreme Court overruled the *Wilcox* decision in *James*, 366 U.S. 213 (1961). The extract from the *RIA Citator* shown in exhibit 5.2, reveals that *Wilcox* was cited on various issues in *James* and that in *James* the court overruled *Wilcox* on issues three, four, nine, and twelve. Thus, reliance on *Wilcox*, simply because it represented a Supreme Court decision, would be ill advised.

Before researchers rely explicitly upon the authority of any particular judicial decision, they should take the few minutes it requires to trace that case through the *RIA Citator* to be sure that

Exhibit 5.2
RIA Citator Extract

WILBUR—WILCOX   3973

WILBUR—Contd.
f-1—Meyer, Leon R. & Lucile H., 46 TC 103, 46 P-H
TC 72
e-1—Niedermeyer, Bernard E. & Tessie S., 62 TC 289, 62
P-H TC 175 [See 31 TC 948]
1—McGah, E. W. & Lucille, 1961 P-H TC Memo
61-862, 863
1—Laidley, Inc., 1961 P-H TC Memo 61-1007
1—Taft, John S. & Virginia M., 1961 P-H TC Memo
61-1241
1—Marin Canalways & Development Co., Inc., 1961 P-H
TC Memo 61-1870
e-1—Lousquisset Golf Club, Inc., 1962 P-H TC Memo
62-1758
e-1—Evwalt Development Corp., 1963 P-H TC Memo
63-257
e-1—Schine Chain Theatres, Inc., 1963 P-H TC Memo
63-565
1—Catalina, Homes, Inc., 1964 P-H TC Memo 64-1496
[See 31 TC 948-952]
1—Brahms, James J., 1964 P-H TC Memo 64-1564 [See
31 TC 948]
e-1—Thomas Machine Mfg. Co., 1964 P-H TC Memo
64-1798, 64-1800 [See 31 TC 948, 950]
1—Smith, George T. & Clela V., 1964 P-H TC Memo
64-1860 [See 31 TC 948]
1—Peco Co., 1967 P-H TC Memo 67-230
e-1—Redak, Hyman R. & Rita F., 1968 P-H TC Memo
68-1161
**WILBUR SECURITY CO. v COMM., 5 AFTR2d 1553,
279 F2d 657 (USCA 9, 5-23-60)**
sa—Wilbur Security Co., 31 TC 938, ¶ 31.92 P-H TC
1959
g—Taft v Comm., 11 AFTR2d 1032, 314 F2d 622
(USCA 9) [See 5 AFTR 2d 1553, 279 F2d 658]
Wood Preserving Corp. of Baltimore, Inc. v U.S., 16
AFTR2d 5042, 347 F2d 119 (USCA 4) [See 5 AFTR
2d 1556, 279 F2d 1556]
Foresun, Inc. v Comm., 16 AFTR2d 5284, 348 F2d 1009
(USCA 6) [See 5 AFTR 2d 1556, 279 F2d 662]
Fors Farms, Inc. v U.S., 17 AFTR2d 226 (DC Wash)
[See 5 AFTR 2d 1556, 279 F2d 662]
e—Foresun, Inc., 41 TC 714, 41 P-H TC 618 [See 5
AFTR 2d 1556, 279 F2d 661]
f—Monon Railroad, 55 TC 356, 55 P-H TC 252 [See 5
AFTR2d 1556, 279 F2d 662]
e—Lancaster, James D. & Marian W., 1964 P-H TC
Memo 64-697 [See 5 AFTR 2d 1556, 279 F2d 662]
Stanchfield, A. L., 1965 P-H TC Memo 65-1853 [See 5
AFTR 2d 1556, 279 F2d 660]
Wynnefield Heights, Inc., 1966 P-H TC Memo 66-1077
[See 5 AFTR 2d 1556, 279 F2d 662]
e—Lupowitz, Joseph, Sons, Inc., 1972 P-H TC Memo
72-1226 [See 5 AFTR2d 1556, 279 F2d 662]
1—P. M. Finance Corp. v Comm., 9 AFTR2d 1457, 302
F2d 789 (USCA 3)
f-1—Consumers Credit Rural Elec. Coop. Corp. v
Comm., 12 AFTR2d 5092, 319 F2d 478 (USCA 6)
1—Lustman v Comm., 12 AFTR2d 5465, 322 F2d 256
(USCA 3)
g-1—J. S. Biritz Constr. Co. v Comm., 20 AFTR2d
5896, 387 F2d 457 (USCA 8)
n-1—Fin Hay Realty Co. v U.S., 22 AFTR2d 5009, 398
F2d 700 (USCA 3)
q-1—Bordo Products Co. v U.S., 31 AFTR2d 73-1121,
201 Ct Cl 502, 476 F2d 1324
1—Utility Trailer Mfg. Co. v U.S., 11 AFTR2d 1122,
1123, 212 F Supp 784, 785 (DC Calif)
1—Gyro Engrg. Corp. v U.S., 20 AFTR2d 5650, 276 F
Supp 467 (DC Calif)
e-1—Hall Paving Co. v U.S., 33 AFTR2d 74-1199 (DC
Ga)
e-1—Universal Castings Corp., 37 TC 114, 37-1961 P-H
TC 84
f-1—Consumers Credit Rural Elec. Coop. Corp., 37 TC
143, 37-1961 P-H TC 106
f-1—Meyer, Leon R. & Lucile H., 46 TC 103, 46 P-H
TC 72
e-1—Zilkha & Sons, Inc., 52 TC 616, 52 P-H TC 438
e-1—Niedermeyer, Bernard E. & Tessie S., 62 TC 289, 62
P-H TC 175
1—McGah, E. W. & Lucille, 1961 P-H TC Memo
61-862, 863

WILBUR—Contd.
1—Laidley, Inc., 1961 P-H TC Memo 61-1007
1—Taft, John S. & Virginia M., 1961 P-H TC Memo
61-1241
1—Marin Canalways & Dev. Co., Inc., 1961 P-H TC
Memo 61-1870
e-1—Lousquisset Golf Club, Inc., 1962 P-H TC Memo
62-1758
e-1—Evwalt Development Corp., 1963 P-H TC Memo
63-257
1—Earenco Truck Co., The, 1963 P-H TC Memo 63-334
e-1—Schine Chain Theatres, Inc., 1963 P-H TC Memo
63-565
e-1—Schine Chain Theatres, Inc., 1963 P-H TC Memo
63-567
1—Merlo Builders, Inc., 1964 P-H TC Memo 64-209
1—Gen. Alloy Casting Co., 1964 P-H TC Memo 64-987
f-1—Gardens of Faith, Inc., 1964 P-H TC Memo 64-1161
1—Catalina, Homes, Inc., 1964 P-H TC Memo 64-1496
[See 5 AFTR 2d 1556, 279 F2d 661-662]
1—Brahms, James J., 1964 P-H TC Memo 64-1564
e-1—Thomas Machine Mfg. Co., 1964 P-H TC Memo
64-1798, 64-1800
1—Smith, George T. & Clela V., 1964 P-H TC Memo
64-1860
1—Barclay Co., 1964 P-H TC Memo 64-1877
f-1—Rouse, Randolph D., 1964 P-H TC Memo 64-2021
[See 5 AFTR 2d 1556, 279 F2d 662]
1—Old Dominion Plywood Corp., 1966 P-H TC Memo
66-784, 66-785
1—Peco Co., 1967 P-H TC Memo 67-230
1—Jaffee, Leon S. & Fern, 1967 P-H TC Memo 67-658
e-1—Redak, Hyman R. & Rita F., 1968 P-H TC Memo
68-1161
WILCOX, C. B., 27 BTA 580
e—Newton, Joel & Clara Mae, 1970 P-H TC Memo
70-527 [See 27 BTA 584]
1—Baltimore, Stuart L. & Glennis M., 1958 P-H TC
Memo 58-336
e-1—Strandquist, Albin J. & Carol E., 1970 P-H TC
Memo 70-442 [See 27 BTA 584]
e-1—Nelson, Harry A., 1974 P-H TC Memo 74-996 [See
27 BTA 583]
1—Letter Ruling 3-6-57, 1957 P-H 76,371
**WILCOX, CO-EXEC. v U.S., 5 AFTR2d 1949, 185 F
Supp 385 (DC Ohio, 5-27-60)**
WILCOX; COMM. v, 327 US 404, 34 AFTR 811
o-3—James v U.S., 7 AFTR2d 1362, 366 US 257, 81 S
Ct 1053, 6 L Ed 2d 251, 1961-2 CB 11
o-3—Rev. Rul. 61-185, 1961-2 CB 9
o-4—James v U.S., 7 AFTR2d 1362, 366 US 249, 81 S
Ct 1053, 6 L Ed 2d 251, 1961-2 CB 11
o-4—Rev. Rul. 61-185, 1961-2 CB 9
o-9—James v U.S., 7 AFTR2d 1362, 366 US 249, 81 S
Ct 1053, 6 L Ed 2d 251, 1961-2 CB 11
o-9—Alper, Louis, Est. of, 1961 P-H TC Memo 61-1786
o-9—Rev. Rul. 61-185, 1961-2 CB 9
o-12—James v U.S., 7 AFTR2d 1376, 366 US 249, 81 S
Ct 1071, 6 L Ed 2d 270
James v U.S., 7 AFTR2d 1380, 366 US 257, 81 S Ct
1075, 6 L Ed 2d 275
g—Prokop v Comm., 1 AFTR2d 1430, 254 F2d 555
(USCA 7)
Dixie Machine Welding & Metal Works, Inc. v U.S., 11
AFTR2d 1083, 315 F2d 440 (USCA 5) [See 327 US
408, 34 AFTR 814]
q—Kahr, Est. of v Comm., 24 AFTR2d 69-5337, 414
F2d 626 (USCA 2)
e—Pitoscia; U.S. v, 15 AFTR2d 271, 238 F Supp 140
(DC NJ) [See 327 US 408, 34 AFTR 814]
Stromberg, Isaac, Est. of, 1962 P-H TC Memo 62-1455
[See 327 US 405-407, 34 AFTR 813]
g—Nelson, Frederic A. & Doris R., 1964 P-H TC Memo
64-658
1—Mandel v Comm., 229 F2d 387, 48 AFTR 909
(USCA 7)
1—Smith v U.S., 2 AFTR2d 5525, 257 F2d 134 (USCA
10)
1—Piel v Comm., 15 AFTR2d 256, 340 F2d 890 (USCA
2)
e-1—Buder, Exec. v U.S., 17 AFTR2d 069, 071, 354 F2d
944 (USCA 8)
q-1—Huelsman v Comm., 24 AFTR2d 69-5645, 416 F2d
478 (USCA 6)

subsequent developments did not render the case invalid for their purposes.

In addition to the *RIA Citator*, Shepard's McGraw-Hill, Inc., publishes a comprehensive legal citator that can assist tax researchers in tracing the history and current status of any case.[31] Since *Shepard's Citations* includes almost all federal and state cases, the publication consists of numerous volumes, requiring extensive space. While it may not be economically feasible to include Shepard's citator in a typical tax library, it can be found in nearly all law libraries, and the tax researcher may wish to make use of it in unusual circumstances.

---

[31] *Shepard's Citations* (Colorado Springs, Colo.: Shepard's McGraw-Hill, Inc.).

6

People get better at using language when they use it to say things they really want to say to people they really want to say them to, in a context in which they can express themselves freely and honestly.

Communicating Tax Research

Throughout this tax study, we have used the terms *tax researcher* and *tax adviser* synonymously. If a distinction could be made between the two forms of practice, it would be based on the tax *adviser's* task of reporting the conclusion that has been so painstakingly pieced together. While some tax conclusions can be communicated orally, much of the information gathered by tax researchers must eventually be placed in writing. The task of writing introduces two major problems for practitioners. First, the ability to write well is an acquired trait, the result of practice and more practice. Second, communicating the conclusions of tax research requires the ability to perceive how much or how little to express. This task is complicated by the fact that highly technical solutions frequently must be distilled into layman's language. Also, tax advisers often must hedge on their solutions because, as discussed in chapter 5, a definitive answer simply is not available in every case. In addition, tax advisers must, to protect their own professional integrity, foresee potential future claims against them. Like writing skill, the ability to determine precisely what needs to be said usually can be improved through practice. In larger offices, all inexperienced tax researchers should be given an early opportunity to present much of their initial research in written form. New researchers should also be assigned the responsibility of preparing draft copies of correspondence that will subsequently be reviewed by a supervisor for weaknesses in writing style and technical presentation. Experience and assistance can mold good researchers into good advisers with a mastery of writing style and an ability to pinpoint the finer information required in tax documents.

The form of a written tax communication is determined by the audience for which it is intended. Some documents are prepared for internal purposes, or firm use, only. Other documents, such as client letters, protest letters, and requests for rulings, are prepared for an external audience outside the firm. In the following pages, we will illustrate the appropriate formats and procedures; nevertheless, certain basic features are universal to most tax communications.

Internal Communications

Within the accounting firm, the client file is the basic tool used to communicate specific client information between the various levels of the professional staff. Pertinent information concerning each client's unique facts is contained in the file in the form of memos and working papers.

Memo to the File

A memo to the file may be written after any one of several developments. Often such memos are the result of a client's request—in person, over the telephone, or in a letter—for a solution to a tax problem. The importance of facts in tax research was explained in chapter 2; a memo to the file is commonly used to inform the researcher of the underlying facts needed to identify issues, locate authorities, and reach solutions. In most large offices, the partners or managers have the initial contact with the client, while much of the actual research is performed by a staff person. It is critical, therefore, that accurate information be communicated between the various levels of the professional staff. A typical memorandum to the file follows:

April 1, 1993

TO:	Files
FROM:	Tom Partner
SUBJECT:	Potential acquisition by American Rock & Sand, Inc. of Pahrump Ready Mix, Inc.

Today, Ron Jones, financial vice-president of American Rock & Sand, Inc. (ARS), called to request information concerning the tax consequences of a proposed acquisition of Pahrump Ready Mix, Inc. (PRM). ARS is a Utah corporation (organized on October 1, 1962) licensed as a general contractor and specializes in road and highway construction. ARS employs the accrual method of accounting and uses a calendar year end as the basis for maintaining its books. ARS's authorized capital consists of 1,000 shares of voting common stock owned principally by the Jones family.

PRM, the target corporation, is a Utah Corporation organized on June 1, 1970. PRM is engaged in the business of making and delivering concrete. PRM employs the accrual method of accounting and uses a calendar year end as the basis for maintaining its books. PRM's authorized capital consists of 5,000 shares of voting common stock owned principally by the Smith family.

ARS has approached PRM about the possibility of acquiring the assets of PRM. PRM has expressed some preliminary interest if the deal can be structured so that the Smith family is not taxed on the initial sale of PRM. The Smith family has stated that they would consider receiving ARS stock as long as the stock will provide them with an annual income.

Due to a shortage of cash, ARS would like to accomplish the acquisition without the use of cash. Also, the Jones family has stated strenuously that they are not interested in giving up any voting power in ARS to the Smith family. John Jones has requested that we develop, if possible, a proposal of how ARS can structure the transaction to satisfy the requests of both ARS and PRM. Mr. Jones has requested that we present at their May 1, 1993, ARS board meeting our proposal for the acquisition of PRM. If we need further information, we are to contact Mr. Jones directly.

The information contained in the above memo should be sufficient for the researcher to begin work. Furthermore, the memo communicates a specific deadline and indicates that the client is willing to supplement this information with additional facts if necessary.

A less formal procedure is often followed when a long-established client calls the tax adviser for an immediate answer to a routine tax question on a well-defined, noncontroversial topic. If the tax adviser gives an oral reply, the conversation should be placed in writing, thus creating a record for the files. Such a record serves as protection against subsequent confusion or misinterpretation that may jeopardize the tax adviser's professional integrity, and it can serve as a basis for billing the client.[1]

Leaving Tracks

Once the necessary information has been recorded in a memo to the files, the researcher may begin the task of identifying questions and seeking solutions. Supporting documents for conclusions, such as excerpts from or references to specific portions of the Internal Revenue Code, Treasury regulations, revenue rulings, court decisions, tax service editorial opinions, and periodicals, should be put in the files. All questions and conclusions should be appropriately cross-indexed so the information can be retrieved quickly. Pertinent information in supporting documents should be highlighted to avoid unnecessary reading. Examples of the content and organization of a client's file are presented in chapter 7.

Because time is one of the most important commodities that any tax adviser has for sale, a well-organized client file is of the utmost importance: it can eliminate duplication of effort. Supervisory review of a staff person's research can be accomplished quickly, and additional time can be saved if and when it becomes necessary to refer to a client's file months (or even years) after the

---

[1] The question of whether oral advice should be confirmed in writing frequently arises. The AICPA Subcommittee on Responsibilities in Tax Practice makes the following recommendation: "Although oral advice may serve a client's needs appropriately in routine matters or in well-defined areas, written communications are recommended in important, unusual, or complicated transactions. In the judgment of the CPA, oral advice may be followed by a written confirmation to the client." (AICPA, Statement on Responsibilities in Tax Practice [1988 rev.] No. 8, *Form and Content of Advice to Clients* [New York: American Institute of Certified Public Accountants, August 1988]).

initial work was performed. Such a delayed reference to a file may be required because of subsequent IRS audits, preparation of protests, or the need to solve another client's similar tax problem. Because promotions, transfers, and staff turnover are common occurrences in accounting firms, well organized files can be of significant help in familiarizing new staff members with client problems.

Another time-saving device used by practitioners is the tax subject file. To prepare such a system, members of the practitioner's tax staff contribute tax problems together with documented conclusions, which are then pooled and arranged on a subject basis. In a multioffice firm such files are duplicated, in some instances on microfilm or computer databases, and made available to each office. A subject file can eliminate many hours of duplicative research.

External Communications

A tax practitioner's written communication to an audience outside the firm takes on added significance because it demonstrates expertise, renders advice, and demonstrates reputation. Perhaps the most frequently encountered external document in a CPA's tax practice is the client letter. Communications with the Internal Revenue Service on behalf of a client to protest a deficiency assessment or to request a ruling for a proposed transaction are also quite common.

Client Letters

In a client letter, the tax adviser expresses a professional opinion to those who pay for his or her services. Because it is important to clearly communicate a professional opinion, writing the client letter may be the tax adviser's greatest challenge in the entire tax engagement. The format of client letters may vary from one firm to another. However, most good client letters have three things in common.

Style. Like a good speaker, a good writer must know the audience before beginning. Because tax clients and their staff vary greatly in their tax expertise, it is important to consider their technical sophistication when composing a tax opinion letter. The style of a letter may range from a highly sophisticated format, with numerous technical explanations and citations, to a simple composition that uses only layperson's terms. In many situations, of course, the best solution lies somewhere between the two extremes.

Format and Content. Regardless of the degree of technical sophistication, a well-drafted client letter follows a well-planned format. It should begin with an enumeration of the facts upon which the tax adviser's research is based. In conjunction with a statement of the facts, a statement of caution (see "Disclaimer Statements," page 165) should be included to warn the client that the research conclusions stated are valid only for the specified facts. Next, the letter should state the important tax questions implicit in the previously identified facts. Finally, the tax practitioner should list his or her conclusions and the authority for those conclusions. An example of the appropriate form and typical content of a client letter is shown in chapter 7.

A client letter may identify areas of controversy (or questions that are not authoritatively resolved) that might be disputed by the Internal Revenue Service. Some highly qualified tax advisers seriously question the wisdom of including any discussion of disputable points in a client letter because that letter may end up in the possession of a revenue agent at a most inopportune time. Furthermore, by authority of section 7602, the IRS has the right to examine all relevant books, papers, and records containing information relating to the business of a taxpayer liable for federal taxes. Tax accountants are well aware that documents in their possession, relating to the computation of a client's federal tax liability, are not considered privileged communication. Those granted privileged communication are usually based on an attorney-client or Fifth Amendment privilege—never on an accountant-client privilege.[2]

The accountant in tax practice is thus faced with a dilemma. If a client letter discloses both the strengths and weaknesses of the

[2] See *U.S. v. Arthur Young & Co.*, 104 S. Ct. 1495 (1984); James A. Woehlke, "CPA–Client Privilege vs. the Confidentiality Ethics Requirement," *The Tax Adviser* (February 1992):123–125; and Denzil Causey and Frances McNair, "An Analysis of State Accountant–Client Privilege Statutes and Public Policy Implications for the Accountant–Client Relationship," *American Business Law Journal* (Winter 1990):535–551.

client's tax posture, the letter could weaken the client's position (even assist the revenue agent's case) if it were to fall into the agent's hands. On the other hand, if the potential weaknesses of the position are not clearly communicated to the client, the tax adviser exposes himself to potential legal liability for inappropriate advice.

Although many advisers do not agree, the authors believe that client letters should contain comprehensive information, including reference to those factors that could be challenged by the IRS. In our opinion, full disclosure and self-protection against claims by clients, which may endanger the professional reputation of all tax practitioners, is more important than the risk of an IRS challenge. Any disclosure of weaknesses must be carefully worded, and the client should be cautioned in advance to control possession of the letter.

The issue of privileged communication is most frequently raised in connection with tax fraud cases, and, in the long run, a tax practitioner will do his or her practice more good by preserving a professional reputation than by protecting a few clients who may be guilty of tax fraud. If a CPA suspects fraud, the client should be immediately referred to an attorney for all further work. If the accountant may be of assistance, the attorney may reengage the accountant (or another accountant) and thereby possibly extend privileged communication to the accountant's workpapers.[3]

Disclaimer Statements. Tax advisers deal with two basically different situations. In the case of after-the-fact advice, tax practitioners must assure themselves that they understand all of the facts necessary to reach valid conclusions. Incomplete or inaccurate facts may lead advisers to erroneous conclusions. In planning situations, in which many of the facts are still "controllable," tax advisers must assure themselves that they fully understand their clients' objectives and any operational constraints on achieving those objectives. Furthermore, planning situations frequently involve lengthy time periods during which changes in tax laws may occur, thus possibly changing the recommended course of action. Statement on Responsibilities in Tax Practice No. 8, issued by the

---

[3] See Cono R. Namorato and Scott D. Michel, "What to Do When IRS Special Agents Arrive," *The Practical Accountant* (December 1990):29–39.

AICPA Responsibilities in Tax Practice Subcommittee, noted some of the problems associated with new developments in tax matters.

> The CPA may assist a client in implementing procedures or plans associated with the advice offered. During this active participation, the CPA continues to advise and should review and revise such advice as warranted by new developments and factors affecting the transaction.
>
> Sometimes the CPA is requested to provide tax advice but does not assist in implementing the plans adopted. While developments such as legislative or administrative changes or further judicial interpretations may affect the advice previously provided, the CPA cannot be expected to communicate later developments that affect such advice unless the CPA undertakes this obligation by specific agreement with the client. Thus, the communication of significant developments affecting previous advice should be considered an additional service rather than an implied obligation in the normal CPA-client relationship.[4]

On the advisability of including a disclaimer statement in a client letter, the same subcommittee stated:

> The client should be informed that advice reflects professional judgment based on an existing situation and that subsequent developments could affect previous professional advice. CPAs should use precautionary language to the effect that their advice is based on facts as stated and authorities that are subject to change.[5]

In summary, the AICPA subcommittee concludes that a disclaimer statement should be included. In our opinion, the client letter should include a brief restatement of the important facts, a statement to the effect that all conclusions stated in the letter are based on those specific facts, and a warning to the client of the dangers implicit in any changes or inaccuracies in those facts. In the case of tax-planning engagements, we also recommend that the tax practitioner include a warning that future changes in the law could jeopardize the planned end results. An example of such

---

[4] AICPA, Statement on Responsibilities in Tax Practice (1988 Rev.) No. 8.
[5] Ibid.

a disclaimer statement in a compliance (after-the-fact) client letter appears in chapter 7.

Protest Letters

Another external document commonly prepared by the tax practitioner is the "protest" of a client's tax deficiency as assessed by the IRS. A formal written protest is required only if the IRS examination is conducted through correspondence or the proposed tax deficiency originating from a field audit is in excess of $2,500.[6] Some tax advisers feel, however, that a well-written formal protest enhances the chances of resolving a disagreement successfully even in cases resulting from office audits or deficiencies of $2,500 or less. The IRS suggests that a protest include—

1. The taxpayer's name and address.
2. A statement that the taxpayer wants to appeal the findings of the examiner to the Appeals Office.
3. The date and symbols from the taxpayer's letter showing the proposed adjustments and findings that are being protested.
4. The tax periods or years involved.
5. An itemized schedule of the adjustments with which the taxpayer does not agree.
6. A statement of facts supporting the taxpayer's position on any issue with which the taxpayer does not agree.
7. A statement outlining the law or other authority on which the taxpayer is relying. The statement of facts in 6 above must be declared true under penalties of perjury. This may be done by adding to the protest the following signed declaration:

   > Under the penalties of perjury, I declare that I have examined the statement of facts presented in this protest and in any accompanying schedules and, to the best of

---

[6] IRS Publication 556, *Examination of Returns, Appeal Rights, and Claims for Refund*, Washington, D.C.: Government Printing Office (Rev. Nov. 1990).

my knowledge and belief, it is true, correct, and complete.

8. If the taxpayer's representative submits the protest, he or she may substitute a declaration stating:

   a. That the taxpayer's representative prepared the protest and accompanying documents, and

   b. Whether the representative knows personally that the statement of facts contained in the protest and accompanying documents are true and correct.[7]

In principle, the body of a protest follows the format of a client letter in that the protest specifies important facts, delineates contested findings, and lists the authority supporting the taxpayer's position. An example of a typical protest letter follows:

July 14, 1993

[*Full Name*]
District Director of
  Internal Revenue[8]
Federal Building
Salt Lake City, UT 84101

Re: Intermountain Stove, Inc.
  1408 State Street
  Moroni, Utah 84646

Corporate income taxes for
the year ended 12/31/91

Dear Mr. or Ms. [*Last Name*]:

I am writing in reference to your letter of May 23, 1993 (Reference-B:S:59-A:FS:rs), which transmitted a copy of your examining officer's report dated May 8, 1993, covering his examination of Intermountain Stove's corporate income tax return for the year ended December 31, 1991. In the report, the examining officer recommended adjustments to the taxable income (loss) in the following amount:

---

[7] Ibid.

[8] Although a conference is requested with the regional director of appeals, the protest letter is directed to the district director. See IRS publication 556 (note 6, herein).

Tax year	Amount of Increase in Income Reported
December 31, 1991	$42,000

PROTEST AGAINST ADJUSTMENT

Your letter granted the taxpayer a period of thirty days from the date thereof within which to protest the recommendations of the examining officer, which period was subsequently extended to July 22, 1993, by your letter dated June 6, 1993, a copy of which is attached. This protest to the Appeals Office is accordingly being filed within that period, as extended.

The taxpayer respectfully protests against the proposed adjustment stated below.

FINDINGS TO WHICH TAXPAYER TAKES EXCEPTION

Exception is now taken to the following item:

Disallowance of the following expenses of Intermountain Stove, Inc.

Description	Year	Amount
Professional Fees	December 31, 1991	$42,000

GROUNDS UPON WHICH TAXPAYER RELIES

The taxpayer submits the following information to support its contentions:

Expenses of Intermountain Stove, Inc.

Your examining officer contends that fees paid in the amount of $42,000 in connection with the employment of certain individuals who were experienced in various phases of the production and sale of cast iron stoves should be considered as the acquisition costs of assets in connection with expansion of operations and establishment of a new cast iron stove division.

Taxpayer contends, for reasons set forth below, that the examining officer's position is untenable on the facts and in law and that such costs are clearly deductible as ordinary and necessary expenses incurred in its trade or business, deductible in accordance with section 162 of the Internal Revenue Code.

Facts concerning the operations of Intermountain Stove, Inc.

Intermountain Stove, Inc. (ISI) is a manufacturer of campers. Orders for campers in 1991 declined, and ISI decided, in addition to their camper operation, to again produce wood and coal burning stoves, a product ISI had manufactured until the end of World War II and for which a strong demand seemed to exist. To begin immediate operation in a new stove division, ISI contracted with a consulting firm to locate personnel with experience in the production and marketing of cast iron stoves. The fee paid for such services during 1991 amounted to $42,000.

Discussion of authorities

Section 162(a) of the Internal Revenue Code provides:

"There shall be allowed as a deduction all of the ordinary and necessary expenses paid or incurred during the taxable year in carrying on any trade or business...."

To contend, as the examining officer does, that assets were acquired with the employment of the newly acquired employees is not within the usual interpretation of the Internal Revenue Code.

There were no employment contracts purchased, as may sometimes be found in the hiring of professional athletes; the employees were free to sever their employment relationships at any time, and, in fact, certain of these specific individuals have done so. The examining officer's position was considered in *David J. Primuth*, 54 T.C. 374 (1970), in which the court stated:

"It might be argued that the payment of an employment fee is capital in nature and hence not currently deductible. Presumably under this view the fee would be deductible when the related employment is terminated. However, the difficulty with this view is to conjure up a capital asset which had been purchased. Certainly the expense was not related to the purchase or sale of a capital asset.... Certainly in the ordinary affairs of life common understanding would clearly encompass the fee paid to the employment agency herein as "ordinary and necessary expenses in carrying on any trade or business" (section 162) within the usual, ordinary and everyday meaning of the term."

Your examining officer is here attempting to disallow deductions for amounts paid to outside consultants in a situation in which the expenses would clearly be deductible if the work had been performed by the company's own staff. No such distinction should be made. The corporation employed the expertise of a knowledgeable consultant to assist in the location of personnel with specific background and experience. The payment of fees for such assistance may be compared with the direct payroll and overhead costs of operating an "in-house" personnel department.

The examining officer apparently believes that such costs should be capitalized primarily because they might be nonrecurring in nature. This is not the test of whether an expense is ordinary and necessary. As the Supreme Court stated in *Thomas H. Welch v. Helvering*, 290 U.S. 111, 3 USTC ¶1164 (1933), "Ordinary in this context does not mean that the payments must be habitual or normal in the sense that that same taxpayer may make them often." The fees are ordinary and necessary because it is the common experience in the business community that payments are made for assistance in the procurement of personnel. This is emphasized by the Court in *Primuth* by the following statement: " 'Fees' must be deemed ordinary and necessary from every realistic point of view in today's marketplace where corporate executives change employers with a notable degree of frequency."

These expenditures, if paid by the individual employees and reimbursed by the employer, would have been clearly deductible by both the employee and the employer, with the employee having an offsetting amount of income for the reimbursement. [See Rev. Rul. 75-120, 1975-1 C.B. 55 and Rev. Rul. 66-41, 1966-1 C.B. 233 as distinguished by Rev. Rul. 73-351, 1973-2 C.B. 323]. The expense is no less deductible when paid directly by the corporation.

It is, therefore, contended that the disallowance made by the examining officer was in error.

REQUEST FOR CONFERENCE[9]

An oral hearing is requested before the regional Appeals Office.

STATEMENT WITH RESPECT TO PREPARATION

The attached protest was prepared by the undersigned on the basis of information available to him (or her). All statements contained therein are true and correct to the best of his (or her) knowledge and belief.

_____

Signature of Tax Practitioner

---

[9] It is assumed that an appropriate power of attorney has been filed with the IRS. Otherwise, a power of attorney must be attached to the protest.

Requests for Rulings and Determination Letters

Frequently, tax practitioners find it necessary to seek a ruling from the IRS to fix the tax consequences of a client's anticipated business transaction or to settle a disagreement with a revenue agent during an examination. The general procedures with respect to advance rulings (before-the-fact) and determination letters (after-the-fact) are outlined in the first revenue procedure issued each year. (See Rev. Proc. 93-1, 1993-1 I.R.B. 10.) In Rev. Proc. 93-1, the IRS announced that a careful adherence to the specified requirements will minimize delays in processing requests for rulings and determination letters. In addition to Rev. Proc. 93-1, the IRS has, on occasion, issued procedures that govern ruling requests for specific topics. For example, Rev. Proc. 90-39,[10] provides the requirements that must be satisfied to change the method of allocating an affiliated group's consolidated federal income tax liability without obtaining permission from the IRS. Similarly, Rev. Proc. 92-88[11] provides guidance for the classification of limited partnerships. Entities described in this revenue procedure are considered limited partnerships for federal tax purposes and do not ordinarily need to request a classification ruling.

Prior to 1988, the IRS responded to taxpayer inquiries without charge. However, currently, fees are charged ranging from $200 to $5,000 for ruling letters, determination letters, and opinion letters. (For a partial list of user fees, see Rev. Proc. 93-1, Section 8.02.) Requests for rulings, which are addressed to the national office of the IRS, generally take the following format:

March 1, 1993

Internal Revenue Service
Associate Chief Counsel (Domestic)
Attention CC:CORP:T
P.O. Box 7604
Ben Franklin Station
Washington, D.C. 20044

Re: American Rock & Sand Inc., E.I.N. 12-3456789

---

[10] Rev. Proc. 90-39, 1990-2 C.B. 365, as clarified by Rev. Proc. 90-39A, 1990-2 C.B. 367.
[11] Rev. Proc. 92-88, 1992-42 I.R.B. 39.

Dear Sir:

Rulings are respectfully requested as to the Federal income tax consequences of the proposed transaction pursuant to Section 355 of the Internal Revenue Code of 1986, as amended (Code).

FACTS

The American Rock & Sand, Inc. (Distributing), E.I.N. 12-3456789, a Utah corporation, is a privately owned corporation with executive offices located at 1235 N. 1500 W., Provo, UT 84604. As of March 1, 1993, the authorized capital of Distributing consisted of 1,000 shares voting common stock. The issued and outstanding stock of Distributing is held principally by the Jones family. Distributing is engaged in the business of road and highway construction, and has continually been actively engaged in such business for the past 10 years.

Distributing uses the accrual method of accounting and maintains its books of account on a fiscal year ending June 30. Distributing files a consolidated Federal income tax return with its subsidiaries and is subject to examination by the District Director, Salt Lake City, UT.

Pahrump Ready Mix, Inc. (Controlled), E.I.N. 12-9876543, a Utah corporation, was formed on June 1, 1970, in order to purchase the assets of a division of an unrelated company. Since the date of that acquisition, Controlled has been actively involved in the business of making and delivering concrete.

As of March 1, 1993, the authorized capital of Controlled consisted of 1,000 shares of Class A common stock, all of which is issued and outstanding and held by Distributing. Controlled is also authorized to issue 10,000 shares of Class B nonvoting common stock, but no shares are currently issued and outstanding.

BUSINESS PURPOSE

A key employee of Controlled wishes to acquire an equity interest in Controlled, but does not wish to, nor can he afford to, purchase an equity interest as long as Controlled is a wholly owned subsidiary of Distributing. Furthermore, he does not wish to acquire an equity interest in Controlled while it has a corporate shareholder as a result of the following factors:

(1) The parent company could use the earnings and profits of Controlled to invest in other business ventures.

(2) Having a corporate parent-shareholder would give him a minority interest in Controlled with a shareholder whose interest in the future of Controlled may be different than his.

(3) Because the corporate shareholder would be entitled to a dividend received deduction, which is a benefit unavailable to him, the decisions regarding dividend distributions may differ from his.

The key employee has indicated that he would seriously consider terminating employment with Controlled if he is not offered an opportunity to purchase such a stock interest, and that when shares of Controlled stock are offered to him, he will purchase them.

PROPOSED TRANSACTION

Distributing will distribute to its shareholders, on a pro rata basis, all of the Controlled voting common stock. Controlled will then sell to the key employee 100 shares of Class B nonvoting stock within one year of receipt of an IRS ruling letter. This will represent 100 percent of the oustanding shares of this class of stock and will represent 5 percent of all of the outstanding shares of Controlled. The Class B nonvoting common stock will, in all respects, be identical to the outstanding Class A common stock, except that it is nonvoting and will contain a restriction requiring resale of Controlled at fair market value.

REPRESENTATIONS

In connection with the proposed transaction, the following representations are made:

(a) There is no plan or intention by the shareholders or security holders of Distributing to sell, exchange, transfer by gift, or otherwise dispose of any of their stock in, or securities of, either Distributing or Controlled subsequent to the proposed transaction.

(b) There is no plan or intention to liquidate either Distributing or Controlled, to merge either corporation with any other corporation, or to sell, or otherwise dispose of the assets of either corporation subsequent to the transaction, except in the ordinary course of business.

(c) Distributing, Controlled, and their respective shareholders will each pay their own expenses, if any, incurred in connection with the proposed transaction.

(d) Following the proposed transaction, Distributing and Controlled will each independently continue the active conduct of their respective businesses with their own separate employees.

(e) No intercorporate debt will exist between Distributing and Controlled at the time of, or subsequent to, the distribution of Controlled's stock.

(f) No two parties to the transaction are investment companies as defined in Section 368(a)(2)(F)(iii) and (iv) of the Code.

(g) The five years of financial information submitted on behalf of Distributing and Controlled is representative of each corporation's present operations, and, with regard to each corporation, there have been no substantial operational changes since the date of the last financial statements submitted.

(h) Payments made in connection with all continuing transactions between Distributing and Controlled will be for fair market value based on terms and conditioins arrived at by the parties bargaining at arm's length.

(i) No part of the consideration to be distributed by Distributing will be received by a shareholder as a creditor, employee, or in any capacity other than that of a shareholder of the corporation.

Attached hereto as Exhibit ____ is the information required by Revenue Procedure 86-41, 1986-2 C.B.716.

RULINGS REQUESTED

On the basis of the above information and representations, the following rulings are respectfully requested:

(a) No gain or loss will be recognized by Distributing upon the distribution of all of the Controlled stock to the shareholders of Distributing. Section 311(a).

(b) No gain or loss will be recognized to (and no amount will be included in the income of) the shareholders of Distributing upon the receipt of Controlled stock, as described above. Section 355(a)(1).

(c) Pursuant to Section 358(a)(1), the basis of the stock of Controlled and Distributing in the hands of the shareholders of Distributing after the distribution will be the same as the basis of the Distributing stock held immediately before the distribution, allocated in proportion to the relative fair market value of each in accordance with Section 1.358-2(a)(2) of the Regulations.

(d) Provided the Distributing stock was held as a capital asset on the date of the distribution of the Controlled stock, the holding period of the Controlled stock received by each shareholder of Distributing will include the holding period of the Distributing stock with respect to which the distribution was made. Section 1223(1).

(e) As provided in Section 312(h) of the Code, proper allocation of earnings and profits between Distributing and Controlled will be made in accordance with Seciton 1.312-10(a) of the Regulations.

MEMORANDUM OF AUTHORITIES

Section 355 provides for the tax free spin-off of a wholly owned subsidiary. The general rules which are required for the transaction to meet the requirements of Section 355 are:

(a) Immediately before the distribution, the distributing corporation must control the corporation whose shares are being distributed.

The term control is defined by Section 368(c) to mean stock possessing at least 80 percent of the total combined voting power and at least 80 percent of the total number of shares of all other classes of stock. Section 355(a)(1)(A).

(b) Immediately after the distribution, both the distributing and controlled corporations must engage in the active conduct of a trade or business. Section 355(a)(1)(C) and 355(b).

(c) The active conduct of a trade or business is satisfied only if the trade or business was actively conducted throughout the five-year period ending on the date of the distribution with certain limitations. Section 355(b)(2).

(d) The distributing corporation must distribute all of its stock and securities in the controlled corporation, or distribute enough stock to constitute control and establish to the satisfaction of the Commissioner, that the retention of stock in the controlled corporation is not part of a tax avoidance plan. Section 355(a)(1)(D).

(e) The transaction must not be used principally as a device for the distribution of earnings and profits. Section 355(a)(1)(B).

(f) There must be a corporate business purpose for the transaction and continuity of interest. Regulations Section 1.355-2(b) and (c).

The test described in (a) above is satisfied, as Distributing owns 100% of Controlled.

The test in (b) will be satisfied given that both Distributing and Controlled will continue to actively conduct their respective businesses.

The test described in (c) is satisfied. The businesses of both Distributing and Controlled are active trades or businesses that have been carried on for more than five years.

The test described in (d) above will be satisfied because Distributing will distribute 100 percent of the stock of Controlled to its shareholders.

Distributing believes that the test described in (e) above is met because it has no knowledge of any plan or intention on the part of its shareholders to sell or exchange stock of either Distributing or Controlled, or to liquidate or sell the assets of Controlled. Thus, there will be no prearranged disposition of stock by the shareholders, and consummation of the transaction will effect only a readjustment of continuing interest in property under modified corporate form.

The business purpose test described in (f) is satisfied. The sole reason for effectuating the proposed transaction is to enable one of Controlled's key employees to acquire an equity interest in the corporation.

PROCEDURAL STATEMENT

To the best of the knowledge of the taxpayer and the within-named taxpayer's representatives, the identical issues involved in this request for a ruling either are not in a return of the taxpayer (or of a related taxpayer within the meaning of section 267 of the Code, or a member of an affiliated group of which the taxpayer is also a member within the meaning of section 1504) or if they are, then such issues (1) are not under examination by a District Director; (2) either have not been examined by a District Director, or if they have been examined, the statutory period of limitations on either assessment or for filing a claim for refund or credit of tax has expired, or a closing agreement covering the issue or liability has been entered into by a District Director; (3) are not under consideration by an Appeals Office in connection with a return of the taxpayer for an earlier period; (4) either have not been considered by an Appeals Office in connection with a return of the taxpayer for an earlier period, or if they have been considered, the statutory period of limitations on either assessment or for filing a claim for refund or credit of tax has expired, or a closing agreement covering such issues has been entered into by an Appeals Office; and (5) are not pending in litigation in a case involving the taxpayer or a related taxpayer. To the best of the knowledge of the taxpayer and the taxpayer's representatives, the identical or similar issues involved in this ruling request have not been (i) submitted to the Service, but withdrawn before a ruling was issued, or (ii) ruled on by the Service to the taxpayer or predecessor of the taxpayer.

Except as discussed above, the undersigned is not aware of any precedential published authority which is directly contrary to the rulings requested herein.

A conference is requested in the event that the issuance of an unfavorable ruling is contemplated or in the event that such conference would be of assistance to your office in the consideration of this request for a ruling.

Please address your reply and ruling letter to the undersigned, pursuant to the enclosed Power of Attorney. If any additional information is required, please telephone (Mr. or Ms.) _____ ____ at (   )_____-_____, or the undersigned.

Respectfully submitted,
American Rock & Sand, Inc.

by _____
(Signature of Tax Practitioner)

[Attach Section 355–Checklist Questionnaire]

STATEMENT OF PROPOSED DELETIONS
UNDER SECTION 6110

With reference to the attached request for ruling dated _____ _____, relating to _____, no information other than names, addresses, and taxpayer identifying numbers need be deleted under section 6110(c).

(Name of Corporate Officer)   (Date)
(Title)
(Company Name)

DECLARATION UNDER PENALTIES OF PERJURY

Under penalties of perjury I declare that I have examined the request for ruling dated _____ related to _____, including: accompanying documents, and to the best of my knowledge and belief the facts presented in support of the requested ruling or determination are true, correct and complete.

(Name of Corporate Officer)   (Date)
(Title)
(Company Name)

[Enclose User Fee With Request]

As mentioned in chapter 4, under the Freedom of Information Act and section 6110(a) of the Internal Revenue Code, rulings and their associated background files are open for public inspection. However, the IRS is required under section 6110(c) to delete certain information, such as, names, addresses, identification numbers, or any other information that the taxpayer feels would enable someone reading the published private letter ruling to identify the taxpayer that actually received the ruling. For that reason Rev. Proc. 93-1 suggests that a ruling be accompanied by a statement of proposed deletions. This can be accomplished by sending the IRS a copy of the ruling request with brackets around the phrases or words the taxpayer suggests deleting.

As depicted in the sample ruling request, a request should also be signed by the taxpayer or an authorized representative. If signed by an authorized representative, the request should include an appropriate power of attorney and evidence that the representative is currently either an attorney, a certified public accountant, or an enrolled agent in good standing and duly licensed to practice.

7

These examples are the school of mankind, and they will learn at no other.

EDMUND BURKE

Tax Research in the "Closed-Fact" Case: An Example

The preparation of a well-organized working-paper file cannot be overemphasized because it proves that research efforts have been thorough, are logically correct, and are adequately documented. The elements of this chapter comprise a sample client file. The formats of files used in practice vary substantially among firms. The new tax accountant who uses this tax study as a guide for actual research efforts should be prepared to modify this illustration to conform to the format used by his or her employer. It is hoped that the general format suggested here would be approved by most experienced tax advisers, although any employer might disagree with any of several specifics. The sample is based on a relatively simple incorporation transaction. Because the tax problems illustrated are relatively simple, the supporting file would be considered excessive by most advisers. The cost of preparing such an elaborate file would be too great to justify. In this case, the reader should concentrate more on general working paper content and arrangement than on the substantive tax issues illustrated.

However, in more complex problems, this kind of detail would be appropriate.

Throughout this chapter it is assumed that the client has contacted the accountant after all aspects of the incorporation transaction were completed. In other words, the accountant's task in this engagement is restricted to compliance-related tax research. We have combined the information for three clients into one file; that is, that of the new corporate entity and that of its president and vice president. In practice, however, three separate files would be maintained. Finally, in practice a file would very likely include a substantial number of photocopies of excerpts from the Internal Revenue Code, Treasury regulations, revenue rulings, judicial decisions, commercial tax services, and other reference works. We have attempted to simulate a real file by combining script and ordinary type. Anything in script type would be handwritten in a real file. Anything in the reduced type format represents photocopied material.

Red E. Ink, Judith Dixon, Ready, Inc.

Tax File
December 1993

Index to Working Papers

R. U. Partner & Company
Certified Public Accountants
2010 Professional Tower
Calum City, USA 00001

December 24, 1993

Mr. Red E. Ink, President
Ms. Judith Dixon, Vice President
Ready, Incorporated
120 Publisher Lane
Calum City, USA 00002

Dear Mr. Ink and Ms. Dixon:

This letter confirms the oral agreement of December 17, 1993, in which our firm agreed to undertake the preparation of your respective federal income tax returns along with that of Ready, Incorporated, for next year. This letter also reports the preliminary results of our investigation into the tax consequences of the formation of Ready, Incorporated, last March. We are pleased to be of service to you and anticipate that our relationship will prove to be mutually beneficial. Please feel free to call upon me at any time.

Before stating the preliminary results of our investigation into the tax consequences of your incorporation transaction, I would like to restate briefly all of the important facts as we understand them. Please review this statement of facts very carefully. Our conclusions depend on a complete and accurate understanding of all the facts. If any of the following statements is either incorrect or incomplete, please call it to my attention immediately, no matter how small or insignificant the difference may appear to be.

Our conclusions are based on an understanding that on March 1, 1993, the following exchanges occurred in the process of forming a new corporation, Ready, Incorporated. Ms. Dixon transferred two copyrights to Ready, Incorporated, in exchange for 250 shares of common stock. Ms. Dixon had previously paid $200 for filing the copyrights. In addition, the corporation assumed an $800 typing bill, which Ms. Dixon owed for these two manuscripts.

(draft)
FES
12/24/93

Red E. Ink
Judith Dixon
December 24, 1993
Page 2

Mr. Ink concurrently transferred all the assets and liabilities of his former sole proprietorship printing company, Red Publishings, to the new corporation in exchange for 750 shares of Ready, Incorporated, common stock. The assets transferred consisted of $11,700 cash, $10,000 (estimated market value) printing supplies, $50,000 (face value) trade receivables, and $58,300 (tax book value) equipment. The equipment, purchased new in 1991 for $100,000, had been depreciated for tax purposes under the modified accelerated cost recovery system (MACRS) since its acquisition. The liabilities assumed by Ready, Inc., consisted of the $65,000 mortgage remaining from the original equipment purchase in 1991 and current trade payables of $10,000. We further understand that Ready, Inc., plans to continue to occupy the building leased by Red Publishings on May 1, 1991, from Branden Properties until the expiration of that lease on April 30, 1995. Finally, we understand that Ready, Incorporated, has issued only 1,000 shares of common stock and that Mr. Ink retains 730 shares; that Mr. Ink's wife Neva holds ten shares; that Mr. Tom Books, the corporate secretary-treasurer, holds ten shares; and that Ms. Dixon holds the remaining 250 shares. The shares held by Mrs. Ink and Mr. Books were given to them by Mr. Ink, as a gift, on March 1, 1993. It is our understanding that Ready, Inc. will report its taxable income on an accrual method, calendar-year basis.

Assuming that the preceding paragraphs represent a complete and accurate statement of all the facts pertinent to the incorporation transaction, we anticipate reporting that event as a wholly nontaxable transaction. In other words, neither of you, the incorporators (individually), nor your corporation will report any taxable income or loss solely because of your incorporation of the printing business. The trade receivables collected by Ready, Inc., after March 1, 1993, will be reported as the taxable income of the corporate entity; collections made between January 1, 1993, and February 28, 1993, will be considered part of Mr. Ink's personal taxable income for 1993.

There is a possibility that the Internal Revenue Service could argue (1)

(draft)
FES
12/24/93

Red E. Ink
Judith Dixon
December 24, 1993
Page 3

that Ms. Dixon is required to recognize $800 of taxable income and/or (2) that the corporation could not deduct the $10,000 in trade payables it assumed from the proprietorship. If either of you desire, I would be pleased to discuss these matters in greater detail. Perhaps, it would be desirable for Mr. Bent and myself to meet with both of you and review these potential problems prior to our filing the corporate tax return.[1]

If Mr. Tom Books desires any help in maintaining the corporation's regular financial accounts, we shall be happy to assist him. It will be necessary for us to have access to your personal financial records no later than March 1, 1994, if the federal income tax returns are to be completed and filed on a timely basis.

Finally, may I suggest that we plan to have at least one more meeting in my office sometime prior to February 28, 1994, to discuss possible tax-planning opportunities available to you and the new corporation. Among other considerations, we should jointly review the possibility that you may want to make an S election and that you may need to structure executive compensation arrangements carefully and may wish to institute a pension plan. Please telephone me to arrange an appointment if you would like to do this shortly after the holidays.

Thank you again for selecting our firm for tax assistance. It is very important that some of the material in this letter be kept confidential, and we strongly recommend that you carefully control access to it at all times. If you have any questions about any of the matters discussed, feel free to request a more detailed explanation or drop by and review the complete files, which are available in my office. If I should not be available, my assistant, Fred Senior, would be happy to help you. We look forward to serving you in the future.

Sincerely yours,

Robert U. Partner

---

[1] Some advisors would delete this paragraph and handle the matter orally.

(draft)
FES
12/24/93

R. U. Partner & Company
Certified Public Accountants
2010 Professional Tower
Calum City, USA 00001

December 17, 1993

MEMO TO FILE

FROM: R. U. Partner

SUBJECT: Ready, Inc.—Tax Engagement

Mr. Red E. Ink (president) and Ms. Judith Dixon (vice president) this morning engaged our firm to prepare and file their personal annual federal income tax returns and the federal corporate tax return for Ready, Inc. During an interview in my office, the following information pertinent to the first year's tax returns was obtained.

On March 1, 1993, Red E. Ink and Judith Dixon incorporated the sole proprietorship publishing house that Mr. Ink has for two years previously operated as Red Publishings. There were two primary business reasons for incorporating: (1) The incorporators desired to limit their personal liability in a growing business; and (2) greater access to credit was desired, since it was becoming increasingly difficult to obtain credit as individuals or as a partnership because of the prevailing interest rates and the state usury laws.

Judith Dixon is a full-time practicing trial lawyer and has done a substantial amount of work in media law. Several years ago she wrote, on her own time, five articles in various professional journals. Her objective in writing the articles was to establish a reputation among her professional peers and to enjoy such resulting benefits as client referrals and seminar speaking engagements. As a matter of fact, Ms. Dixon obtained such benefits. The articles were written on a gratis basis.

For the past four years, Ms. Dixon has devoted many hours to writing two full-length books, *Trials and Tribulation* and *Media Law: Developing Frontiers*. Ms. Dixon has encountered unexpected difficulty in getting her manuscripts published. This difficulty has been very frustrating to Ms. Dixon.

A-1 (RUP 12/17/93)

Memo to File (R. U. Partner)
Page 2

Ms. Dixon met Mr. Ink at a seminar—entitled "Media and Its Place in Our American Society"—during the fall of 1992. This was one of several seminars at which Ms. Dixon lectured annually on a fee basis. Red Publishings had never been approached by Ms. Dixon because she had wanted to be associated with a larger organization. However, at this point Ms. Dixon was fearing the possibility that her works would never appear in print. Thus, after a period in which Ms. Dixon sold Mr. Ink on the quality of her books and, conversely, Mr. Ink sold Ms. Dixon on the capability and growth potential of his publishing house, they convinced one another that their association would bring adequate returns to all concerned.

The following incorporation transaction was agreed upon: Judith transferred the copyrights to her two manuscripts to Ready, Inc., a newly formed corporation. Judith's tax basis in the two manuscripts was $200, the amount she paid another lawyer to file the copyright papers. She still owed $800 for the manuscript typing. Ready, Inc., agreed to assume this liability and to issue Judith 250 shares of Ready, Inc., common stock.

Red transferred *all* the assets and liabilities of his former proprietorship to Ready, Inc., in exchange for 750 shares of Ready, Inc., common stock. Immediately after receiving the 750 shares, Red gave ten shares to his wife, Neva, and another ten shares to Tom Books, an unrelated and long-time employee who was named the corporate secretary-treasurer. Red stated that these two transfers were intended as gifts and not as compensation for any prior services.

Tom Books provided me with a copy of the balance sheet for Red Publishings just prior to the incorporation. It appears as follows:

Red Publishings
Balance Sheet
February 28, 1993

Assets

Cash	$ 11,700
Supplies on hand	10,000
Trade receivables	50,000
Equipment (net)	58,300
Total assets	$130,000

A-2 (RUP 12/17/93)

Memo to File (R. U. Partner)
Page 3

	Liabilities & Equity	
Trade payables	$10,000	
Mortgage payable	65,000	
Total liabilities		$ 75,000
Red E. Ink, capital		55,000
Total liabilities & equity		$130,000

The balance sheet was prepared at the request of Mr. Hal Bent, who served as legal counsel to Mr. Ink and Ms. Dixon during the Ready, Inc., incorporation. Mr. Bent and Ms. Dixon are members of the same law firm. Incidentally, Mr. Bent recommended to Mr. Ink and Ms. Dixon that our firm be engaged to prepare and to file their federal tax returns.

During our interview Mr. Ink and Ms. Dixon stated that they had always reported their respective personal incomes on a calendar-year, cash basis. It is their intention to report the corporation's taxable income on an accrual basis in the future. They plan to have the corporation use the calendar year.

The $65,000 mortgage payable represents the balance payable on equipment that was purchased in 1991. This equipment has been depreciated under MACRS. The $58,300 shown on the balance sheet is tax book value. Red estimates that the fair market value of the equipment transferred was approximately $75,000 at the time of the incorporation transaction. The trade payables represent the unpaid balances for supplies, utilities, employees' wages, etc., as of the end of February 1993. All of these accounts were paid by Ready, Inc., within sixty days following incorporation. Tom has agreed to provide us with Ready's income statement and year-end balance sheet by no later than February 1, 1994. Mr. Ink and Ms. Dixon will provide us with additional details concerning their personal tax returns in early February.

I have assigned Fred E. Senior the responsibility of investigating all tax consequences associated with the initial incorporation of Ready, Inc. He is immediately to begin preparation of our file, which will be used early next year in connection with the completion of the tax returns for these new clients. All preliminary research should be completed by Fred and reviewed by me before December 31, 1993. I have also asked Fred to prepare a draft of a client letter confirming this new engagement and stating our preliminary findings on the tax consequences of the incorporation transaction.

A-3 (RUP 12/17/93)

R. U. Partner & Company
Certified Public Accountants
2010 Professional Tower
Calum City, USA 00001

December 19, 1993

MEMO TO FILE

FROM: Fred E. Senior

SUBJECT: Additional Information on Ready, Inc.—Tax Engagement

After reviewing Mr. Partner's file memo of December 17, 1993, and subsequently undertaking limited initial research into the tax questions pertinent to filing the Red E. Ink, Judith Dixon, and Ready, Inc., federal income tax returns, I determined that additional information should be obtained. Specifically, I observed that the February 28, 1993, balance sheet included no real property, and I believed that it was necessary for several reasons to confirm all the facts pertinent to this client's real estate arrangements. Accordingly, with R. U.'s approval, I telephoned Tom Books today and obtained the following additional information.

Tom explained that Red had signed a forty-eight-month lease with Branden Properties, Inc., on May 1, 1991, and that Ready, Inc., had continued to occupy the same premises and had paid all monthly rentals due under this lease ($6,000 per month) since March 1, 1993. It is Tom's opinion that Red probably will construct his own building once this lease expires but that he probably will not try to get out of the present lease before its expiration on April 30, 1995. Tom said that the lease agreement calls for a two-month penalty payment (that is, a $12,000 payment) if either party should break the lease prior to its expiration. According to this agreement, whichever party breaks the lease must pay the other the stipulated sum. Tom further stated that the present lease "really is not a particularly good one." In 1991, it appeared to Red that office space in Calum City was going to be scarce, and he thought that the lease then negotiated was a wholly reasonable one. By the spring of 1993, however, the available office space exceeded the demand. Tom suggested (and, based on his square-footage estimates, I agree) that this same lease could now be negotiated for about $5,500 per month. The penalty for breaking the lease would just about equal the savings that could be obtained by renegotiating a new lease today. Under the circumstances, Red has elected to continue with the old lease for the present. This option allows him time to decide whether to build or purchase another building sometime prior to 1995.

A-4 (FES 12/19/93)

Red E. Ink (Personal Account)
Summary of Questions Investigated
December 1993

W.P. Ref.

1. Was the March 1, 1993, incorporation transaction between Red
    E. Ink, Judith Dixon, and Ready, Inc., a tax-free transfer under
    section 351?

    Conclusion: Yes; all of the requirements of section 351 were   C-1 and C-2
    satisfied.

    a. Collateral Question: Do Ms. Dixon's copyrights qualify as
        "property" for purposes of section 351?

        Conclusion: Yes. Substantial authority probably exists to   C-2 thru C-4
        treat Ms. Dixon's copyrights as section 351 property.

    b. Collateral Question: Do Mr. Ink and Ms. Dixon "control"
        Ready, Inc., for section 351 purposes?

        Conclusion: Yes. There are no control problems that would   C-4 and C-5
        preclude the application of section 351.

    c. Collateral Question: Could Ready's assumption of
        liabilities cause partial taxability of the incorporation
        transaction in regard to Mr. Ink?

        Conclusion: No. Mr. Ink receives full nontaxable treatment   C-6 thru C-9
        pursuant to section 357(c)(3).

    d. Collateral Question: Will Ms. Dixon recognize taxable
        income as a result of Ready Inc.'s assumption of the
        $800 typing bill?

        Conclusion: No. Ms. Dixon will not recognize any taxable   C-9 thru C-14
        income because of Ready Inc.'s assumption of the $800
        typing bill.

B-1 (FES 12/21/93)

Red E. Ink (Personal Account)
Working Papers
December 1993

W.P. Ref.

2. *Are collections of the trade receivables transferred by Mr. Ink*
to Ready, Inc., the taxable income of Mr. Ink, or of Ready,
Inc.?

    <u>*Conclusion:*</u> *The trade receivables collected after incorporation*   *C-15*
    should be the taxable income of Ready, Inc.

3. *What is Mr. Ink's tax basis in the 730 shares of Ready, Inc.,*
common stock that he retained?

    <u>*Conclusion:*</u> *In our opinion, Mr. Ink's basis in 730 shares is*   *C-15 thru C-18*
    $4,867.

Red E. Ink (Personal Account)
Working Papers
December 1993

W.P. Ref.

1. *Was the incorporation of Red Publishings on 3/1/93 a tax-free transaction?*

Conclusion: Yes; the incorporation of Red Publishings should be treated as a tax-free transaction pursuant to section 351 which reads as follows:

For facts, see W.P. A-1 thru A-4.

SECTION 351. TRANSFER TO CORPORATION
CONTROLLED BY TRANSFEROR.

See collateral question 1(a).

(a) General Rule.—No gain or loss shall be recognized if property is transferred to a corporation by one or more persons solely in exchange for stock in such corporation and immediately after the exchange such person or persons are in control (as defined in section 368(c)) of the corporation.

See collateral question 1(b).

(b) Receipt of Property.—If subsection (a) would apply to an exchange but for the fact that there is received, in addition to the stock or securities permitted to be received under subsection (a), other property or money, then—

(1) gain (if any) to such recipient shall be recognized, but not in excess of—

(A) the amount of money received, plus

(B) the fair market value of such other property received; and

(2) no loss to such recipient shall be recognized.

N/A (No boot received by Mr. Ink or Ms. Dixon.)

(c) Special Rule.—In determining control, for purposes of this section, the fact that any corporate transferor distributes part or all of the stock which it receives in the exchange to its shareholders shall not be taken into account.

N/A

C-1 (FES 12/20/93)

Red E. Ink (Personal Account)
Summary of Questions Investigated
December 1993

(d) Services, Certain Indebtedness, and Accrued Interest Not Treated as Property.—For purposes of this section, stock issued for—

(1) services,

(2) indebtedness of the transferee corporation which is not evidenced by a security, or

N/A

(3) interest on indebtedness of the transferee corporation which accrued on or after the beginning of the transferor's holding period for the debt,

shall not be considered as issued in return for property.

(e) Exceptions.—This section shall not apply to—

(1) Transfer of property to an investment company.—A transfer of property to an investment company.

(2) Title 11 or similar case.—A transfer of property of a debtor pursuant to a plan while the debtor is under the jurisdiction of a court in a title 11 or similar case (within the meaning of section 368(a)(3)(A)), to the extent that the stock or securities received in the exchange are used to satisfy the indebtedness of such debtor.

N/A

(f) Treatment of Controlled Corporation.—If—

(1) property is transferred to a corporation (hereinafter in this subsection referred to as the "controlled corporation") in an exchange with respect to which gain or loss is not recognized (in whole or in part) to the transferor under this section, and

(2) such exchange is not in pursuance of a plan of reorganization,

N/A

section 311 shall apply to any transfer in such exchange by the controlled corporation in the same manner as if such transfer were a distribution to which subpart A of part I applies.

(g) Cross References.—

(1) For special rule where another party to the exchange assumes a liability, or acquires property subject to a liability, see section 357.

See W.P. C-6 thru C-14.

C-2 (FES 12/20/93)

Red. E. Ink (Personal Account)
Working Papers
December 1993

W.P. Ref.

(2) For the basis of stock, securities, or property received in an exchange to which this section applies, see sections 358 and 362.

} *See W.P. C-15 thru C-18.*

(3) For special rule in the case of an exchange described in this section but which results in a gift, see section 2501 and following.

(4) For special rule in the case of an exchange described in this section but which has the effect of the payment of compensation by the corporation or by a transferor, see section 61(a)(1).

(5) For coordination of this section with section 304, see section 304(b)(3).

} *N/A*

(a) *Collateral Question: Are Ms. Dixon's copyrights considered "property" for section 351 purposes?*

Conclusion: The term "property" as used in section 351 is neither statutorily defined (the definition in section 317(a) is applicable only to part 1 of subchapter C and does not apply to section 351) nor interpreted by Treasury regulations. The problem here is determining whether Ms. Dixon has transferred intangible property or services to the corporation. In Rev. Rul. 64-56, 1964-1 C.B. 133, the service indicates that transfers of intangibles such as "know-how" will qualify as transfers of property under section 351 if they meet certain requirements:

(1) Is the item transferred inherently considered property?

(2) Does the property have legal protection?

(3) Were all substantial rights to the property transferred?

C-3 (FES 12/20/93)

Red. E. Ink (Personal Account)
Working Papers
December 1993

(4) If the transferor agrees to perform services in connection with the transfer, are the services merely ancillary and subsidiary to the transfer?

The transfer of the copyright by Ms. Dixon appears to meet all of these requirements:

(1) Rev. Rul. 53-234, 1953-2 C.B. 29, held that the sale of a manuscript would qualify as a casual sale of personalty eligible for installment sale reporting. In Rev. Rul. 68-194, 1968-1 C.B. 87, a taxpayer produced and copyrighted a manuscript. Later, he sold the manuscript to a publisher granting sole and exclusive rights to the manuscript. The ruling held that the transfer was a sale of the literary property. Furthermore, in Rev. Rul. 64-56, it states that, "Once it is established that 'property' has been transferred, the transfer will be tax-free under section 351 even though services were used to produce the property." This is the case unless the property transferred was specifically produced for the transferee. This is not the case with Ms. Dixon.

(2) & (3) In a telephone conversation with Ms. Dixon on Dec. 19, 1993, she indicated that the copyright had been properly filed giving exclusive U.S. protection to the property. Furthermore, she indicated that she had transferred all rights in the copyright to Ready, Inc.

(4) In the same telephone conversation with Ms. Dixon on Dec. 19, 1993, she indicated that, under the terms of the transfer, no further services were required with regard to the copyrighted manuscript.

C-4 (FES 12/20/93)

Red. E. Ink (Personal Account)
Working Papers
December 1993

(b) *Collateral Question: Do Mr. Ink and Ms. Dixon have any*
"control" requirement problems under section 351(a)?
Specifically, since Mr. Ink individually owns only 75%
Ready, Inc., common stock, is the section 351(a) control
requirement met?

Conclusion: There are no problems. The section 351(a)
control requirement is met.

In order for the general rule of section 351(a) to apply,
the shareholders involved in the transfers must be in
control of the corporation immediately after the exchange.
Section 351 "control" is statutorily governed by the
definition of "control" contained in section 368(c). The
requisite ownership percentage in section 368(c) is 80%.
This control requirement is met if, in the words of both
the statute and the regulations, "immediately after the
exchange such person or persons are in control" (emphasis
added).

In our case Mr. Ink and Ms. Dixon are the "persons,"
and they own 98% of the Ready, Inc., stock. "Control"
does not have to be maintained by a sole shareholder.
Treas. Reg. Sec. 1.351-1(a)(2) example (1) illustrates a
situation that contains an ownership structure almost
identical to our case, that is, two shareholders, one
owning 75% and one owning 25%. The example states that
no gain or loss is recognized by either shareholder.

C-5 (FES 12/20/93)

W.P. Ref. _____

TREAS. REGS. SEC. 1.351-1. TRANSFER TO
CORPORATION CONTROLLED BY TRANSFEROR.

(a)(1) Section 351(a) provides, in general, for the nonrecognition of gain or loss upon the transfer *by one or more persons* of property to a corporation solely in exchange for stock or securities in such corporation, *if immediately after the exchange, such person or persons are in control* of the corporation to which the property was transferred. As used in section 351, the phrase *"one or more persons"* includes individuals, trusts, estates, partnerships, associations, companies, or corporations (see section 7701(a)(1)). To be in control of the transferee corporation, *such person or persons* must own immediately after the transfer stock possessing at least 80 percent of the total combined voting power of all classes of stock entitled to vote and at least 80 percent of the total number of shares of all other classes of stock of such coporation (see section 368(c)). . . .

(2) The application of section 351(a) is illustrated by the following examples:

Example (1). C owns a patent right worth $25,000 and D owns a manufacturing plant worth $75,000. C and D organize the R Corporation with an authorized capital stock of $100,000. C transfers his patent right to the R Corporation for $25,000 of its stock and D transfers his plant to the new corporation for $75,000 of its stock. No gain or loss to C or D is recognized.

Identical to our case

c. *Collateral Question: Could Ready's assumption of liabilities cause partial taxability of the incorporation transaction in regard to Mr. Ink?*

Conclusion: The assumption by Ready, Inc. of Red Publishing's liabilities does not cause partial taxability to Mr. Ink. Section 357 deals with the assumption of liabilities in a section 351 transaction, and reads as follows:

C-6 (FES 12/20/93)

Red. E. Ink (Personal Account)
Working Papers
December 1993

SECTION 357. ASSUMPTION OF LIABILITY.

(a) General Rule.—Except as provided in subsections (b) and (c), if—

    (1) the taxpayer receives property which would be permitted to be received under section 351 or 361, without the recognition of gain if it were the sole consideration, and

    (2) as part of the consideration, another party to the exchange assumes a liability of the taxpayer, or acquires from the taxpayer property subject to a liability,

then such assumption or acquisition shall not be treated as money or other property, and shall not prevent the exchange from being within the provisions of section 351 or 361, as the case may be.

(b) Tax Avoidance Purpose.—

    (1) In general.—If, taking into consideration the nature of the liability and the circumstances in the light of which the arrangement for the assumption or acquisition was made, it appears that the principal purpose of the taxpayer with respect to the assumption or acquisition described in subsection (a)—

        (A) was a purpose to avoid Federal income tax on the exchange, or

        (B) if not such purpose, was not a bona fide business purpose

then such assumption or acquisition (in the total amount of the liability assumed or acquired pursuant to such exchange) shall, for purposes of section 351 or 361 (as the case may be), be considered as money received by the taxpayer on the exchange.

    (2) Burden of proof.—In any suit or proceeding where the burden is on the taxpayer to prove such assumption or acquisition is not to be treated as money received by the taxpayer, such burden shall not be considered as sustained unless the taxpayer sustains such burden by the clear preponderance of the evidence.

The rule

N/A

N/A

C-7 (FES 12/20/93)

W.P. Ref.

(c) Liabilities in Excess of Basis.—

(1) In general. In the case of an exchange—

(A) to which section 351 applies, or

(B) to which section 361 applies by reason of a plan of reorganization within the meaning of section 368(a)(1)(D)

☆

Exception to rule in section 357(a)

if the sum of the amount of the liabilities assumed, plus the amount of the liabilities to which the property is subject, exceeds the total of the adjusted basis of the property transferred pursuant to such exchange, then such excess shall be considered as a gain from the sale or exchange of a capital asset or of property which is not a capital asset, as the case may be.

(2) Exceptions. Paragraph (1) shall not apply to any exchange—

(A) to which subsection (b)(1) of this section applies,

N/A

(B) which is pursuant to a plan of reorganization within the meaning of section 368(a)(1)(G) where no former shareholder of the transferor corporation receives any consideration for his stock.

(3) Certain liabilities excluded.

(A) In general. If a taxpayer transfers, in an exchange to which section 351 applies, a liability the payment of which either—

(i) would give rise to a deduction, or

(ii) would be described in section 736(a),

See collateral question (d) regarding Ready's assumption of Ms. Dixon's typing bill of $800.

then, for purposes of paragraph (1), the amount of such liability shall be excluded in determining the amount of liabilities assumed or to which the property transferred is subject.

(B) Exception. Subparagraph (A) shall not apply to any liability to the extent that the incurrence of the liability resulted in the creation of, or an increase in, the basis of any property.

N/A

Red. E. Ink (Personal Account)
Working Papers
December 1993

Under section 357, the transfer of liabilities in a section
351 transaction will cause the recognition of gain only if
either (1) there is a tax-avoidance purpose (section
357(b)), or (2) the liabilities transferred exceed the basis
of all the assets transferred (section 357(c)). Section
357(b) is inapplicable here since, pursuant to the facts,
there is a valid purpose for the transaction and no tax
avoidance motive is present. According to Rev. Rul.
66-142, 1966-1 C.B. 66, section 357(c) is to be applied
separately to each transferor.

Per R. U. Partner's memo to file (12/17/93), p. 2, the
assets transferred to Ready, Inc., by Red E. Ink were as
follows:

Asset	FMV	Basis
Cash	$11,700	$11,700
(1) Supplies	10,000	-0-
(2) Trade receivables	50,000	-0-
(3) Equipment	75,000	58,300
Total basis of assets		$70,000

FOOTNOTES:
(1) In response to my telephone inquiry of today, Tom Books
confirmed that Mr. Ink has always expensed all supplies for tax
purposes when paid.
(2) Mr. Ink has always reported his taxable income on a cash basis.
(3) Value estimated; adjusted basis is tax basis.

Liabilities of Red Publishings assumed by Ready, Inc., were

Mortgage payable of Red Publishings	$65,000
Trade payables of Red Publishings	10,000
	$75,000

C-9 (FES 12/20/93)

Red. E. Ink (Personal Account)
Working Papers
December 1993

*In the incorporation transaction, Ready, Inc., assumed all
the liabilities of Red Publishings in the amount of
$75,000. However, pursuant to section 357(c)(3), the
trade payables of $10,000 may be excluded in applying
section 357(c) since the payment of these liabilities would
give rise to a deduction. Thus, for purposes of section
357(c) the total basis of the assets transferred is
$70,000 and the total liabilities transferred is $65,000.
Mr. Ink is not taxable on the transaction because of the
transfer of the liabilities.*

d.   *Collateral Question: Will Ms. Dixon recognize taxable
income as a result of Ready's assumption of her $800
typing bill?*

*Conclusion: No. Ms. Dixon will not recognize any taxable
income because of Ready, Inc.'s assumption of the $800
typing bill Here again, section 357(b) does not apply
since there is a valid business purpose for the transaction
and no tax avoidance motive is present. For purposes of
section 357(c), if the $800 expense must be capitalized
rather than being deductible, the basis of the copyright
transferred to Ready is $200 (rather than $1,000) and
the liability transferred ($800) is greater than the basis
of the copyright ($200). However, pursuant to section
357(c)(3), if the liability is deductible, it is not counted
for purposes of section 357(c), the liability transferred is
not greater than the basis of the asset transferred, and
Ms. Dixon does not recognize any taxable income. Pursuant
to section 263A(h), the $800 typing expense is not
required to be capitalized under section 263A as long as
it was incurred in Ms. Dixon's trade or business (other
than an employee) of being a writer. The pertinent parts
of section 263A are as follows:*

C-10 (FES 12/20/93)

Red. E. Ink (Personal Account)
Working Papers
December 1993

W.P. Ref. _____

SECTION 236A.   CAPITALIZATION AND INCLUSION IN INVENTORY COSTS OF CERTAIN EXPENSES.

(a) Nondeductibility of Certain Direct and Indirect Costs.—

(1) In general.—In the case of any property to which this section applies, any costs described in paragraph (2)—   } *The rule*

(A) in the case of property which is inventory in the hands of the taxpayer, shall be included in inventory costs, and

(B) in the case of any other property, shall be capitalized.

(2) Allocable costs.—The costs described in this paragraph with respect to any property are—

(A) the direct costs of such property, and

(B) such property's proper share of those indirect costs (including taxes) part or all of which are allocable to such property.

Any cost which (but for this subsection) could not be taken into account in computing taxable income for any taxable year shall not be treated as a cost described in this paragraph.

(b) Property to Which Section Applies.—Except as otherwise provided in this section, this section shall apply to—

(1) Property produced by taxpayer.—Real or tangible personal property produced by the taxpayer.

(2) Property acquired for resale.—

(A) In general.—Real or personal property described in section 1221(1) which is acquired by the taxpayer for resale.

(B) Exception for taxpayer with gross receipts of $10,000,000 or less.—Subparagraph (A) shall not apply to any personal property acquired during any tax-

C-11 (FES 12/20/93)

Red. E. Ink (Personal Account)
Working Papers
December 1993

able year by the taxpayer for resale if the average annual gross receipts of the taxpayer (or any predecessor) for the 3-taxable year period ending with the taxable year preceding such taxable year do not exceed $10,000,000.

(C) Aggregation rules, etc.—For purposes of subparagraph (B), rules similar to the rules of paragraphs (2) and (3) of section 448(c) shall apply.

For purposes of paragraph (1), the term "tangible personal property" shall include a film, sound recording, video tape, book, or similar property. . . .

(h) Exemption for Free-lance Authors, Photographers, and Artists.—

Exception to Gen. Rule, see W.P. C-10.

(1) In General.—Nothing in this section shall require the capitalization of any qualified creative expense.

(2) Qualified Creative Expense.—For purposes of the subsection, the term "qualified creative expense" means any expense—

(A) which is paid or incurred by an individual in the trade or business of such individual (other than as an employee) of being a writer, photographer, or artist, and

(B) which, without regard to this section, would be allowable as a deduction for the taxable year.

Such term does not include any expense related to printing, photographic plates, motion picture files, video tapes, or similar items.

(3) Definitions.—For purposes of this subsection—

(A) Writer.—The term "writer" means any individual if the personal efforts of such individual create (or may reasonably be expected to create) a literary manuscript, musical composition (including any accompanying words), or dance score.

(B) Photographer.—The term "photographer" means any individual if the personal efforts of such indi-

Red E. Ink (Personal Account)
Working Papers
December 1993

W.P. Ref. _____

vidual create (or may reasonably be expected to create) a photograph or photographic negative or transparency.

(C) Artist.—

(i) In general.—The term "artist" means any individual if the personal efforts of such individual create (or may reasonably be expected to create) a picture, painting, sculpture, statue, etching, drawing, cartoon, graphic design, or original print edition.

(ii) Criteria.—In determining whether any expense is paid or incurred in the trade or business of being an artist, the following criteria shall be taken into account:

(I) The originality and uniqueness of the item created (or to be created).

(II) The predominance of aesthetic value over utilitarian value of the item created (or to be created).

The deductibility of this $800 typing expense depends upon whether or not Ms. Dixon was in the business of being a writer. This is a question of fact, and I believe that the facts certainly justify treating Ms. Dixon as being in the business of writing. Pursuant to the memo dated December 17, 1993, Ms. Dixon had devoted many hours to writing these two full-length books. Even though Ms. Dixon was also a practicing attorney at the time she wrote the books, it is well established that an individual may be engaged in more than one business at the same time.
Furthermore, the Tax Court also ruled in Fernando Faura et al. v. Comm'r., *73 T.C. No. 68 (1980) that an author was engaged in a business and had the right to deduct nearly $5,000 in prepublication costs (rent, postage, telephone, transportation, etc.)*

C-13 (FES 12/20/93)

Red E. Ink (Personal Account)
Working Papers
December 1993

<u>W.P. Ref.</u>

The service could counter that the typing bill was a nondeductible capital expenditure or that it was a personal expenditure incurred in a transaction where profit had not been expected (that is, a hobby expenditure).

Revenue Ruling 68-194, 1968-1 C.B. 87, involved a taxpayer not engaged in a trade or business. It held that various expenses (including expenses for secretarial help, art work, supplies, and postage) incurred in producing and copyrighting a manuscript of a literary composition were directly attributable to the producing and copyrighting of the manuscript. Accordingly, the service said the expenses were not deductible for federal income tax purposes.

The service reaffirmed this position in Rev. Rul. 73-395, 1973-2 C.B. 87. The latter ruling also stated that the service would not follow the decision in <u>Stern</u> v. <u>U.S.</u>, 27 AFTR 2d 71-1148 (D. Cal. 1971).

The taxpayer in <u>Stern</u>, a Los Angeles resident, had spent considerable time in New York preparing a book. The necessary material for this book could be obtained only in New York. The taxpayer claimed his travel expenditures were deductible under section 162. The service claimed that the expenditures were nondeductible capital expenditures. The court, while holding in favor of the taxpayer, summarily stated, "Nor were they expenses for securing a copyright and plates which remain the property of the person making the payments," referring to Treas. Reg. Sec. 1.263(a)-2(b).

In summary, although the treatment would not be free from attack from the service, I feel Ms. Dixon should not recognize taxable income as a result of Ready's assumption of her typing liability. This result flows from the characterization of her typing bill as fitting within the exception to the exception contained in section 357(c)(3).

C-14 (FES 12/20/93)

Red E. Ink (Personal Account)
Working Papers
December 1993

2. *Is collection of the trade receivables transferred by Mr. Ink to Ready, Inc., to be considered the taxable income of Mr. Ink or of Ready, Inc.?*

    Conclusion: For many years, relying on the "assignment-of-income" doctrine, the courts held that an individual transferor, rather than the controlled corporate transferee, was taxable on the inchoate income items transferred in a section 351 transaction (Brown v. Comm'r., 115 F.2d 337 (CA-2, 1940), and Adolph Weinberg, 44 T.C. 233 (1965), aff'd per curiam 386 F.2d 836 (CA-9, 1967)).

    The Tax Court was finally persuaded, however, to allow a cash basis taxpayer to transfer accounts receivable tax free under Sec 351 (Thomas Briggs, T.C.M. 1956-86). Since Briggs at least two cases, Hempt Bros., Inc. v. U.S., 354 F.Supp. 1172 (D. PA. 1973), and Divine, Jr. v. U.S. 1962-2 USTC para. 85,592 (W.D. Tenn. 1962), have argued that the assignment-of-income doctrine is inapplicable in such situations. In addition, Rev. Rul. 80-198, 1989-2 C.B. 113, supports the Tax Court's decision. The ruling concludes that the transfer of accounts receivable to a controlled corporation qualifies as an exchange within the meaning of Sec. 351(a) and that the transferee corporation will report in its income the accounts receivable as collected. Under the circumstances of Ink's case, there seems to be good authority to argue that any receivables collected by Ready, Inc., should be treated as the taxable income of the corporation and not that of Mr. Ink individually.

3. *What is Mr. Ink's tax basis in the 730 shares of Ready, Inc., stock that he retained?*

    Conclusion: Section 358 determines the adjusted basis of stock and securities received in a section 351 transaction. It reads as follows:

Red E. Ink (Personal Account)
Working Papers
December 1993

SECTION 358. BASIS TO DISTRIBUTEES.

(a) General Rule.—In the case of an exchange to which section 351, 354, 355, 356, 361 applies—

(1) Nonrecognition property.—The basis of property permitted to be received under such section without the recognition of gain or loss shall be the same as that of the property exchanged—

} *Here, $7,000. See C-8.*

(A) decreased by—

(i) the fair market value of any other property (except money) received by the taxpayer,

} *None*

(ii) the amount of any money received by the taxpayer, and

} *$65,000. (See section 358(d).)*

(iii) the amount of loss to the taxpayer which was recognized on such exchange, and

} *N/A*

(B) increased by—

(i) the amount which was treated as a dividend, and

(ii) the amount of gain to the taxpayer which was recognized on such exchange (not including any portion of such gain which was treated as a dividend).

} *N/A*

(2) Other property.—The basis of any other property (except money) received by the taxpayer shall be its fair market value.

} *N/A*

(b) Allocation of Basis.—

(1) In general.—Under regulations prescribed by the Secretary, the basis determined under subsection (a)(1)(I) shall be allocated among the properties permitted to be received without the recognition of gain or loss.

} *N/A*

(2) Special rule for section 355.—In the case of an exchange to which section 355 (or so much of section 356 as relates to section 355) applies, then in making the allocation under paragraph (1) of this subsection, there shall be taken into account not only the property so permitted to be received without the recognition of gain or loss, but also the stock or securities (if any) of the distributing corporation which are retained, and the allocation of basis shall be made among all such properties.

} *N/A*

Red E. Ink (Personal Account)
Working Papers
December 1993

(c) Section 355 Transactions Which Are Not Exchanges.—For purposes of this section, a distribution to which section 355 (or so much of section 356 as relates to section 355) applies shall be treated as an exchange, and for such purposes the stock and securities of the distributing corporation which are retained shall be treated as surrendered, and received back, in the exchange.

N/A

(d) Assumption of Liability.—

(1) In general.—Where, as part of the consideration to the taxpayer, another party to the exchange assumed a liability of the taxpayer or acquired from the taxpayer property subject to a liability, such assumption or acquisition (in the amount of the liability) shall, for purposes of this section, be treated as money received by the taxpayer on the exchange.

For result, refer to section 358(a)(1) (A)(ii), above

(2) Exception.—Paragraph (1) shall not apply to the amount of any liability excluded under section 357(c)(3).

Thus, N/A to any lease obligation or trade payables

(e) Exception.—This section shall not apply to property acquired by a corporation by the exchange of its stock or securities (or the stock or securities of a corporation which is in control of the acquiring corporation) as consideration in whole or in part for the transfer of the property to it.

N/A

(f) Definition of Nonrecognition Property in Case of Section 361 Exchange.—For purposes of this section, the property permitted to be received under section 361 without the recognition of gain or loss shall be treated as consisting only of stock or securities in another corporation a party to the reorganization.

N/A

Red E. Ink (Personal Account)
Working Papers
December 1993

According to section 358(a), therefore, Mr. Ink's basis in the 750 shares he initially received would be $5,000 (that is, $70,000 basis transferred less $65,000 liabilities assumed by Ready, Inc.).

Because Mr. Ink gave ten shares to Mrs. Ink and ten shares to Mr. Books, the basis in his remaining 730 shares would be $4,867 (730/750 x $5,000). Each donee would have a basis of $67 in the ten shares received per section 1015.

Judith Dixon (Personal Account)
Summary of Questions Investigated
December 1993

W.P. Ref.

1. **Was the March 1, 1993, incorporation transaction between**
    Ready, Inc., and Judith Dixon, tax-free transfers under section
    351?

    Conclusion: Yes; all of the requirements of section 351 were   *See again C-1 and*
    satisfied.   *C-2.*

    a. *Collateral Question: Do Ms. Dixon's copyrights qualify as*
        "property" for purposes of section 351?

        Conclusion: Yes. Authority probably exists to treat Ms.   *See again C-2 thru*
        Dixon's copyrights as section 351 property.   *C-4.*

    b. *Collateral Question: Do Mr. Ink and Ms. Dixon "control"*
        Ready, Inc., for section 351 purposes?

        Conclusion: Yes. There are no control problems that would   *See again C-4 and*
        preclude the application of section 351.   *C-5.*

    c. *Collateral Question: Could Ready's assumption of*
        liabilities cause partial taxability of the incorporation
        transaction in regard to Mr. Ink?

        Conclusion: Although the issue is not totally free of   *See again C-6 thru*
        doubt, there is strong authority for characterizing Ms.   *C-9.*
        Dixon's incorporation as fully nontaxable.

    d. *Collateral Question: Will Ms. Dixon recognize taxable*
        income as a result of Ready Inc.'s assumption of the
        $800 typing bill?

        Conclusion: No. Ms. Dixon will not recognize any taxable   *See again C-9 thru*
        income because of Ready Inc.'s assumption of the $800   *C-14.*
        typing bill.

D-1 (FES 12/20/93)

Judith Dixon (Personal Account)
Summary of Questions Investigated
December 1993

2. *What is Ms. Dixon's tax basis in the 250 shares of Ready,*
Inc., common stock that she obtained in the incorporation
transaction?

Conclusion: In our opinion, Ms. Dixon's basis in her 250 shares   *See C-13 thru C-15*
is $200. Ms. Dixon's basis in this case is determined by   *for a copy of section*
section 358. According to section 358(a), Ms. Dixon's basis in   *358.*
her 250 shares would be $200 (that is, the basis of the
copyrights she transferred in exchange for the stock).

Ready, Inc. (Corporate Account)
Summary of Questions Investigated
December 1993

	W.P. Ref.

1. *Must Ready, Inc., report any taxable income in its first tax year because of its exchange of previously unissued stock for either the assets of Red Publishings or Ms. Dixon's copyrights?*

   Conclusion: No (section 1032).   F-1

2. *Can Ready, Inc., claim a tax deduction under section 162 for the $10,000 expended within sixty days following incorporation in payment of the trade payables it assumed from Red Publishings and the $800 expended in payment for the typing bill assumed from Ms. Dixon?*

   Conclusion: The officers of Ready, Inc., should be alerted to   F-1 and F-2
   the remote possibility that the IRS might challenge the propriety of the corporation's deducting these expenditures. We believe, however, that they are properly deductible.

3. *Are the $50,000 trade receivables transferred by Mr. Ink to Ready, Inc., and collected by the corporation after the incorporation, properly deemed to be the taxable income of the corporation?*

   Conclusion: The receivables collected should be the taxable   *See again C-14 and*
   income of Ready, Inc.   *C-15.*

4. *What is Ready's adjusted tax basis in the various assets it received on 3/1/93?*

   Conclusion: F-3

Cash	*$11,700*
Supplies	*-0-*
Receivables	*-0-*
Equipment	*58,300*
Copyrights	*200*

E-1 (FES 12/19/93)

Ready, Inc. (Corporate Account)
Working Papers
December 1993

1. *Must Ready, Inc., report any taxable income in its first tax*
year because of its exchange of previously unissued stock for
either the assets of Red Publishings or Ms. Dixon's copyrights?

Conclusion: No; see section 1032 below.

SECTION 1032. EXCHANGE OF STOCK FOR PROPERTY.

(a) Nonrecognition of Gain or Loss.—No gain or loss shall be
recognized to a corporation on the receipt of money or other
property in exchange for stock (including treasury stock) of
such corporation. No gain or loss shall be recognized by a
corporation with respect to any lapse or acquisition of an
option to buy or sell its stock (including treasury stock).

(b) Basis.—For basis or property acquired by a corporation in
certain exchanges for its stock, see section 362.

The rule

2. *Can Ready, Inc., claim a tax deduction under section 162 for*
the $10,000 it expended within sixty days following
incorporation in payment of the trade accounts it assumed from
Red Publishings and the $800 expended in payment for the
typing bill assumed from Ms. Dixon?

For facts, see W.P.
A-1 thru A-3.

Conclusion: Early court decisions have denied a deduction for
ordinary (section 162) expenses incurred by the transferor but
paid by the corporate transferee following a section 351
incorporation. As recently as 1972 the Tax Court declared:

It is well settled that an expenditure of a preceding owner of
property which has accrued but which is paid by one acquiring that property is a part of the cost of acquiring that property, irrespective of what would be the tax character of the
expenditure to the prior owner. Such payment becomes part
of the basis of the property acquired and may not be deducted
when paid by the acquirer of that property.

[*M. Buten and Sons, Inc.*, T.C.M. 1972-44]

F-1 (FES 12/19/93)

Ready, Inc. (Corporate Account)
Working Papers
December 1993

Thus, the Tax Court in Buten indicates that a definite uniformity of application exists in this area. Despite the cases supporting that conclusion, however, it may be significant that in Peter Raich, 46 T.C. 604 (1966), the parties stipulated that the accounts payable were deductible by the transferee corporation. Furthermore, in Bongiovanni, 470 F.2d 921 (CA-2, 1972), the second circuit court in 1972 noted that "where the acquiring corporation is on an accrual basis, such accounts are also deductible in its initial period." (Note: Ready, Inc., will be an accrual basis taxpayer.) Also, in U.S. v. Smith, 418 F.2d 589 (CA-5, 1969), the court noted, "If this factual inquiry reveals a primary purpose other than acquisition of property, the court may properly allow a deduction to the corporation if all the requirements of Title 26 USC, section 162, are met...." Finally, in Rev. Ruls. 80-198, 1980-2 C.B. 113 and 80-199, 1980-2 C.B. 122, the service has indicated that payment of the liabilities by the transferee is deductible if there was a valid business purpose for the transfer and the transferor did not defer collection of the accounts receivable or prepay the accounts payable.

In Ink's incorporation it appears that the liabilities of Red Publishings were assumed by Ready, Inc., solely for business convenience reasons and not for the acquisition of property and that there has been no accumulation of the accounts payables. I feel that Ready, Inc. should be able to deduct the payment. However, the officers of Ready, Inc., should be alerted to a possibility of an IRS challenge. See Magruder v. Supplee, 316 U.S. 394 (1942); Holdcraft Transportation Co., 153 F.2d 323 (CA-8, 1946); Haden Co. v. Comm'r., 165 F.2d 588 (CA-5, 1948); and Athol Mfg. Co., 54 F.2d 230 (CA-1, 1931).

3. *Are the $50,000 trade receivables transferred by Mr. Ink to Ready, Inc., and collected by the corporation after the incorporation properly deemed to be the taxable income of the corporation?*

F-2 (FES 12/19/93)

Ready, Inc. (Corporate Account)
Working Papers
December 1993

Conclusion: Yes. The collection of the receivables should be the taxable income of Ready, Inc.

See again C-14 and C-15.

4. *What is Ready's adjusted tax basis in the various assets it received on 3/1/93?*

Conclusion: The basis of the assets received by a corporate transferee in a section 351 transaction are determined by section 362(a), which reads as follows:

SECTION 362. BASIS TO CORPORATIONS.

(a) Property Acquired by Issuance of Stock or as Paid-In Surplus.—If property was acquired on or after June 22, 1954, by a corporation—

(1) in connection with a transaction to which section 351 (relating to transfer of property to corporation controlled by transferor) applies, or

(2) as paid-in surplus or as a contribution to capital,

then the basis shall be the same as it would be in the hands of the transferor, increased in the amount of gain recognized to the transferor on such transfer.

The rule

Accordingly, Ready's adjusted tax basis of assets received is as follows:

See W.P. A-1 thru A-3.

Supplies	*-0-*
Receivables	*-0-*
Equipment	*$58,300*
Copyrights	*200*

Red E. Ink, Ms. Dixon, Ready, Inc.
Suggestions for Client's Future Consideration
December 1993

If Mr. Ink or Ms. Dixon desire any assistance in future tax planning we should discuss with either of them, in the near future, the following matters:

1. *"S" election*
    a. *The circumstances under which this would be desirable or undesirable.*
    b. *When the decision must be made.*
    c. *Need for every shareholder's approval.*
    d. *Need for buy-out agreements.*

2. *Executive compensation possibilities.*
    a. *Group-term life insurance (section 79(a)).*
    b. *Health and accident insurance (section 106).*
    c. *Death benefits (section 101).*
    d. *Travel and entertainment (requirements and advantages).*

3. *Pension plans (costs and benefits).*

4. *Future contributions to capital.*
    a. *Consider advantages of securities.*
    b. *Section 1244.*

8

It is too well settled to need citation of authorities that it is no offense nor is it reprehensible to avoid the attachment of taxes. One may employ all lawful means to minimize taxes.

JUDGE WALTER A. HUXMAN

Research Methodology for Tax Planning

This chapter examines the research methodology appropriate to tax planning. It considers (1) the general role of tax planning in the CPA firm and (2) the technical differences between research methodologies for tax planning and tax compliance.

A survey by an AICPA committee contained several observations about the role of tax practice in the CPA firm.[1] First, the survey clearly established the fact that tax practice represents an important source of revenue for the CPA. (Tax work accounts for between 21 and 40 percent of the total billings in nearly 46 percent of the responding firms.) Second, although the preparing of returns accounted for the largest portion of the tax work revenues, consulting and planning ranked second—ahead of representing clients before government bodies. Third, the larger practice units

---

[1] Jerome P. Solari and Don J. Summa, "Profile of the CPA in Tax Practice," *The Tax Adviser* (June 1972): 324–28.

tended to generate a larger proportion of their total tax work revenues from consulting and planning than did the smaller practice units. Fourth, most of the respondents anticipated that consulting and planning would account for a greater proportion of future tax work fees.

Although the AICPA has not yet replicated its study, other studies confirm the projections of the AICPA.[2] All of this suggests, of course, that the CPA who limits his or her tax practice to compliance work is not taking full advantage of available opportunities. CPAs who want to expand their practices will likely discover that tax-planning work is a latent source of major growth. The continuing relationship that CPAs have with their clients ordinarily provides them with a sufficient knowledge of facts to make tax-planning proposals with minimal additional input from the client.

As we noted in chapter 2, a final tax liability depends on three variables: the facts, the law, and an administrative process. A change in any one of these variables is likely to change a client's tax liability. To devise a tax plan that relies for its success on an amendment to the Internal Revenue Code is usually unrealistic. Very few taxpayers wield that much influence, and, even if they did, the response of Congress in tax matters typically is unpredictable and slow. Attempts to change the administrative process would be equally ineffective for similar reasons. Good tax planning always gives adequate consideration to the administrative process, but it does not rely on changes in that process for its success. Thus, tax plans generally must be based on the existing law and administrative processes because only the facts are readily modified. The ultimate significance of those facts stems, of course, from options already in the code.

Tax-Planning Considerations

The fundamental problem encountered in tax planning might be compared to those inherent in, say, a decision to transport an

---

[2] Texas Society of CPAs, "How Does Your Firm Compare," *The Practical Accountant* (April 1984): 43–45; *Public Accounting Report*, Vol. X, No. 6 (March 15, 1987): and *Public Accounting Report*, Vol. X, No. 24 (December 15, 1987).

object from New York City to Atlanta. Momentarily ignoring operational constraints, there are many ways to achieve the objective. That is, the object could be shipped by a commercial carrier (with air, rail, ship, or surface carrier possibilities); it might be personally delivered, or a friend might deliver it. However, only a few transportation methods are realistic because of various operational constraints, such as time (the object must be delivered before 9 A.M. on Monday morning), cost (the object must be shipped in the most inexpensive manner possible), or bulk (the size of the object may exclude all but a few possibilities). The transportation decision can be managed successfully only if the decision maker (1) knows which options actually exist and (2) understands the constraints. A tax problem has very similar boundaries.

Statutory Options

The Internal Revenue Code already contains many options from which a taxpayer must select alternative courses of action. For example, a taxpayer generally can choose to operate a business as a sole proprietorship, as an S corporation, or as a regular corporation. By exercising any option, a taxpayer automatically causes several different portions of the code to apply to the business operations, any one of which may create a drastically different tax result. In addition to selecting a basic business form, a taxpayer may also have an opportunity to select a tax year, choose certain accounting methods, determine whether the entity selected should be a "foreign" or "domestic" one, choose between a "taxable" and a "nontaxable" incorporation transaction, or decide whether or not to capitalize certain expenditures. Selecting the most advantageous combination of statutory tax options is obviously a difficult task: the decision maker's knowledge of the very existence of those options is critical.

Client Constraints

In addition to understanding all of the options implicit in the Internal Revenue Code, a tax planner must also understand the objectives and constraints inherent in the client's activities. Typically, those are a combination of personal, financial, legal, and social considerations. For example, such personal objectives as a desire to increase wealth, to control the distribution of property after death, to drive a competitor out of business, or to retire with minimal financial concerns may dictate certain actions. Personal objectives are often constrained by financial and legal obstacles. A tax planner can understand a client's objectives only if the client is willing to confide in the adviser; therefore, it is absolutely essential that mutual trust and openness exist between the client and the tax adviser before a tax-planning engagement is undertaken.

Because tax plans often necessarily involve very significant financial and legal implications, generally more tax planning is better achieved through a team effort than through individual work. For example, in an estate-planning engagement, it is not unusual to include the taxpayer's attorney, the insurance agent, and a trust officer, as well as the CPA on the tax-planning team. By combining the special expertise of several individuals, the client is better served. More importantly, the team approach generally protects the client from the danger of "secondary infection," that is, from the danger of putting into operation a plan that may succeed from a tax standpoint but that may have undesirable legal or financial consequences.

Creativity

Even if a tax adviser knows all the pertinent code provisions and fully understands all the client's objectives and constraints, the best tax plan may not be obvious. The best plan depends on the creative resources of the planner. Using all of his or her knowledge, the tax adviser must test tentative solutions in a methodical process that rejects some alternatives and suggests others. Without a systematic method of considering and rejecting the many alternatives, the tax planner is likely to overlook the very alternative being sought. As suggested earlier in this study, one common reason for overlooking a good alternative is simply the tax adviser's failure to think long or hard enough about the problem. There is the tendency to rush to the books or to another person for help, hoping that the best solution will automatically surface, when what is really needed is more creative thought on the subject. The authors' recommendation is not that books and consultants be avoided, but rather that the ideas obtained from these sources be given an opportunity to mature in quiet contemplation.

Tax-Planning Aids

Books

Tax library materials can help generate successful tax-planning ideas. Most of the commercial tax services include, in some form or another, tax-planning ideas intended to assist the CPA in his or her practice.[3] For example, the *Standard Federal Tax Reporter*, published by Commerce Clearing House (CCH), contains a tax-planning section, organized on a topical basis, in its index volume. The editorial comments found there are sufficiently detailed for addressing the easier tax-planning problems; they are cross-referenced to other CCH paragraphs that aid in the solution of the more difficult problems. In addition, Research Institute of America provides similar materials in its *Federal Tax Coordinator*, 2d. Volume 3 of this service has a section entitled "Tax Savings Opportunities Checklist," which provides both guidance for basic transactions and cross references to the other volumes of the service for more detailed transactions.

Warren Gorham & Lamont publishes a separate, two-volume *Tax Ideas* service. This service provides insights into tax planning that can be accomplished in a variety of areas, such as individual and family, retirement, forms of business, transfers and disposition of assets, and investments. Matthew Bender provides a six-volume service, *Modern Estate Planning*, which is devoted entirely to myriad issues that face professionals who work in the estate planning area. Although the *Tax Management Portfolios*, published by the Bureau of National Affairs, do not contain tax-planning volumes per se, the portfolios include tax-planning recommendations throughout the commentary of the tax issue to which they relate.

---

[3] For additional details concerning the publishers of the several commercial tax services, see exhibit 4.12, pages 122 through 124.

The AICPA publishes *Tax Practice Guides and Checklists* which provides extensive review checklists that are useful in dealing with the different tax entities, for example, individuals, regular corporations, S corporations, partnerships, estates, and trusts. Many other books, with varying degrees of sophistication, have been written on tax planning; it simply is not practical to mention each of them individually. Suffice it to note that readers should not be misled by all of the titles that include the phrase *tax planning*. Many of these publications are intended for specific taxpayers and their unique tax problems, for example, tax planning for professionals, for real estate transactions, for closely held corporations, or for international operations. Topics covered in one publication are often duplicated in another. Before deciding to purchase such a book, a practitioner would be well advised to examine it in detail to make certain that it actually adds something to the material already available in his or her library. Although many of these publications can be useful in tax-planning work, there is no good substitute for the ability that comes only from years of experience.

Continuing Education

The extension of formal classroom instruction beyond the college campus is partially due to the accounting profession, which requires continuing education. For tax practitioners, however, tax institutes provided continuing professional instruction long before it became mandatory in any state.

Today, continuing education programs are a second major source of assistance in successful tax planning. Well-developed courses are readily available from national, state, and local professional societies, universities and colleges, and private organizations. The American Institute of Certified Public Accountants annually publishes a catalog describing most of the continuing education programs offered by the CPE Division of the AICPA. The annual catalog includes descriptions of different courses in taxation. These courses generally last one to two days and are most often scheduled during the summer and fall, throughout the United States.

Information about other tax courses can frequently be found in tax periodicals. Some courses are designed for the beginner; others for an advanced audience. Some cover specific subjects; others are of general interest. Some are well-developed and taught by highly qualified instructors; others have been hastily prepared and are poorly presented. Obviously, the caveat "let the buyer beware" is applicable in the selection of any course.

Tree Diagrams

In tax-planning work, the alternatives that an adviser must consider multiply quickly. After clearly identifying a general course of action (based on an understanding of the client's objective and knowledge of the code), and before reaching a conclusion, an adviser might consider structuring the possible solutions to the problem in the form of a "tree diagram." Such a method ensures a thorough and systematic consideration of each alternative, because it focuses on the critical questions in sequence. The branches of the tree represent different options existing in the tax law, any one of which can achieve the client's objective. After ordering the options in this fashion, the adviser should quantify the tax result implicit in each alternative. This quantification will facilitate discovery of many of the risks and constraints that, in turn, eliminate some alternatives and favor others. For an example of a tree diagram, see figure 8.1 (page 226).

As noted above, a tree diagram cannot be prepared for a tax problem until a tax adviser fully understands the client's objectives and determines the tax rules applicable to each available method of achieving those objectives. Knowledge of the client's objectives can come only from a complete and open discussion of the transaction with the client. In tax planning, objectives and constraints are determined in the same way in which facts are established in compliance engagements. Determining the possible alternatives stems from a unique blend of prior experience, reading, and thinking about the problem. Ascertaining the tax outcome for each alternative is based on the same research techniques described in the earlier chapters of this study. In summary, the major differences between the tax research methods applicable to compliance work and to planning work are in the adviser's ability to identify possible alternatives and in the method for selecting the best of the several alternatives considered. In an attempt to focus on these aspects of tax planning, the following pages illustrate the process involved in a relatively simple planning engagement. We will not

Figure 8.1
Tree Diagram

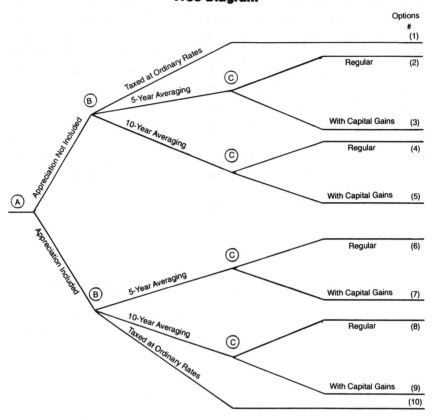

	Options #
	(1)
Regular	(2)
With Capital Gains	(3)
Regular	(4)
With Capital Gains	(5)
Regular	(6)
With Capital Gains	(7)
Regular	(8)
With Capital Gains	(9)
	(10)

examine in detail the procedures by which the tax adviser determines the tax result implicit in each option, since they are the same as those followed in a "closed-fact" situation (see chapter 7).

A Tax-Planning Example

To illustrate the procedures that might be used in a tax-planning engagement, assume that Joe Retiree comes to you for advice. Joe is retiring this year (19X2) and has to make a decision concerning the potential distribution of his retirement savings from a qualified pension plan. Joe's employer instructs him that he can do any of the following: (1) receive the benefits as an annuity over his life or the combined lifespan of both him and his wife, (2) receive the benefits as a lump-sum distribution and roll over the proceeds into an Individual Retirement Account (IRA), (3) leave the funds with the employer and allow his retirement savings to continue to grow tax-free until Joe wants to take a distribution or until he reaches seventy-and-one-half years of age, or (4) receive the benefits as a lump-sum distribution and pay the tax currently.

Joe feels that through social security and other resources he will have adequate funds to live comfortably during his retirement years. However, he is interested in purchasing a retirement home in Scottsdale, Arizona. Joe and his wife reside in Wyoming and would prefer to spend the cold winter months in Scottsdale.

To purchase a home in Scottsdale, Joe needs a considerable amount of cash. Joe is not interested in creating any liabilities in his old age and would like to purchase the Scottsdale home for cash. Consequently, Joe has ruled out options (1) through (3) because they do not generate enough immediate cash. Since Joe's distribution will consist of stock of his corporate employer, Joe has decided to take the lump-sum distribution and immediately thereafter sell the stock. Joe consults with you to help plan how to maximize the amount of cash that will be available after the receipt of the 19X2 lump-sum distribution and subsequent sale of the stock.

In your interview, you obtain the following information:

1. Joe is married and will be filing a joint federal income tax return for 19X2 and 19X3. Joe is sixty-four years of age in 19X2.

2. Joe's lump-sum distribution will consist of stock of his employer. The stock is readily marketable and has a fair market value of $100,000 and an adjusted basis to the pension plan of $30,000.

3. Joe has not made any contributions to the pension plan.

4. Sixty percent of the distribution is attributable to Joe's pre-1974 participation in the plan.

5. For 19X2, Joe has a salary of $53,000, a capital loss carryover from 19X1 of $13,000, a standard deduction of $7,400, and is entitled to two personal exemptions.

6. Based on the information provided by Joe, and ignoring the tax consequences of the lump-sum distribution, his 19X3 taxable income will be zero (i.e., his gross income will equal his itemized deductions and personal exemptions).

Joe may elect to include the entire $100,000 in gross income in 19X2. If so, Joe will have a $100,000 basis in the stock. If Joe does not make the election, only $30,000 will be includable in 19X2 gross income and Joe will have a $30,000 basis in the stock.

In addition to the foregoing facts, four assumptions are made for purposes of this illustration. First, to obtain the necessary cash that Joe needs, the stock will be sold on January 3, 19X3. Thus, if any income is generated by the sale of the stock, it will be recognized in 19X3. Second, several of the elections generate long-term capital gains. In some of the available options, these capital gains will be offset by capital loss carryovers. Third, the income tax rates for 199X will be used to calculate the tax liabilities for 19X2 and 19X3. Fourth, since the more relevant method of tax analysis involves comparing current cash flows, the net present value of the tax costs of each option will be computed. This requires that any tax consequences in 19X3 that affect cash flows be discounted back to 19X2. The discount rate used for these computations is 10 percent.

In a more practical setting, a tax professional would probably consider a much broader range of possibilities. For example, some additional questions to consider are: (1) What is the amount of the annuity, and what would Joe's projected tax bracket be in future years? (2) If Joe's wife outlives him, is an annuity necessary in order to provide sufficient support for his wife upon Joe's death? (3) If the funds are left with the pension plan, does a significant difference exist between the earnings from the pension plan and what Joe feels he can earn if the funds were self-invested? However, to limit the size of this illustration, it is assumed that the only viable option is a lump-sum distribution. As will be illustrated, limiting the planning possibilities to a lump-sum distribution provides enough planning options to sufficiently demonstrate the tax-planning function (see figure 8.1, page 226).

Tax Consequences of Different Options

The primary purpose of this illustration is to show the character-istics of a planning engagement and the usefulness of a tree diagram, rather than to present a detailed treatise on lump-sum distributions. A crucial element of any tax-planning engagement is to determine from the facts the possible options available to the client. As mentioned previously, if there are numerous options, a tree diagram may prove helpful in organizing the tax-planning process.

For purposes of this illustration, figure 8.1 (on page 226) summarizes the different options available to Joe. These options are numbered one through ten for easy reference. Without detail-ing the procedures used to determine the tax results implicit in each of the ten options, figure 8.2 (on page 233) provides the total tax costs inherent in each option.

The subsequent discussion focuses on each of the basic deci-sions that Joe must make to arrive at the ultimate option selected. For easy reference, each "decision point" is identified in figure 8.1 by the capital letters A, B, and C. Therefore, even though ten possible options exist, these options can effectively be discussed by analyzing each of the three decision points.

Unrealized Appreciation in the Employer's Stock (Decision A). As the tree diagram in figure 8.1 illustrates, the first option available to Joe is whether to include the stock appreciation as part of the lump-sum distribution. The stock Joe received as part of a lump-sum distribu-tion must either be included as part of his regular taxable income or is taxed under the applicable lump-sum distribution rules. Howev-er, absent an election by Joe, any net unrealized appreciation in the employer's stock is excluded from the Joe's gross income.

If Joe elects to include any net unrealized appreciation as part of the lump-sum distribution, the obvious question is why he would choose to recognize income currently when the option to defer exists? Some of the possible reasons are: (1) significant net operat-ing or capital losses may be available in the current year, (2) tax rates may be legislatively scheduled to increase, or (3) for various reasons the taxpayer's marginal tax rates may be higher in the future. In our example, it is assumed that a capital loss carryover of $13,000 exists. Therefore, a decision by Joe to include the unrealized appreciation in his 19X2 income may allow him to utilize more of the $13,000 capital-loss carryover.

In contrast, the most significant reason for not accelerating the net unrealized appreciation into 19X2 is the opportunity to defer the income recognition into the future. Due to the time value of money, the longer the recognition of the unrealized appreciation can be postponed, the smaller the total tax effect. However, since in our example Joe is planning to sell the stock in 19X3, the potential deferral of the recognition of the net unrealized appreciation is for only one year. Thus, the deferral option will not be a major factor.

The decision to include the appreciated stock in Joe's 19X2 income cannot be effectively evaluated without considering each of the remaining options. Regardless of whether or not Joe decides to include the appreciation in the stock as part of the lump-sum distribution, he must next choose between the following three alternatives (see point B in figure 8.1 on page 226): (1) tax the entire lump-sum distribution at ordinary rates, (2) elect the 5-year averaging provision, or (3) elect the 10-year averaging provision.

Tax Entire Lump-Sum Distribution at Ordinary Rates. The first option (at point B in figure 8.1), and probably the least desirable, is to simply tax the entire lump-sum distribution in 19X2 at ordinary income rates. This option results in the highest overall tax cost (see the total tax costs of options 1 and 10 in figure 8.2). However, this option cannot be ignored. If Joe fails to do any tax planning, by default, this is the option that would apply even though better alternatives may exist.

Five-Year Averaging Provision. The second alternative available (at point B in figure 8.1) is the 5-year averaging provision. To alleviate the harsh results of taxing the entire distribution in one year, section 402(e) allows a 5-year averaging election. If the regular 5-year averaging convention is elected, the entire amount of the lump-sum distribution is excluded from the normal taxable income computation. Instead, a separate tax is determined on the lump-sum distribution that is independent of the taxpayer's regular tax liability. This separate tax on the lump-sum distribution is computed using a two-step process. First, one-fifth of the taxable amount of the distribution is multiplied by the 19X2 tax rates for a single taxpayer. Second, this amount is then multiplied by five, resulting in the separate tax due on the lump-sum distribution. The separate tax on the lump-sum distribution is then added to the taxpayer's regular tax to determine the taxpayer's total 19X2 federal income tax liability.

Ten-Year Averaging Provision. Due to special transition rules contained in the TRA '86, the 10-year averaging provision that existed for pre-1987 lump-sum distributions is also available to Joe [Act Sec. 1122(h)(3)]. The computation for the 10-year averaging provision is basically the same as the computation for the 5-year averaging provision, except that in calculating the separate tax, a "10" is substituted for the "5." It would seem reasonable that when a choice is available, the taxpayer should always choose to average a lump-sum distribution over 10 years rather than 5 years. However, the possible flaw in this conclusion is that for the 10-year averaging provision, the separate tax is figured using 1986 rather than 19X2 single taxpayer rates. As a result of the TRA '86, the maximum individual tax rates were reduced from 50 percent for 1986 to 31 percent for 19X2. Therefore, only after actually calculating the tax under both the 5-year and 10-year averaging conventions can the most advantageous alternative be determined.

Another option also is available to Joe (see point C in figure 8.1): The portion of the lump-sum distribution attributable to pre-1974 years can be treated as long-term capital gains.

Capital Gains Treatment. If a portion of the distribution is attributable to contributions made in pre-1974 years, that portion of the distribution can be treated as a long-term capital gain and is taxed at a flat 20 percent. In our example, we assume that 60 percent of the distribution is attributable to pre-1974 contributions and is, therefore, eligible for the 20 percent rate. The long-term capital gain cannot be used to offset capital losses from other sources and is not eligible for either of the averaging provisions. The remaining 40 percent of the distribution, representing ordinary income, is taxed under either the 5-year or 10-year averaging rules. This option is especially attractive when the marginal tax rate applicable to the regular averaging provisions for the lump-sum distribution exceeds 20 percent.

Each of the options available to Joe are summarized in figure 8.1. Once the alternatives have been formulated, all that remains for the tax adviser is to compute the total tax costs of each option. When the least cost alternative is identified, other tax consequences, such as, which options result in greater capital loss carryovers, may need to be considered. Finally, there may be nontax considerations that are also an integral part of determining the overall best alternative.

Summary

If the decision is based solely on which option provides the greatest amount of after-tax cash, option 8 is clearly the best choice (see figure 8.2 on page 233 for a summary of the tax costs for each of the 10 options). Option 8 involves the regular 10-year averaging convention coupled with an election to include the built-in appreciation of the stock in Joe's 19X2 gross income. In our illustration, averaging the lump-sum distribution over ten years results in a lower tax than the capital gain election. In fact, the effective tax rate on the lump-sum distribution for option 8 is 14.47 percent. Option 8 not only provides the lowest overall tax cost, but it is also one of the options that retains the added tax benefit of a $10,000 capital loss carryover available for future years.

Once the options are understood and the corresponding tax results have been computed, the decision becomes fairly simple. However, without the detailed analysis provided in this illustration, it would be impossible to systematically determine the best tax result. Likewise, other tax-planning issues require a similar type of approach to effectively evaluate each of the possible alternatives.

The tax adviser needs to be aware that other issues may not provide such a clear-cut result as the issue in this example. Often,

Figure 8.2
Tree Diagram

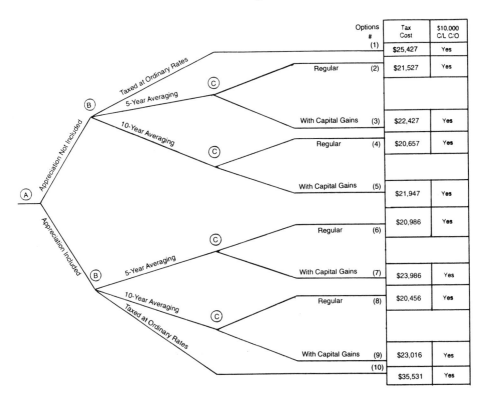

the various options and courses of action have questionable outcomes and a certain element of risk. The client may opt for a solution that does not provide the lowest tax liability, but that does provide him or her an acceptable level of risk.

Once all of the reasonable alternatives have been researched and their tax results determined, a tax adviser should recommend a course of action to the client. In some circumstances, the client may elect to ignore tax results and base a decision on other completely unrelated considerations. In the final analysis, only the client can determine which alternative is best. However, when the qualified tax adviser gives the client all the information needed to make an intelligent decision, in most instances, the client will accept the adviser's recommendation.

The foregoing example demonstrates a systematic approach to the research of alternative courses of action available to a taxpayer. This tax-planning process represents a serial rearrangement of facts over which a client can still exercise control. Such a systematic creation and evaluation of alternative strategies is the key to profitable tax planning.

Tax-Planning Communications

Practitioners should recognize distinct differences between communicating research conclusions in a tax-compliance problem and making recommendations in a tax-planning engagement. In tax compliance work, the facts and the law pertinent to the solution are generally fixed. Therefore, once the appropriate statute and all related authorities have been identified and evaluated, the researcher generally can offer a conclusion to the client with reasonable certainty that it is "correct."

Reaching an optimal conclusion in a tax-planning engagement is much less certain. The "facts" are merely preliminary proposals based on many estimates and assumptions. Furthermore, the enactment of a proposed plan is not fixed in time. It may occur the following week, the following month, or two years hence. Consequently, at the time the plan is finally executed, even the tax statutes upon which it is based may have changed, and the tax alternative originally recommended may no longer be the preferred one. Because of these uncertainties, the tax adviser should prepare for the client a written memorandum containing a statement of the assumptions and the recommended plan of action, qualified as follows:

1. A statement should be included emphasizing the fact that, unless the plan is actually implemented as originally assumed, the tax results may be substantially altered.

2. It should be stressed that the recommendations are based on current tax authority and that possible delays in implementation may change the result because of changes in the law during the interim period.

The foregoing recommendations concur with the opinion expressed in the AICPA Statement of Responsibilities in Tax Practice No. 8, as quoted in chapter 6, herein. Tax advisers should seriously consider the adoption of such standard disclaimer statements in their tax-planning engagements.

9

...in the library—a big 10-story library, with books floor to ceiling. There's a young associate in there and an older attorney is saying, "The answer is somewhere in this room. You find it." You don't have to do that anymore. Now the answer is somewhere on that screen, in that terminal.

PETER ELINSKY

Computer-Assisted Tax Research

One of the greatest challenges for any tax adviser is keeping abreast of the ever-changing body of tax law. In the past decade, Congress has revised the Internal Revenue Code at an unprecedented rate. In addition, court decisions, treasury regulations, revenue rulings, revenue procedures, and private letter rulings are proliferating at a staggering rate. How does the tax professional tap all of these sources of tax law in conducting tax research?

In previous chapters, we have discussed basic research methods and how these methods are applied to conventional research services (hard-copy services such as CCH's *Standard Federal Tax Reporter*, RIA's *Federal Tax Coordinator 2d*). This chapter explores the use of the computer in researching the diverse sources of the tax law by looking specifically at "computer-assisted tax research" (CATR).

For many tax professionals, the use of computer technology is an integral part of tax research. The development of sophisticated on-line systems has for some time been an option for the larger

CPA firms. Nevertheless, with the development of the compact-disk read-only memory (CD-ROM) technology, the availability of a CATR system has become affordable for even the smallest of CPA firms.

A detailed discussion of CATR and each of the current services available to perform this type of research is beyond the scope of this book. What we hope to provide is an introduction to the concepts used in performing CATR, a discussion of possible benefits of CATR, and a brief introduction to several of the major CATR services. Our discussion of the different CATR systems will begin with direct on-line CATR systems and will be limited to the services of LEXIS, ACCESS, and WESTLAW. Next, we will focus on several of the available CD-ROM CATR systems.

In our discussion of CATR, one important clarification should be made. As implied by the term *computer-assisted tax research*, the computer is a supplement to the researcher rather than his or her replacement. When used correctly, CATR offers the researcher a valuable tool. Conversely, when used incorrectly, CATR can result in a loss of both time and money.

Characteristics of a CATR System

A CATR system generally is described as a large database. A database is an organized set of data files that can be accessed in a number of ways. A database creates its own index whereby it can locate any file entered into the system.

In a CATR system, the files of the database are nothing more than full-text copies of judicial cases or documents in the tax environment. These files are then grouped together in libraries within the database. In using the database, the user must (1) determine which library is likely to contain the material he or she is searching and (2) enter the appropriate search request. The search request includes any words or phrases that the user expects to find in the relevant documents. Based on the words or phrases that the researcher supplies the computer, the system searches all files in the selected library for those particular words. Any document that includes the specific terms in the correct grammatical relationship is accessed by the computer and placed in its memory. After all user-specified constraints (to be discussed later) have been applied to the documents, the computer informs the user of the number of documents that satisfy the research query. The user can then have these documents either displayed on the computer screen or sent to a printer.

The specific features of a CATR system were defined in the late 1960s by a task force formed by the Ohio State Bar Association. The task force was formed to study the possibility of computer-assisted legal research (CALR), which was defined as "...a nonindexed, full-text, on-line, interactive, computer-assisted legal research service."[1]

Nonindexed

The conventional tax services that have previously been discussed rely heavily on a topical index created by the editor of the service. The researcher who uses conventional research methods is required to guess which subject file the editor of the service used in indexing the document. Clearly, a conventional tax service relies heavily on the human judgment used when referencing the document into the tax service. An example of these differences in indexing is found in chapter 4, herein.

One advantage of a CATR system is that the tax researcher creates his or her own index. Documents in the CATR system are accessed by a literal word search conducted by the computer after a "query formulation" or "search request" is provided by the researcher. Therefore, the researcher relies on an index created specifically for the factual situation rather than a subject index created by someone else.

Full-Text

CATR systems generally contain the full text of such items as the Internal Revenue Code, Treasury regulations, judicial cases, revenue rulings, various editorial services, and so on. Nevertheless, each service contains slightly different materials. Additional information pertaining to the specific contents of these databases will be provided in the discussion of each of the CATR services.

---

[1] William G. Harrington, "A Brief History of Computer-Assisted Legal Research," *Law Library Journal* (Vol. 77, 1984–85): 541–556.

Interactive

The researcher is interactive with the computer rather than running in a batch mode. In the case of the on-line systems, this may result in the retrieval of recent documents that are not yet available in conventional tax libraries. Because new CD-ROM disks must be provided for each update, CD-ROM systems face more of a challenge in supplying current updates than do on-line CATR systems. Nevertheless, both on-line and CD-ROM services allow the user to interact with the database as the research is being performed in order to modify search requests, change the scope of the materials being searched, or scan portions of the documents retrieved. This ability to modify either the search request or the libraries being accessed allows the researcher to narrow or broaden his or her search in an attempt to retrieve the most relevant documents from the database.

Formulating a Search Request

A CATR system allows the user to determine the actual words and topics to be searched. This is done using a search query written by the researcher. In formulating a good search request, a process entitled "TIPS" provides a helpful framework.[2] TIPS is an acronym for TERMS, ISSUES, PROXIMITY, and SCOPE. Each of these characteristics of a good search query will be subsequently discussed. A user ill-informed of efficient search techniques runs the risk of accessing many irrelevant documents or of passing up relevant documents.

Issues

As in any method of tax research, the success of a search in a CATR system is largely dependent on how well the user has defined the tax issues. For illustration purposes, assume the following situation:

---

[2] The "TIPS" terminology is suggested in chapter 11 of Terry Thomas and Marlene G. Weinstein, *Computer-Assisted Legal and Tax Research* (Englewood Cliffs, NJ: Prentice Hall, 1986).

Example 9.1. A client has approached a tax adviser with a question relating to periodic payments that she receives from her former spouse pursuant to a divorce settlement. The payments appear to be partially for the support of the client and partially for the support of the client's child. The tax adviser is asked to determine the appropriate tax treatment for the receipt of the payments.

The first step in researching this case is to properly define the issues. Defining the issues is simplified when the issues are couched in question form. For example, the issues in the preceding situation could be stated as follows: (1) What portion of the payments are alimony, and what portion of the payments are child support? (2) What is the correct tax treatment of alimony? (3) What is the correct treatment of child support payments? When the issues have been sufficiently defined, the tax adviser can begin to choose the terms or phrases that best describe the issue.

Terms or Phrases

Because CATR is a nonindexed system, the tax adviser is not forced to rely on a topical index provided by an editor to initiate the research process. However, the researcher is still dependent on the words and phrases used by the author of the particular document. The database will only retrieve those documents that exactly match the search request. Thus, perhaps the greatest challenge to the effective use of a CATR system is developing the ability to formulate a meaningful research query.

Since a more detailed example of developing a research query is part of the LEXIS presentation (later in this chapter), we will provide only a very basic discussion of a possible query formulation for this illustration. Some of the possible components of a research request have already been identified in our discussion of the tax issues. For example, in writing a tax opinion of a case dealing with periodic payments to a divorced spouse, a judge would most likely use the term *alimony*. However, a manual or computer-assisted search of a tax library that is based solely on the term "alimony" will yield far too many tax documents, many of which may be irrelevant to our situation. Alimony, therefore, is probably not a good choice of terms when used in isolation. The use of the term *child support* by itself will likely produce similar results. The researcher, by using both *alimony* and *child support* as terms, can reduce the amount of irrelevant documents accessed by the system. The search request **"CHILD SUPPORT AND ALIMONY"** yields fewer irrelevant documents. To further narrow the number of documents retrieved by the CATR system, the researcher may add additional terms, such as gross income, property settlement, periodic, divorce decree. However, the researcher also must be aware that if the research query is too exclusive, relevant documents may be missed. Formulating a good search query is a process of stringing together the appropriate words or phrases in the correct grammatical relationship that identify a manageable number of relevant documents.

Proximity of Terms and Phrases

Another element of formulating a good search request is to identify how close together the words in the search request must be in order for the document to be relevant. It is possible that a document that discusses alimony on the first page of the document and child support on the twentieth page of the document may not be relevant to our research. However, if the two terms are discussed in the same paragraph, it is more likely that the document is relevant.

Proximity in CATR systems is specified with the use of *connectors*. Connectors are terms or words used to link together the key words or phrases in the search request. Connectors allow the researcher to specify the distance between the terms that he or she will allow in order for a document to be retrieved. In our example, suppose the tax adviser decides that any document that contains the terms *alimony* and *child support* within twenty words of each other should be examined. By using the proper connectors (or combination of connectors), the researcher can custom-fit the search request and examine only those documents where the occurrence of alimony and child support meets the specified requirements. This search request is likely to produce a substantial number of documents that could be referenced in answering the client's question.

Some may argue that conventional research methods can produce the same documents as the CATR system. This may be true owing to the simplicity of our illustration. The power of CATR lies in its ability to efficiently locate documents that deal with more complex tax questions.

Scope

The initial search may still yield too many documents. The researcher should then identify those specific libraries within the database that will yield the most pertinent documents. For example, if the researcher is interested in judicial cases, and the client resides in New York, the number of retrieved documents may be reduced by accessing only the judicial-cases library and identifying only those court cases that will provide direct precedent. Therefore, the researcher may limit the scope of his or her search to cases decided in the Supreme Court, the Second Circuit Court of Appeals (in which New York is located), the district courts located in the Second Circuit, and any Tax Court cases originating in the same jurisdiction.

Perhaps the researcher is most interested in IRS pronouncements relating to alimony and child support. Since the statutory provisions dealing with alimony were changed by the Deficit Reduction Act of 1984, the researcher may be interested only in documents for post-1984 years. By limiting the scope of the search to IRS pronouncements issued after 1984, the number of retrieved documents is reduced to a more manageable size. Since CATR systems are interactive, the researcher has the ability to either reduce or expand the scope of the search depending on the desired results.

Computer Hardware Needed for a CATR System

On-line Systems

For most professionals interested in acquiring an on-line CATR system, a significant capital investment is not necessary. There are essentially two ways a firm can gain access to an on-line CATR. One means of access is through the use of dedicated terminals. These terminals are produced specifically for tax and legal research and are connected directly to the database. Presently, LEXIS and

WESTLAW offer their own dedicated terminals for sale to interested firms. A second, and less expensive choice, involves the use of a microcomputer. With the use of a microcomputer, a modem, and the appropriate application software, the firm can interact with the databases over common telephone lines. LEXIS, ACCESS, and WESTLAW all offer this alternative. Since most firms are already using microcomputers, this method does not require a substantial capital investment.

CD-ROM Systems

A CD-ROM user needs to have a CD-ROM player and a controller card for the player in addition to a basic microcomputer. CD-ROM players are available in sufficient variety to satisfy both the novice user and the more advanced tax professional. The specific needs of each user will dictate the type of player required.

CD-ROM technology needs a base software program to allow the system to function. This software is much like disk operating systems for microcomputers. The software controls the functions of the CD-ROM player and its interaction with the computer. A service may use a third-party software program or it might use its own program. Each CD-ROM service is unique and should be reviewed before a purchase decision is made.

Possible Benefits of a CATR System

Cost

It may seem odd to mention cost as one of the benefits of an on-line CATR system when many firms have used cost as a major argument against adopting an on-line CATR system. Although it may be true that CATR is not cost effective for all tax offices, it can be a valuable tool in reducing research costs and increasing efficiency in firms that frequently deal with complex tax questions. These cost savings are possible because of faster, more efficient research than is generally possible with conventional research methods. With the introduction of CD-ROM CATR systems, the cost may not be greater than the cost of the traditional hard-copy editorial services.

The true cost of these systems, however, can only be measured when analyzed in conjunction with the associated benefits. In reality, much of the cost of a CATR service stems from inappropriate use. The researcher can eliminate much of the time and cost associated with tax research by learning how to create more efficient search requests.

The initial introduction to an on-line CATR system ought to be through training sessions provided by a representative of the CATR system being considered. In addition to this initial tutoring, a potential user should invest some time in studying the written documentation of the particular system. Individuals who are determined to learn how to use an on-line CATR system by simply sitting down at the computer may find themselves unnecessarily frustrated in addition to generating a rather large bill.

Another possible aspect of cost savings is that a CATR system may make some hard-copy services redundant, thus allowing the office to eliminate them from the library. For example, on occasion, access to private letter rulings (PLRs) and general counsel memorandums (GCMs) is very important in doing tax research. Yet, the cost of a hard-copy service of these documents is relatively high. With a CATR system, both the PLRs and the GCMs are available and may be accessed as part of any research query.

Completeness

Through the use of CATR, tax professionals can quickly access documents that are not available or that are difficult to locate in hard-copy services. As mentioned previously, many tax libraries may have a hard-copy of either the PLRs or the GCMs. Even if these documents are available through hard-copy services, these services do not contain adequate indexing systems because of the large numbers of PLRs being issued each week. With the use of a CATR system, private letter rulings are easily located in the same way as any other tax document in the system. Because of the difficulty in referencing PLRs through a hard-copy service, many larger tax offices may consider this single factor sufficient justification for the acquisition of a CATR system.

Occasionally, a tax researcher may need access to non-tax law or state-tax law, such as bankruptcy or antitrust statutes and judicial law. Most CPA tax libraries cannot afford extensive hard-copy services of either of these items. However, several CATR systems have at least some coverage of these sources of the law in their database. As the demand increases, the CATR systems will certainly continue to expand the number of different items included in their databases.

Timeliness

On-line CATR systems usually are updated daily, whereas hard-copy and CD-ROM services are updated less frequently. Some tax researchers use an on-line CATR system to both verify their hard-copy research results and to conduct a final "current matters" search to ensure that recent tax documents relevant to the research project are identified.

On-line CATR Systems: LEXIS, ACCESS, and WESTLAW

The discussion of the on-line CATR systems in this chapter is limited to three services: LEXIS, ACCESS, and WESTLAW. LEXIS, published by Mead Data Central, was the first CATR system on the market and the offspring of a project initiated in the mid-1960s by the Ohio State Bar Association. It was first introduced to the public in 1973.

WESTLAW, published by West Publishing Company, was initially introduced in April 1975. However, the original version of the WESTLAW database consisted solely of West headnotes. In 1976, WESTLAW began a program of conversion to a full-text database. By 1984, virtually all the software problems had been solved, and WESTLAW was a viable computer-assisted research system.[3]

Most recently, Commerce Clearing House (CCH) introduced ACCESS On-line (ACCESS), a database that includes the usual full-text related documents as well as a considerable amount of CCH's federal and state tax materials. Even though ACCESS is the newest of the on-line computer systems, it has been adopted by numerous tax professionals.

Since LEXIS is the oldest CATR system, this chapter will focus on LEXIS as a basic illustration of some of the specific characteristics of a CATR system. For more detailed information, the researcher should consult the written documentation for each service.

---

[3] For a detailed history of the origins of CATR, see Harrington, supra note 1.

LEXIS

The Mead Data Central Database. LEXIS is just one of several services contained in the Mead Data Central database. Additional services that may be of interest to CPAs include: (1) NEXIS—a worldwide news and wire service covering over 1,300 newspapers, magazines, journals, and newsletters; and (2) NAARS (National Automated Accounting Research System)—a financial accounting database that contains annual reports for more than 4,200 companies. NAARS is made available by agreement with the AICPA.

The information available in LEXIS is divided into **libraries**. A library is a collection of related material for a given area of research. An example of the types of libraries contained in LEXIS are BKRTCY, LABOR, BANKNG, and FEDTAX. The library used most frequently by someone involved in tax research is the FEDTAX library. Located in the FEDTAX library are a number of different **files**. A file is a separately searchable group of related documents. Exhibit 9.1 lists some of the more commonly used files in the FEDTAX library of LEXIS.

From the partial list of files provided in exhibit 9.1, it is readily apparent that, through this CATR system, the researcher has access to most of the materials available in the more traditional hard-copy tax library. In fact, the sources of the tax law discussed in chapter 4 are all available in the above listed files; that is, (1) the Internal Revenue Code and accompanying legislative history, (2) administrative authorities, such as revenue rulings, revenue procedures, Treasury regulations, general counsel memoranda, and private letter rulings, (3) judicial tax cases decided in the Supreme Court, the circuit courts of appeal, the Claims Court, the Tax Court, and the various district courts, and (4) even certain editorial authority, such as RIA's *Federal Tax Coordinator 2d* and Tax Analysts' *Tax Notes*. Clearly, the files contained in exhibit 9.1 would contain all the information necessary for the majority of tax research performed by tax advisers.

Certain of the files in the FEDTAX library are combined to allow the user to efficiently search larger portions of the database with a single search. For example, the RELS file is a combination of the CBPLR and MEMOS files. By accessing the RELS file, the user is able to search most of the available administrative authority in a single search.

The basic unit of information within a file is a **document**. The

Exhibit 9.1
Selected Files From the LEXIS FEDTAX Library

US	United States Supreme Court Reports from 1790
USAPP	United States Circuit Court of Appeals from 1789—United States Court of Appeals for the Federal Circuit from October 1982
DIST	United States District Courts from 1789
CLAIMS	United States Court of Federal Claims from November 1992—United States Claims Court from October 1982—United States Court of Claims from January 1864 to September 1982
TC	United States Tax Court Opinions from November 1942; Commissioner's Acquiescence and Non-Acquiescence Tables from the Cumulative Bulletin
BTA	Board of Tax Appeals (predecessor to the Tax Court) from July 1924 to November 1942
TCM	United States Tax Court Memorandum Decisions from October 1942
CASES	Combined US, USAPP, CAFC, CLCT, TC, TCM, DIST, BANKR, BTA, CIT, and CUSTCT files
CODE	RIA's Internal Revenue Code of 1986, as amended—Title 26, USC
REGS	Final and Temporary Treasury Regulations Published in Federal Register and Code of Federal Regulations
P—REGS	Proposed Treasury Regulations Published in Federal Register
ALLREG	Combined REGS and P—REGS Files
LEGIS	Legislative History File from 1954
TREATY	United States Tax Treaties
CB	Cumulative Bulletin, Internal Revenue Bulletin, Revenue Rulings, Revenue Procedures, Announcements, Notices, News Releases, Treasury Department Orders, Prohibited Transactions Exemptions, Executive Orders, Findings Lists of Current Action on Previously Published Rulings, Acquiescence and Non-Acquiescence Tables
PLR	Private Letter Rulings and Technical Advice Memoranda from January 1954
CBPLR	Combination of the CB and the PLR Files
GCM	General Council Memoranda from May 1967
TM	Technical Memoranda from July 1967

AOD	Actions on Decisions from October 1963
MEMOS	Combined GCM, AOD, and TM Files
RELS	Combined PLR, CB, GCM, AOD, and TM Files
TNT	Tax Analysts' *Tax Notes Today* from January 1984
TXNOTE	Tax Analysts' Weekly *Tax Notes* Magazines from January 1982
TAXRIA	*Federal Tax Coordinator 2d*, published by RIA

result of a successful search request is a manageable number of pertinent documents. Actual court cases, revenue rulings, or news articles that are retrieved in a LEXIS search are referred to as documents.

A further refinement of the LEXIS materials is that each document is divided into separate **segments**. The segments consist of separable portions of a document such as titles, dates, dissents, opinions, and so on. The nature of segments varies with each document. For example, the following are some of the segments in a typical court case:

- name
- court
- citation

- date
- judges
- counsel

- opinion
- concur
- dissent

Understanding how a document is subdivided into segments can be beneficial in structuring a LEXIS search. For instance, if the researcher is looking only for cases decided after 1980, he or she could limit the scope of the search to the "date" segment and formulate a search request (**"date aft 1980"**) that would include only post-1980 cases. As a result, the number of documents retrieved by LEXIS is reduced significantly.

Formulating a Search Request. As previously demonstrated, the proper formulation of the search request is perhaps the most critical part of CATR. The order and relationship of the words in the query have a profound effect on the success of the search query. Therefore, the user must be sure to properly link the key words and phrases. This linkage is accomplished through the use of connectors.

Connectors allow the search terms to be arranged so that only relevant documents are retrieved by the computer. LEXIS provides eight connectors that a researcher may use to arrange his or her search query in the desired order. The eight connectors are: **OR, W/n, AND, PRE/n, AND NOT, W/SEG, NOT W/SEG,** and **NOT W/n**. A simple example illustrates the use of several of the preceding connectors.

> *Example 9.2.* Suppose that for a period of time after moving from one principal residence to another, a client is unsuccessful in his attempts to sell the former home. During the time that the home is listed for sale, the client decides to rent it out in order to defray the costs of making payments on two homes. When the home finally sells, the client would like to defer the gain as allowed by section 1034. All section 1034 requirements are met. The client wants to know if he can deduct the expenses of renting the home while, at the same time, taking advantage of section 1034. The tax adviser is aware that expenses associated with rental property are deductible according to sections 168 and 212.

The OR Connector. The OR connector instructs the LEXIS system to search for documents in which either or both of the search words occur. Usually the OR connector is used to link synonyms, but OR can link antonyms or alternative words as well. Using the example above, the researcher may use the OR connector as follows:

rent! or lease!

expense! or deduct!

168 or §168

The exclamation point (!) truncates the root of a word and instructs the computer to include any alternative form of the root word in the search request. For example, if the root word "depreciat" is used in a search request, the computer will retrieve all documents that contain any of the following forms of the root word: depreciate, depreciates, depreciated, depreciating, depreciation, and so on.

In the first example, LEXIS will search for documents that contain either the root word "rent" or the root word "lease" or both. The second example instructs LEXIS to search for documents that contain either the root word "expense" or the root word "deduct" or both. The third example allows LEXIS to retrieve documents that discuss section 168.

For obvious reasons, the researcher would not want to perform a search using just the queries as written above. If the researcher were to use these queries, he or she would retrieve far too many documents. Other connectors may be used in conjunction with the OR connector to formulate a more precise query.

The W/n Connector. The W/n connector instructs the LEXIS system to search for documents that are within "n" searchable words of each other. LEXIS treats certain words as "noise" words and ignores them when performing a search. A complete list is beyond the scope of this book, but a few of the more common noise words are: and, or, if, because, therefore, whether, and which.

When using the W/n connector, both words or phrases must be in the same segment. The W/n connector generally is used to connect words that describe two closely related ideas. In the example, the W/n connector may be used as follows:

residence or home W/10 sale

rent! W/15 expense! or deduct!

depreciat! W/10 deduct! or expense!

In the first example, LEXIS will search for documents that contain either the word "residence" or "home" within ten searchable words of the word "sale." In the second example, LEXIS will search for documents that include the root word "rent" within fifteen searchable words of either the root word "expense" or the root word "deduct" or both. In the third example, LEXIS will search for documents that include the root word "depreciat" within ten words of either the root word "deduct" or the root word "expense," or both. With the use of this connector, the ordering of the words in the document is not important. Thus, in the first example, the computer will retrieve documents where the word "sale" occurs either before or after "residence" or "home," just as long as they occur within ten searchable words.

Generally, a number between five and twenty will retrieve most of the relevant documents. As was mentioned previously, if too many or too few documents are retrieved, the researcher may modify the request by either increasing or decreasing the "n" number used in the connector or by changing the words or phrases used in the request.

The AND Connector. The AND connector instructs the LEXIS system to search for documents that contain both search words or phrases linked by AND. Usually the AND connector is used to link two separate ideas or concepts together. In contrast to the OR connector which tends to expand the number of documents retrieved, use of the AND connector would decrease the number of documents retrieved since both words must be present somewhere in the document. Unlike the W/n connector, the proximity of the search words is irrelevant when using the AND connector as long as the words are contained somewhere in the same document.

By referring to the example above, the following requests containing the AND connector may be used:

rent w/5 expense! and 1034 or §1034

212 or §212 and 1034 or §1034

The first example will instruct LEXIS to search for documents that both (1) contain the word "rent" within five searchable words of the root word "expense" and (2) also refer to section 1034. The second query will cause LEXIS to search for documents that mention both sections 212 and 1034.

The PRE/n Connector. The PRE/n connector instructs the LEXIS system to locate documents in which the first search word precedes the second search word by no more than "n" searchable words. This connector is extremely useful where it is known that the key words will be in a specific order. For example, if the researcher is looking for the case citation—420 F.2d 107—the "**420 PRE/5 107**" search request should locate those documents that contain this exact citation without retrieving other irrelevant documents.

The AND NOT Connector. The AND NOT connector instructs the LEXIS system to search for documents in which a certain word or phrase appears and a second word or phrase does not. For example, the search request **"expense AND NOT disallowed"** tells LEXIS to search for documents in which the word "expense" occurs and the word "disallowed" does not. This connector applies for the entire document. Therefore, a document would not be retrieved if the word "expense" occurs on the first page and the word "disallowed" occurs on the last page. As can be seen, this connector is very restrictive and should be used with care.

The W/SEG Connector. The W/SEG connector instructs the LEXIS system to search for documents in which the search words appear within the same segment. The W/SEG connector does not require that both of the search words appear in a specific segment, as long as they appear in the same segment.

The NOT W/SEG Connector. The NOT W/SEG connector instructs the LEXIS system to search for documents that have at least one segment in which the first search word appears, but not the other search word. Again, this connector is very restrictive and should be used cautiously.

The NOT W/n Connector. The NOT W/n connector instructs the LEXIS system to search for documents in which the first search word is found. If the second word is found in the document, it cannot appear within "n" searchable words of the first search word. Due to the exclusive nature of this connector, if it is not used judiciously, pertinent documents may be excluded from the search results.

Combination and Priority of Connectors. Formulating a fairly complicated search request will normally require the use of several connectors. LEXIS has assigned a priority to the connectors that determine the order in which the system will perform the search request. The priority LEXIS has assigned to the connectors is:

1. **OR**
2. **W/n, PRE/n, NOT W/n**
3. **W/SEG**

4. NOT W/SEG
5. AND
6. AND NOT.

To illustrate how LEXIS treats multiple connectors used in the same search request, assume the following search request:

charitable w/3 contribution! and religious or education!

The OR connector has the highest priority and forms the search unit

religious or education!

The W/n connector has the next highest priority. The W/3 connector forms a second search unit

charitable w/3 contribution!

The AND connector forms the last search unit by combining the two search units described above. The **religious or education!** search unit is now connected to the **charitable w/3 contribution** search unit by the AND connector.

If the same connector is used more than once in the same search request, LEXIS processes the request from left to right. If more than one **W/n**, **PRE/n**, and **NOT W/n** are used in the same search request, LEXIS gives the highest priority to the connector with the smallest "n." If the researcher wishes to change the priority assigned by LEXIS to the connectors, parentheses may be used. If parentheses are placed around a portion of the search request, that portion of the search will be performed first.

Using LEXIS as a Citator. Once a researcher has identified what appears to be the relevant tax authorities that deal with the tax question being examined, the authority needs to be reviewed to confirm that the cited authority is still a valid precedent. Judicial cases are often appealed and overturned. More recent court cases may be decided that disagree with the case that the researcher has identified. Revenue rulings and revenue procedures are often superseded or revoked. The steps of good tax research should always include updating one's research results.

Using a CATR system as a citator can result in significant time savings. LEXIS has two different features that can serve as citators. Auto-Cite is a LEXIS feature that deals with court cases, revenue rulings, and revenue procedures. When Auto-Cite is used to check a court case, this special feature: (1) verifies the correctness of the citation, (2) provides a history of the case, and (3) provides citations of other cases that may disagree with the decision of the cited case.

LEXIS also possesses the capability of "shepardizing" a judicial case. Shepard's Citations has traditionally been a complex citation service used predominantly by lawyers. Using the Shepard's function in LEXIS provides the following information: (1) parallel citations, (2) case history, and (3) a list of all cases that cite the case in question. Auto-Cite provides the same basic information except that the list of related cases provided by Shepard's should be a complete list, whereas the list provided by Auto-Cite is only a partial list.

Generally, to manually obtain the information provided by Auto-Cite or Shepard's is a slow and tedious process. LEXIS can perform this valuable research function almost instantaneously. Both these citing functions can be accessed while viewing a case or by providing the computer with a correct citation of the case.

Although LEXIS contains additional important and useful functions that go beyond the scope of this particular text, this chapter has provided sufficient background information to enable the reader to appreciate the possible use of LEXIS in computer-assisted tax research. Before attempting to use LEXIS, the researcher should review the various LEXIS manuals to become familiar with all of its capabilities.

ACCESS

As mentioned previously, no attempt is made here to discuss ACCESS in any real detail. Even though CCH uses different terms to describe its database, different connectors to facilitate search requests, and a different menu-driven operating system, the basic features of ACCESS are similar to those of LEXIS and WESTLAW.

ACCESS is dedicated strictly to providing a comprehensive tax database. Thus, unlike LEXIS and WESTLAW, ACCESS does not contain databases that address other law, such as criminal procedure or bankruptcy. Although this feature makes ACCESS simpler to use, it reduces the overall breadth of this database as compared with those of LEXIS and WESTLAW. For example, suppose the tax researcher needs nontax federal statutes or judicial cases. ACCESS cannot provide these materials, whereas both LEXIS and WEST-LAW can.

ACCESS includes seven libraries: (1) User Services, (2) News, (3) Federal Taxes, (4) Federal Archives 1986–1990, (5) Federal Archives 1978–1985, (6) State Taxes: Alabama–Montana, (7) State Taxes: Nebraska–Wyoming. As previously mentioned, the libraries cover the offerings of CCH's printed service. Daily updates from both the federal and state levels are available on ACCESS.

WESTLAW

The WESTLAW computerized service is marketed by West Publishing Company. The WESTLAW central computer database is located in St. Paul, Minnesota. The mechanics of the operations of WESTLAW are similar to that of LEXIS and will not be discussed in detail. Even though the WESTLAW connectors are somewhat different and WESTLAW refers to its databases using different terminology, the basic approach to performing CATR on WEST-LAW is the same as it is on LEXIS. Also, it is important to note that the WESTLAW database (like the LEXIS database, but unlike the ACCESS database) provides a great deal more information than merely tax-related materials.

One feature that differentiates WESTLAW from LEXIS and ACCESS is worth highlighting. WESTLAW offers a "full-text plus" CATR system. The "plus" refers to the inclusion in its judicial case databases of certain editorial information pertaining to each case. In all West judicial cases, the editors provide a headnote, a general topical index, and a more specific keynumber index.

As discussed previously, a limitation of a traditional indexing system is the reliance on editors to reference the case in the index most likely accessed by the researcher. This constraint applies equally to the traditional West indexing system that exists for its judicial case law. However, through the use of WESTLAW, a tax researcher can utilize the West keynumber indexing system in conjunction with the "literal word search" capabilities of the computer. Since West Publishing Co. is the largest publisher of U.S. judicial case law, this aspect of WESTLAW may prove to be very beneficial, particularly if a tax researcher does extensive judicial case law research.

To illustrate the possible benefit of this WESTLAW feature, assume that the tax researcher is interested in cases dealing with home office expenses. Searching the West Digest index (either in WESTLAW or hard-copy service), the tax researcher finds the topic number and name "220—Internal Revenue." Within the general topic of Internal Revenue, the index shows a key number for "home office expenses" of 3355. Therefore, a possible search query for cases relating to this topic could be **220k3355** (k indicates the keynumber). Without looking at the actual body of the judicial case, the computer will search all Internal Revenue cases that have been assigned the key number 3355. However, if the researcher does not want to rely on the West editors for proper classification, the research query could be restructured as follows:

Topic (220) /p home /p office /p expense or deduction

The computer will now look for all tax cases that have the words "home" and "office" and "expense or deduction" in the headnotes of the judicial cases within the "Internal Revenue" topic. This search request also can be expanded to include certain additional word searches in the actual text of the case.

This feature of WESTLAW is somewhat similar to both LEXIS and ACCESS in that these CATR systems have the advantages of a full-text retrieval system in addition to certain editorial information. To enhance its editorial coverage, WESTLAW has added CCH's *Standard Federal Tax Reporter* to its database. In the hands of an experienced user, the additional editorial information contained in the databases can be very helpful.

Cost of On-Line CATR Systems

The issue of actual costs of the respective on-line CATR systems needs to be addressed. The total cost of an on-line CATR system is difficult to pinpoint because it changes so frequently and is often subject to a certain amount of negotiation. However, the total costs of an on-line CATR system usually consist of: (1) initial cost outlay (hardware, software, and hook-up costs), (2) monthly charges, (3) charges for actual use of the system, and (4) cost of the time of the tax researcher.

Item (1) largely depends on what hardware is already available to the firm. If a microcomputer is available and can be assigned to the CATR system, the initial outlay costs can be dramatically reduced.

Item (4) is a variable cost that depends on the skill of the tax researcher and to what degree the CATR system is "user friendly." Assuming that each CATR system is comparable in ease of use, item (4) does not differentiate between the three CATR systems.

Items (2) and (3) are more easily identified and differences do exist between the CATR systems. Ignoring items that are necessary for each system (such as telecommunication charges), the following is a summary of actual costs of engaging in a search on each of the three CATR systems:[4]

ACCESS

Registration fee	$250
Connect time	$100 per hour[5]

LEXIS

Monthly subscription access charge	$125 per month
Connect time	$.77 per minute
Cost of each search	$6–$55 per search

WESTLAW[6]

Subscription charge	$125 per month
Database charge	$160–$195 per hour[7]
Connect time/Communication charges	$48 per hour

---

[4] These charges are current as of March 1993. However, they are subject to frequent change.

[5] This amount varies depending on which option the subscriber uses. There is a pay-as-you-go option of $100 per hour, or a block pricing option in which the subscriber buys blocks of time from 6 hours to 240 hours with prices ranging from $600 to $20,160.

[6] WESTLAW provides another fee structure that may be attractive to tax practitioners who want access to WESTLAW, but anticipate minimal usage. This pricing structure does not have a monthly charge. The database charge is $4 per minute and the connect time is 34 cents per minute. There is a twenty minute minimum usage requirement per month.

[7] These hourly rates vary depending on the amount of usage. The $195-per-hour rate applies to the first 50 hours used per month. The $160-per-hour rate is available only when monthly usage is in excess of 200 hours. WESTLAW requires a minimum of three hours of usage per month.

LEXIS also can be acquired through the AICPA's TOTAL (Total On-line Tax and Accounting Library). TOTAL represents a special contract negotiated with Mead Data Central where AICPA members can have access to all LEXIS/NEXIS libraries without the monthly $125 charge. In addition to the regular connect time and per-search fees, LEXIS charges an additional $3 per search. Therefore, if an AICPA member wishes to have access to LEXIS, but does not plan to use it extensively, the AICPA arrangement may be attractive.

CD-ROM CATR SYSTEMS

CD-ROM CATR systems are fast-growing, compact tools for doing tax research. Enormous amounts of information are stored on compact disk—the same types of disks used in the music industry—and accessed by a desktop computer. Each disk has the capacity of tens of thousands of printed pages; for example, an entire encyclopedia set can be stored on one compact disk.

Tax, with its vast amount of researchable, widely used data, is an area that lends itself to the use of CD-ROM technology. The mechanics of how to structure research queries in a CD-ROM system are similar to those used in an on-line CATR system and will not be discussed in detail in this section. The principle difference between the two systems is that for an on-line system, the user is dependent on a central database that is accessed through a telephone link. A CD-ROM system is contained on a series of disks maintained on the premises of the user. Generally, the CD-ROM systems are less expensive. However, the on-line systems contain more information and have the ability to be updated on a more timely basis.

Our discussion of CD-ROM CATR systems will be limited to four services: CCH's ACCESS CD-ROM, RIA's ONPOINT, WEST's CD-ROM LIBRARY, and BNA's TAX MANAGEMENT PORTFOLIOS PLUS.

CCH's ACCESS CD-ROM

CCH offers a complete line of CD-ROM offerings. The publications—each an independent CD or set of CDs—include the Standard Federal Tax Reporter; the Federal Estate & Gift Tax Reporter;

the Federal Excise Tax Reporter; IRS Letter Rulings, including TAMs, TMs, GCMs, and AODs; Revenue Rulings and Revenue Procedures; IRS Publications (selected); Internal Revenue Manual; U.S. Tax Cases; Tax Court Regulars; Tax Court Memoranda; and Board of Tax Appeals Regulars and Memoranda. CCH updates the disks either monthly, quarterly, or annually, depending on the CD.

Along with the CD-ROM service, CCH also provides the user with the option of accessing its on-line database through a software product called ACCESS PLUS. This option allows the user to query and retrieve information from either platform without first exiting and entering the other program. At this writing, CCH had recently acquired the CD-ROM products of Matthew Bender. It is not clear at this point whether these systems will be integrated or whether they will continue to be marketed as separate CD-ROM systems.

RIA's ONPOINT

ONPOINT consists of one CD containing its complete Federal Tax Coordinator 2d; complete Internal Revenue Code and Treasury Regulations; the Master Federal Tax Manual; the Weekly Alert; RIA Special Problems; Current-year IRB documents; IRS Taxpayer Information Publications; Revenue Rulings and Procedures from 1954; Selected Notices, Announcements, Treasury Decision Preambles, and Commissioner Delegation Orders from 1954; and a master index to the entire ONPOINT Library.

If users of RIA's ONPOINT are interested in accessing additional tax databases, the ACCESS PLUS software allows the user of ONPOINT to access the full text of documents through a link with the LEXIS on-line system. This option has the potential to make LEXIS's more extensive databases available to the user of ONPOINT. For those who are considering a CD-ROM system, the possibility of a link with LEXIS offers some exciting possibilities.

West's CD-ROM Library

West's CD-ROM LIBRARY is divided into four sets: Code and Regulations, Letter Rulings, Administrative Materials, and Taxation Cases. The Code and Regulations set includes the Federal

Taxation Code and Regulations, BNA Abstracts, Rules of the Tax Court and Claims Court, International Tax Agreements from 1955, Federal Taxation Legislation, and Federal Taxation Legislative History.

The Administrative Materials set includes Revenue Rulings from 1954, Revenue Procedures from 1954, Administrative Orders from 1954, Actions on Decisions from 1967, and General Counsel Memoranda from 1967. The Letter Rulings set contains the Letter Rulings from 1954. The Taxation Cases set includes the Federal Tax Cases from 1924.

BNA's Tax Management Portfolios Plus

BNA offers its portfolio series on CD-ROM. BNA allows the user to customize its CD platter by selecting from: U.S. Income Portfolio Series; Estates, Gifts and Trust Portfolio Series; Foreign Income Portfolio Series; Tax Practice Series; Journals and reports; and BNA software spreadsheets used for tax planning. Again, the user is faced with the decision of whether to retain his or her hard-copy portfolio series or obtain the entire series on CD-ROMs plus other BNA computer products.

Cost of CD-ROM CATR Systems

The relative costs of the various CD-ROM systems are hard to compare because each service contains different amounts of information. In addition, most publishers provide their electronic tax materials on a piecemeal basis so the user can select various options within each service. This makes it difficult to quote meaningful prices for competing CD-ROM services. However, the following represents a range of prices[8] for each service:

	Price
CCH's ACCESS CD-ROM	$1,420–$7,070 per year
RIA's ONPOINT	$1,475 per year
WEST's CD-ROM LIBRARY	$1,500–$4,500 per year
BNA's TAX MANAGEMENT PORTFOLIOS PLUS	$700–$1,700 per year

---

[8] These prices are current as of March 1993. However, they are subject to frequent change.

Summary

To effectively and efficiently deal with the variety and complexity of tax questions that arise daily, a tax adviser must be able to utilize all the available tax research tools. This book has suggested certain steps that should be followed to approach and solve tax questions. In earlier chapters, the use of traditional hard-copy tax services in performing tax research has been discussed. In this chapter, the tax adviser was introduced to CATR systems. A CATR service allows the tax researcher to perform in a matter of minutes a comprehensive search of a vast tax database. This search is not constrained by a predetermined index, but has the flexibility of allowing the researcher to construct his or her own index through the formulation of a personalized search query. The use of computers unquestionably will continue to expand in all facets of tax practice. Consequently, a tax adviser must learn to tap the tremendous capabilities of the computer in order to continue to provide the best possible client services at the most reasonable costs.

Index

DATE		